CW00558087

Merchants on the Mediterranean

Merchants on the Mediterranean

Ottoman–Dutch Trade in the Eighteenth Century

Despina Vlami

I.B.TAURIS

LONDON • NEW YORK • OXFORD • NEW DELHI • SYDNEY

I.B. TAURIS
Bloomsbury Publishing Plc
50 Bedford Square, London, WC1B 3DP, UK
1385 Broadway, New York, NY 10018, USA
29 Earlsfort Terrace, Dublin 2, Ireland

BLOOMSBURY, I.B. TAURIS and the I.B. Tauris logo are trademarks of Bloomsbury
Publishing Plc

First published in Great Britain 2023
Paperback edition published 2025

Copyright © Despina Vlami 2023

Despina Vlami has asserted her right under the Copyright, Designs and
Patents Act, 1988, to be identified as Author of this work.

For legal purposes the Acknowledgements on p. x constitute an extension
of this copyright page.

Cover design by Holly Capper
Cover image: Amsterdam Port Entrance by Abraham Storck (1644–1708).
(© INTERFOTO/Alamy Stock Photo)

All rights reserved. No part of this publication may be reproduced or transmitted
in any form or by any means, electronic or mechanical, including photocopying,
recording, or any information storage or retrieval system, without prior
permission in writing from the publishers.

Bloomsbury Publishing Plc does not have any control over, or responsibility for, any third-
party websites referred to or in this book. All internet addresses given in this book were
correct at the time of going to press. The author and publisher regret any inconvenience
caused if addresses have changed or sites have ceased to exist, but can accept no
responsibility for any such changes.

A catalogue record for this book is available from the British Library.

A catalog record for this book is available from the Library of Congress.

ISBN: PB: 978-0-7556-4889-4
ePDF: 978-0-7556-4886-3
eBook: 978-0-7556-4887-0

Typeset by Deanta Global Publishing Services, Chennai, India

To find out more about our authors and books visit www.bloomsbury.com
and sign up for our newsletters.

For my parents,
Dimitri and Susana

Contents

Tables

Acknowledgements

The study of the letters from the Dutch merchant Thomas De Vogel to his Greek Ottoman clients Bartholo and Raphael Cardamici during their ten-year collaboration will always remain an important moment of my academic career. When read through the magnifying lens of microhistory, De Vogel's letters reveal all the individual characteristics, risks and impasses that Ottoman trade faced as it expanded into Western markets in the long eighteenth century. They also highlight the everyday anxieties, rewards and worries that accompanied business collaborations at the time: importantly, they show how the pursuit of profit could coexist with a relationship of trust between merchants and in what way a business strategy might include a variety of mechanisms to deal with unpredictable, unfamiliar and threatening situations. Finally, they confirm the imperative significance of timing, climate and geography in long-distance trade. De Vogel's business transactions emerge as a '*jeu multiple de la vie*' with '*tous ses movements, toutes ses durées, toutes ses ruptures, toutes ses variations*', to use Fernand Braudel's metaphor from the distant 1958. Throughout the writing of the book, I had the warm encouragement of my colleagues in the Research Centre for Medieval and Modern Hellenism of the Academy of Athens, where I have the honour to serve as a senior researcher for the last twenty years. I am also indebted to the Netherlands Institute at Athens for encouraging my research and partly supporting the cost of copy-editing the manuscript. Above all, I would like to express my gratitude to the institute's secretary, Emmy Mestropian-Makri. A special thanks goes to Damian Mac Con Uladh for undertaking the copy-editing. My dear colleague Thierry Allain provided me with valuable archival material from the Dutch Consulate of Smyrna, which I had the opportunity to elaborate and incorporate in my research. He also provided me with important bibliographical material and references: I cannot thank him enough. Through research and writing, my daughters Stefania and Maria have been a constant source of support and delight, reminding me relentlessly of the self-evident truth that love is really what makes life beautiful. It is for their unconditional love, as for so many other reasons, that the book is dedicated to my parents.

Preface

The eighteenth century, mainly characterized as the 'Age of Enlightenment and Reason', coincided with the final phase of the era of 'merchant capitalism': a period of unprecedented growth in the volume, geographical range and value of international trade, which had begun in the sixteenth century.[1] For at least two centuries, the movement of goods, services and money had a dramatic impact on the development of the world economy, politics and society – an impact which culminated in the eighteenth century, when, according to contemporary historians, international trade developed into a 'supernatural wheel' that 'moved the engine of society'.[2] And yet the most significant attribute of the eighteenth century, whether it concerned international politics, society or the economy, was its highly transitional character.

As a period of relative stability marked by traditional values and age-old practices, the ancien régime was succeeded by a period of great upheaval, in which society, economy, politics and ideology underwent significant changes. Political and social turmoil was combined with an ideological stir ignited by the European Enlightenment.[3] The outbreak of the French and American revolutions had a decisive influence on the balance of international relations, leaving an important imprint on modern Western civilization. Calling into question the legitimacy of monarchical and aristocratic power structures, the two revolutions highlighted new models of political, social and ideological values.[4] In the field of international relations, important dynastic wars, such as those over succession in Spain, Austria and the Seven Years' War, underscored geopolitical competition and alliances between European states and challenged regimes that had survived since the ancien régime era. A series of bilateral conflicts, such as the English–Dutch and Russian–Turkish wars, were economically motivated and led to significant territorial rearrangements.

In the eighteenth century, international trade entered a key period of transition. Change came, above all, with growth. Demographic expansion increased the volume of international trade transactions and their geographical range incorporated new distant areas. European discoveries and the formation of colonial empires had already expanded and boosted the international system of commercial transactions, while at the same time new commodities had been introduced to Europe and the rest of the world through colonial trade. Meanwhile the development of the transport industry and the improvement of financial techniques allowed for long-distance, more efficient and faster deals. As the prevalent ideas of mercantilism were slowly replaced by liberalism and laissez-faire, a variety of business associations and partnerships, from regulated and joint stock companies to individual and family firms, appeared in the eighteenth-century international markets. Methods and techniques of the past blended with new strategies and tactics, as commercial firms combined direct trade with various forms of indirect and transit trade while offering commission agency, insurance and financial services to clients. To cope with the ordeals of war, increasing international antagonism and the necessity to achieve a quick turnover, many merchants turned to other merchant houses and brokers to buy information, intermediation and credit. This practice assigned the management and responsibility of different phases of an enterprise to commercial correspondents on commission and created large mercantile networks based on relations of trust and common interest.

The shift from old techniques, strategies and ideas to modern ones was accomplished in different geographical regions to varying degrees. Even though in some European regions new trends and methods appeared quite early, in other parts of western and south-eastern Europe the organization and techniques of international trade remained entrenched in traditional merchant capitalist practices into the nineteenth century. This distinct juncture of the dynamic coexistence of theories, strategies and merchant routines was particularly visible in bilateral economic relations between Europe and the Ottoman Empire and the associations between Ottoman and European merchants.[5]

Levantine trade, although less significant in volume and geopolitical importance than its contemporary Atlantic and South Pacific equivalent, represents an ideal research laboratory for the study of the methods, relationships, ideas and everyday life of the members of an Ottoman merchant milieu who in the eighteenth century expanded their business transactions to the West. This development was closely related to a European penetration of the Ottoman market economy. Trade transactions between Europe and the Ottoman Empire had increased from the sixteenth century. The Ottoman Empire was a natural gate to the East and a huge market for the distribution of European products and colonial goods traded by European merchants. It was also a vast country producing high-quality raw materials and foodstuffs as well as serving as an outlet for Levantine products and goods arriving from the East. However, from the eighteenth century, and as Europe entered the turmoil of war, there was an intensification of trade flows, accompanied by a significant increase in the number of European and other foreign merchants setting up business in Ottoman markets. The arrival of merchants and factors from England, France and Holland, as well as Italian and German cities, to Ottoman ports and commercial centres enhanced an already intense traffic of people, products and services carried out through various intersecting maritime and land routes. The economic strategy and trade methods of those willing to set up business in the Levant were more complicated and very different than the 'colonial model' adopted by Europeans to penetrate and manipulate colonial markets under their rule. Establishing commercial relations with the Ottoman Empire required coming to terms with the organization of the Ottoman economy, its management, infrastructure, resources and market organization. Daily business was determined by the government's strategy and its implementation by the public administration as well as bureaucratic turmoil, organization and the institutions of a complex multi-ethnic society. Having to deal with a despotic ruler, rigid officialdom and a public administration prone to corruption, European and foreign officials were obliged to adopt discreet and conciliatory ways in approaching the Ottoman authorities with the intention of guaranteeing safety and free enterprise for their subjects. Therefore, since the sixteenth century, many European governments had developed a form of trade diplomacy, using political arguments and diplomatic means, in their dealings with the Ottoman authorities in order to attain trade agreements and special privileges.[6] For their part, European and foreign merchants hired factors and representatives in Ottoman markets and built partnerships with local trade operators. These alliances between Europeans and Ottomans were based on common interest and led to an exchange of protection, the distribution of special privileges and the delivery of confidential information and services. They eventually gave to many Ottoman subjects, mostly Christians and Jews, the opportunity, and the incentive, to transfer their business to commercial centres and ports all around the Mediterranean basin, in central and western Europe and later across the Atlantic. As it appears, Ottoman merchants in expanding their trade business outside the Ottoman Empire had to reconsider their strategy and embrace those methods and techniques that would allow them to place themselves within the international business milieu, a setting very different from the cosmopolitan Ottoman markets where they had started out in the first place.

The flows and traits of Ottoman trade with the West during this turbulent period have been investigated extensively, and many studies have focused on the common strategies and performance of ethnic and religious minorities – Greeks,

Armenians and Jews – who led the way. Less common has been an analysis at a microhistory level, to examine how Ottomans and foreigners, strangers and 'friends', individuals of different faiths and cultural backgrounds, joined forces, worked together or competed within an international business setting. The book attempts to contribute to this end through a study of the collaboration between two Ottoman Greeks, Bartholo Cardamici and his nephew Raphael, and a Dutch merchant, Thomas De Vogel, who, from 1760 to 1771, acted as their commercial correspondent in Amsterdam.

Reconstructing a business relationship

Bartholo and Raphael Cardamici were Ottoman subjects of Greek origin who ran a family trading business in Smyrna and Constantinople. Their association with Thomas De Vogel is revealed in the letters the Dutch merchant addressed to them throughout their collaboration. The content of the letters allows us to discern the main characteristics of an early expansion of Ottoman trade in the West; it shows the means and methods employed by Ottoman merchants to infiltrate Western markets, the responsibilities they assumed to promote their business transactions and, finally, the experts and trusted parties they chose to include in their business networks as consultants, employees and partners. It also reveals through a microhistory lens the operation of European and Levantine trade networks in the Ottoman Empire, as well as the broader Mediterranean area.

The association between Cardamici and De Vogel reveals a type of Ottoman–European collaboration in the sectors of trade and finance that has not featured in the relevant bibliography. And in doing so it describes a situation that overturns prevalent perceptions of the standard roles and responsibilities assumed by European and Ottoman merchant entrepreneurs in the Levantine import–export business. It shows, in other words, that the renowned eighteenth-century European infiltration of the Ottoman market economy combined with and complemented an opposite tendency, since Ottoman merchants were already expanding their trade business into Western markets by utilizing similar strategies to their European counterparts. As has already been mentioned, in order to promote their business pursuits in Ottoman markets efficiently, Europeans needed the expertise and connections of local merchants, agents and brokers to serve as local footholds in unknown and hazardous environments. Their partnership with Greeks, Armenians and Jews was based on a mutual understanding and profit-seeking agreement, leading to an exchange of privileges, confidential information and services. Eventually, it encouraged many Ottoman subjects to exploit European protection and connections and expand their business abroad. This perception of a linear association of events, bringing Ottoman merchants from Ottoman commercial centres, where they successfully acted as agent-intermediaries of Europeans, to the major trading and financial centres of the West, where they followed autonomous careers, has dominated the bibliography at least since the 1960s.[7] However, some recent studies have indicated that already from the early eighteenth century, Ottoman commercial firms, like the Cardamici, embarked on autonomous careers in Europe; to realize this project, they collaborated with European commercial firms, which acted as their local agents in European markets. To gain access to Amsterdam's commercial, mercantile and financial market, Bartholo and Raphael Cardamici did not hire, as anticipated, another Ottoman enterprise from their business and ethnic milieu as their main correspondent on the ground but chose to appoint an experienced insider from the Amsterdam market. The Cardamici–De Vogel partnership, described in this book, represents therefore an interesting deviation from the 'European merchant–Ottoman commercial agent' pattern that dominates the analysis of Levantine trade; instead, it portrays a reverse model, one where the Cardamicis are the principals/clients wishing to expand their business from their operational base in Smyrna and Constantinople to a major Western commercial and financial market. De Vogel is instead their local representative/correspondent, providing various market, maritime, insurance and financial services under commission.

Thomas De Vogel's business letters

The following study is the outcome of an in-depth analysis of De Vogel's letters addressed to Bartholo and Raphael Cardamici between 1760 and 1771. In the analysis we have also considered and made the most of information coming from De Vogel's letters to other well-known Ottoman merchants of the period, including, most notably, Ambrosio Mavrogordatos and Apostolos Demestikas, Ottoman merchants of Greek origin who were involved in the Amsterdam–Smyrna Ottoman trade network of the period. We have also relied upon İsmail Hakkı Kadı's study for an assessment of De Vogel's extensive correspondence with members of his family and other Dutch merchants established in the major Ottoman commercial centres of the period. Our analysis of De

Vogel's correspondence considers each letter both as the ultimate tool for the achievement of a commercial/financial transaction and as an illustration of an individual conducting a business operation – his behaviour, thoughts and personality.[8] Each letter is enlightening and instructive, unveiling the reasoning behind each commercial transaction and the procedure necessary to fulfil it.[9]

This is by no means an innovative method, as historians have made extensive use of business correspondence as a valuable tool for the reconstruction and analysis of international trade in the modern period.[10] Despite the fact that business letters do not usually contain quantitative data, as registers and ledgers do for individual enterprises, they nevertheless provide important information, which enables the reconstruction of a fascinating narrative of mercantile trade. The casual, contractual and, at the same time, personal character of the business letters are qualities that establish them as valuable pieces of evidence in the hands of historians. They also distinguish them from other means of information, such as the various types of pamphlets, almanacs and commercial guides and manuals that circulated extensively in Europe from the seventeenth century onwards.[11]

Correspondence by letter remained the fundamental means of communicating and sharing information for merchants throughout the eighteenth century.[12] Knowledge of its techniques and a fluency in writing business letters constituted, for all the above reasons, a very important skill.[13]

But was there perhaps a more 'suitable' way of corresponding through business letters,[14] some more appropriate merchant style which corresponded to the different languages spoken by the parties concerned and allowed obligations and contracts to be understood by all?[15] In their recent study, Bartolomei et al. mention, among others, that the capacity of merchants to compose letters developed and improved substantially during the eighteenth and the nineteenth centuries.[16] The style and wording of letters was elaborated through centuries of practice. Each letter retained a very personal form of expression and wording that reflected the distinctive personality and will of its author. It seems that letters retained this particular character despite the fact that until the late eighteenth century, manuals had been published in many different languages throughout Europe, containing models of business letters, together with commercial guides for the profession.[17] These manuals contained methods for keeping accounts, transacting with bills of exchange and money, and also commercial laws.[18]

Through their letters, merchants were able to design, organize and advance their business enterprise.[19] At the same time each letter depicted and served the character, mentality, strategy and priorities of a specific merchant; as such it represented his personality and also the way he chose to create and develop his personal business network. Business letters responded to vital, everyday necessities and demands and were exchanged within an environment of mutual commitment and trust, familiarity and sentiment, something that rendered the correspondence reliable and trustful.[20] The form and style of De Vogel's letters to the principals of the firms he collaborated with reflected a savoir faire of the merchant profession and the business correspondence of the period, conveying a sense of mutual trust and respect for associates, collaborators and colleagues. The business-like and, at the same time, intimate character of his correspondence with the Cardamicis reveals their personal liaison and their perpetual discourse, which referred primarily to business and profit, and then also to subjects like trust, skills, efficiency, solidarity and confidence. References to family, religion, social relations, culture and everyday life are also contained in the texts as well.

The control mechanisms to assess a merchant's reliability and the efficiency of a collaboration functioned through repetition – the constant flow of transactions, common projects that were repeated and the confronting and jointly dealing with common crises. Merchants chose eventually to collaborate with those merchants, representatives and agents they considered could help and serve them in the best way possible without being influenced, at least decisively, by references, acquaintances and advice from members of their extended family, social and religious-ethnic environment. This conclusion seems to question the opinion that business enterprises in the eighteenth century were more intrapersonal and less informal than modern enterprises. It also allows us to better understand the way in which eighteenth-century merchants, like the Cardamicis, chose their representatives and shaped business collaboration networks, which were based more on knowledge and instinct and will and less on kinship-social relations and references.

Thomas De Vogel was an eighteenth-century Dutch merchant entrepreneur based in Amsterdam whose international business network allowed him to operate all around the world. By the mid-eighteenth century, De Vogel had already expanded his business to the Ottoman Empire and had an intensive collaboration with Ottoman, Dutch and foreign commercial houses established in Constantinople, Smyrna, Ankara and Aleppo. His business correspondence includes letters addressed to the principals of some of these companies.

De Vogel's association with Bartholo and Raphael Cardamici in the 1760s and 1770s formed part of the wider spectrum of his business activity in the Ottoman Empire. De Vogel's business correspondence and business archive is part of the De Vogel family's records conserved in the Amsterdam City Archives.[21] The records comprise personal correspondence, notarial acts, contracts and genealogical trees, business correspondence, ledgers, letterbooks, contracts and agreements concerning the family's business transactions. As it stands, De Vogel's business archive has a unique value considering that it appears to be the only personal archive of an eighteenth-century Dutch merchant that has survived in such good condition and can be consulted by researchers.[22] The letters addressed by De Vogel to his various partners and associates were copied and preserved in large letterbook volumes. In this series, volumes 44–52 contain copies of the letters sent by De Vogel to the principals of foreign commercial houses in Belgium, France, Spain, Portugal, Italy, the Habsburg and Ottoman Empires from 1760 to 1771. The letters are written in French, Italian or Spanish Ladino. Each volume corresponds to a specific year. The copies of the letters are classified in chronological order, and an alphabetic index of addressees appears at the start of each volume.

From 1760 to 1764 Thomas De Vogel sent letters to both Bartholo and Raphael Cardamici in Smyrna and Constantinople. Bartholo was the director of the Bartholo Cardamici & Co, and his nephew Raphael represented the firm in Constantinople. From 1764, following Bartholo's death, Raphael took the reins of the family enterprise and until 1771 collaborated with Thomas De Vogel & Son under the name Raphael Cardamici & Co.

Based on this valuable material of 253 business letters sent to their addressees between 1760 and 1771, we investigate a number of important issues related to Ottoman–Dutch trade of the period. How easy and uncomplicated was it for a medium-sized eighteenth-century Ottoman trade company, such as the

Table 1 Letters from Thomas De Vogel to Bartholo and Raphael Cardamici, 1760–71

Year	Bartholo Cardamici	Raphael Cardamici	Average Letters/Year
1760	12	7	1.58
1761	19	13	2.66
1762	15	14	2.41
1763	13	14	2.25
1764	2	21	1.91
1765	–	21	1.75
1766	–	23	1.91
1767	–	21	1.75
1768	–	21	1.75
1769	–	17	1.41
1770	–	17	1.41
1771	–	3	0.25
Total	61	192	

Source: Stadsarchief Amsterdam [StdAm], 332, Thomas De Vogel, Kopieboek, vol. 44–52, 1760–71.

Cardamicis, to expand its business to the West? What were the decisions to be made and the setbacks to overcome? Which kind of resources, in terms of knowledge, information, experience, contacts and capital, could guarantee its successful passage from the business environment of a precapitalist oriental market to that of a major western European commercial and financial centre? Following the venture of the Cardamicis, who in 1760s traded goods between Smyrna, Constantinople and Amsterdam, we investigate various aspects of the organization and strategy necessary for such an important transition. To expand their wholesale trade business to Amsterdam, the Cardamicis chose as their local correspondent the experienced and strong-minded De Vogel. De Vogel's letters to his Ottoman-based clients reveal the course of their business dealings and the making of their personal relationship. At the same time, they are comprehensive and efficient tutorials on the trade business and strategy that guided the Cardamicis in an eighteenth-century international business universe that was unpredictable and mainly unfamiliar to them.

Chapter 1 presents a brief account of Dutch–Ottoman trade relations and sketches the historical context within which the De Vogel–Cardamici association came into being and developed. Chapter 2 describes the organization and strategy of the Dutch and the Ottoman enterprises and depicts the immediate, common, business-social milieu in which their partnership and joint ventures were staged. Chapters 3–5 present the various domains of the De Vogel–Cardamici association, namely the buying and selling of products in various markets, the organization of the Mediterranean passage of the commodities, the procedure for arranging cargo insurance and the foundation of credit and monetary exchange systems that supported the business. The De Vogel letters to Cardamici reveal all the concrete and psychological tools utilized by the Dutch merchant to establish a relationship of trust with his principals and to overcome the difference of provenance, culture, language and religion and collaborate for the sake of business profit. Chapter 6 analyses De Vogel's rhetoric on trust and confidence that he used to convince his Ottoman partners. The letters show how this collaboration worked and developed into a personal exchange of information, advice and demands. As De Vogel's archive does not include incoming letters, our picture of this exchange replies on his monologue. However, the wide range of issues addressed in the letters, the detailed narrative and intensity of expression allow us to compose an imaginary dialogue between De Vogel and the recipients of his letters – a synthesis of spoken or unsaid ideas, opinions, instructions and requests, of deeds and delays.

Dutch merchants in the east, Ottoman merchants in the west

The venture of the Greek Ottoman Cardamici in the West, and the collaboration with the Dutch Thomas De Vogel, developed within the context of the Dutch–Ottoman commercial relations as they evolved in the eighteenth century. By the mid-eighteenth century De Vogel already had dealings with Ottoman and other foreign commercial houses in Smyrna, Constantinople, Aleppo and Ankara. During the same period, Bartholo and Raphael Cardamici attempted, through De Vogel, to build an entrepreneurial bridge that would connect them directly with the international market of Amsterdam and would give them the opportunity to buy and sell merchandise in the geographical triangle of Smyrna, Constantinople and Amsterdam. They also intended to expand their business into other international markets at a later stage. In what follows, we portray the historical environment of Dutch–Ottoman commercial and maritime relations and underline those structural parameters that determined the course of those Ottoman enterprises that sought to expand their transactions to the Netherlands.

Amsterdam: From the golden age to the eighteenth century of transformation

The seventeenth century is considered the golden age of economy, society and civilization of the Dutch Republic. It was the century of the 'Dutch miracle', of unprecedented progress in Dutch shipping and trade all around the world. This development was closely related to conditions innate to the Dutch economy, society and politics and to some others that were connected to the global development in the areas of international commerce and the economy. The Dutch would later bring this miracle to other parts of the world. Among the conditions inherent to the Dutch economy and society that contributed to the development of commerce and shipping was urbanization, which resulted in an extraordinary population density, with almost half of the Dutch population living in urban areas – the highest share in Europe. These conditions explain the continuous traffic in the ports and markets, the regular transports and the need to exploit, to the greatest extent possible, the rivers, channels and sea to facilitate more effective transports.[1] The state of Holland was at the centre of this activity, with Amsterdam being the principal international port. Situated along the Dutch coast, Zeeland, Friesland, Groningen and part of Utrecht were also open to the sea and they also participated in this activity.[2]

The international growth in Dutch trade and shipping was first evident in the Baltic Sea trade and then in Iberia. In fact, since the seventeenth century the principal foreign trade transactions of the Dutch were in grain, raw materials and commodities shipped in from the Baltic countries. This activity accounted for 60 per cent of the circulating capital of the Low Countries and almost 800 ships.[3] Dutch ships and Dutch merchants were active in a geographical area that extended from the Baltic, Flanders, France and Germany in the North to the Iberian Peninsula in the South, with Seville being the centre of commodity and monetary traffic and representing an opening to the Americas. Through the Dutch, Spain imported grain, raw materials and manufactured products and exchanged them for coins, which the Dutch used to pay off their debits in the North. The exchange of Baltic grain for American gold, silver and coins that arrived in large quantities in Seville and Cadiz constituted the principal transaction on which the seventeenth-century Dutch miracle was founded.[4]

In this dynamic conjuncture Amsterdam played a leading role as the centre of Dutch and international trade and a major entrepôt. The port was the principal entrepreneurial junction in an international network of ports and commercial centres serving maritime transports from the North and Baltic Seas to the Atlantic and Mediterranean.[5] The port and its extensive storage facilities gave rise to considerable commercial and maritime activities.[6] On Amsterdam's market wheat, corn, timber and minerals from northern and western Europe, salt from the Bay of Biscay, and wool and silver from Spain, arrived and were exchanged for herrings from the Atlantic Ocean, and wine and textiles from various Mediterranean countries.[7] The creation of a powerful and technically advanced Dutch commercial navy that was as big as, according to contemporaries, all the European navies put together played a major contribution to the development of Dutch trade. This navy was manned with a high number of efficient sailors.[8] According to French calculations, at the end of the seventeenth century the Dutch merchant marine comprised around 6,000 vessels, each of which weighed

100 tons and had an average crew of eight sailors; a 600,000-ton and 48,000-man merchant marine seems a huge number for that period, but as Braudel maintains, it probably reflected reality.[9] According to various other calculations, in this period the Dutch merchant marine comprised twice as many vessels as the English and nine times as many as the French.[10] An additional advantage of the Dutch navy, which made it unbeatable by the others, was that it comprised large vessels that could be chartered at relatively low freights and could therefore transfer large cargoes at a very low cost. Chartering Dutch ships was therefore extremely profitable, especially for foreign merchants, given that the additional duties charged by the Dutch consular authorities were also very low. Therefore, European, English and Ottoman merchants chose Dutch vessels to transfer their merchandise in Europe.[11] By 1615, 100 Dutch ships were participating in the Levantine trade, many of which carried English cargoes to Ottoman ports.[12]

During the 'golden' seventeenth century, the Dutch trade expanded from the Rhine to the Alps, in Germany, France, Poland, Scandinavia and Russia. And yet, as R. T. Rapp maintains, the Dutch, as the English, found in the Mediterranean Sea a real gold mine which they sought to exploit.[13] Already from the end of the sixteenth century, and throughout the famines, Dutch vessels loaded with grain crossed the Gibraltar straits and were directed to the Eastern Mediterranean to the countries of North Africa, Livorno (Leghorn) and the Ottoman ports. Expanding their transactions to southern Europe and the East, Dutch merchants and shipowners developed into major carriers of merchandise from Europe to the Ottoman Empire and back. At the same time, they carried through commercial enterprises for their own account or for the account of other Dutch and foreign commercial houses; they sometimes sailed under a foreign flag and under foreign protection.[14] During the same period Dutch vessels reached some new exotic destinations in South Africa, India, Sri Lanka, Java, Suriname, China and Japan.[15]

From the second half of the seventeenth century this particularly positive circumstance gradually reversed. The enactment of the English Navigation Laws in 1651 and 1660 excluded Dutch ships from English commerce, with particularly negative consequences for the activity of many Dutch commercial enterprises[16] as with the new legislation England sought to block all foreign merchant fleets from its trade.[17] This new situation obliged the Dutch to utilize almost permanently the port of Livorno as an intermediary station in their itineraries: in the port of Tuscany they loaded English textiles and other commodities and they transported them to Smyrna.[18] The English–Dutch wars, the outcome of Anglo–Dutch rivalry in the markets and the sea, exhausted even further the dynamism of the Dutch merchant navy and interrupted drastically its momentum.[19] The involvement of the Netherlands in the European wars against France contributed to the enfeeblement of Dutch economy at the end of the seventeenth century and constrained the Dutch to diminish commercial transactions with the English and the French merchants. By the end of the eighteenth century, the conditions that had prevailed a century before had been modified dramatically: England and France had become European and colonial superpowers, and they dominated the Mediterranean maritime commerce and navigation. The position of the Dutch had weakened considerably.[20] For the two rival European powers, the Ottoman Empire represented an invaluable market for the distribution of European textiles, manufactured commodities and colonial goods; in the Ottoman markets the European merchants could buy raw silk, cotton, leathers, dyes, products for pharmaceutical use and the necessary raw materials for the developing manufacture and industrial sectors of the two countries.[21]

Under the pressure of the Anglo–French commercial rivalry, the Dutch trading activity languished definitively. According to Andrea Metrà, the crisis of Dutch commerce and navigation since the eighteenth century was also related to three very important structural factors of the country's economy. First, the Dutch Republic lacked natural resources that would allow local industries to thrive; second, the government's customs policy was directed steadily towards the support of commerce and imports against local manufacture and industry. Finally, the Dutch Republic had known great progress as the 'broker' and the 'carrier' of Europe. The maritime and financial market of Amsterdam, in particular, was very vulnerable to the protectionist policies adopted by many European countries. The aforementioned English navigation laws, and the customs policies adopted by not only France and Britain but also other lesser countries like Sweden, gave a very strong blow to the Netherlands by not allowing it to continue to operate as Europe's intermediary, a role it had operated with great success.[22] Until the mid-eighteenth century, the ports of North Germany, Bremen, Altona, but mostly Hamburg, gradually replaced Amsterdam. As has already been mentioned, in 1750 the volume of sugar, coffee and indigo arriving to Hamburg from France was three times greater than that arriving to the Dutch port. The same applied to overland trade, as the old commercial routes passing through the Netherlands were replaced by others connecting commercial centres directly with ports. The advanced Dutch shipping industry was no longer a Dutch achievement and for what concerned the cost of the freights, since the mid-eighteenth-century French and British merchant ships were offering equally low prices with the Dutch to those merchants who wished to charter their ships to carry their merchandise.[23] From this period a gradual decrease of the number of Dutch merchants who were established in various cities of the Ottoman Empire was evident – with the exception of Smyrna, which remained the centre of Dutch trade and navigation in the Eastern Mediterranean.

Recent studies have questioned the image of a sharp, complete and definite retreat of the Dutch from the area of international trade and sea transport, in particular from the Eastern Mediterranean.[24] For what concerns the Dutch economy, in particular, it appears that the Dutch continued to play a significant role in the area of international trade and, in any case, retained control of the international banking and financial transactions by investing in the public and the private sectors of several countries. If the eighteenth-century Amsterdam had lost its paramount position as a commercial, maritime and financial centre of Europe and was replaced by London, Hamburg and even Paris,[25] it did not cease to be a point of reference for the international commercial and maritime transactions. In 1735, a traveller counted two thousand vessels anchored in the port, a port full of life, glutted with vessels of all different types and flags.[26] Meanwhile, Amsterdam's banking sector developed even more in order to respond to the great financial and credit needs of Europe, particularly during war, and to the great increase of the volume of bills transacted globally.[27] In 1728, William Defoe wrote that the Dutch were still 'the Carryers of the World, the middle Persons in Trade, the Factors and Brokers of Europe'.[28]

Dutch merchants in the Ottoman Empire: The institutional context

Dutch awareness of Levantine commerce was first manifested in the late sixteenth century, when, as it has been maintained, some Dutch merchants from Antwerp were established in Constantinople.[29] At that time the government of the seven independent states that had founded the confederation of the Low Countries following the treaty of Utrecht in 1579 had not established diplomatic relations with the Ottoman Porte.[30] Dutch subjects, merchants, shipowners and marines were constrained to travel and transact within the empire under the protection of some other European power. Already from 1569, when the Low Countries were under Habsburg rule, the Dutch traded in the East under French protection and their vessels sailed in the Eastern Mediterranean under French flags.[31] This special relationship between the Low Countries and France was mentioned in the French capitulations of 1597, signed by France and Sultan Mehmed III.[32] As anticipated, the progress of Dutch commercial transactions and navigation in the Eastern Mediterranean under French protection[33] stimulated the reaction of English merchants; in 1580 English merchants established diplomatic and commercial relation with the Ottoman Empire, formally through the English-chartered Levant Company.[34] The English ambassador in Constantinople, Sir Edward Barton, in one of his letters to the Levant Company in London, mentioned Dutch attempts to approach England and operate under English protection; it also relayed the concern that the presence of Dutch merchants in the Levant had caused to members of the company. As Barton mentioned, 'some Dutch' had arrived in Constantinople, had presented themselves to him as travellers and asked him for his protection in order to proceed with some commercial transactions. The incident elicited a very strong reaction from some members of the Levant Company, but its administration responded with composure, deciding that since it was pointless to obstruct the advance of Dutch merchants in the East, it would be ultimately wiser to offer them the possibility to operate under English protection, motivating them to pass under the control of the English authorities.[35] To carry through this resolution, orders were sent to the company's officials and members in the Ottoman Empire asking them to treat the Dutch merchants with kindness and generosity.[36]

In the following years, as it is revealed by a later letter of the English ambassador, Henry Lello, to Robert Cecil (14 November 1599), Dutch merchants and shipowners showed a very explicit preference for English protection, which guaranteed them the support of the Levant Company, the English diplomatic authorities, and free use of the English flag.[37] This preference was connected to the fact that a very significant field of Dutch trade in the East had been in the traffic of commodities from and to English ports, an activity interrupted only when the English government enacted the first navigation law.[38] The special relationship between Dutch and English merchants in the East brought mutual benefits. The high taxes and duties the Dutch merchants and shipowners paid to Levant Company officials in return for their protection were a very important source of revenue for the English chartered-company and enabled it to cover part of its expenses. For this reason, until the signing of separate Dutch capitulations by the Dutch government and the Ottoman Porte, the English diplomatic authorities strove to retain the right to protect Dutch subjects, despite the severe reactions of France.

In 1612 Cornelis Haga, special envoy of the Low Countries, arrived in Constantinople, with the mission to promote the signing of a capitulation agreement with the Ottoman authorities.[39] In July of that year, Haga succeeded in signing an agreement with Sultan Ahmed I;[40] the agreement bore many similarities to the French and English capitulations.[41] The Dutch were guaranteed permission to trade in cotton, cotton yarn, leather, wax and silk from Aleppo (article 3). They could import lead, iron, steel and tin (articles 43 and 46) to be utilized as raw material in the Ottoman armament industry. In 1634, a new capitulation agreement signed by Sultan Murad IV repeated the privileges and benefits bestowed to the Dutch under the previous 1612 capitulations.[42]

Even after the signing of the Dutch capitulations, Dutch merchants and shipowners continued to utilize the English protection and the flag in order to travel in the Mediterranean and to safely and easily operate in Ottoman markets. In the English capitulations of 1675,[43] an article stated that Dutch merchants operating under the protection of the Queen of England would be recognized by the Ottoman authorities with the status of English subjects in Ottoman territory.[44] As England's protegees, they would pay consular duties to the English ambassador and consuls.[45] This meant, among others, that they would benefit from all the tax exemptions offered to English merchants by the Ottoman authorities and that they would pay the Ottoman customs a duty of 3 per cent on the value of all the merchandise imported into the Ottoman Empire, similar to the English merchants.[46] This issue, as anticipated, created friction between England and France and negatively influenced the diplomatic relations between the two countries for a long period.[47] The collaboration of the Dutch and English, which continued into the eighteenth century, also took the form of business associations.[48] This particular relationship of friendship, collaboration and competition was furthered by the establishment of family relationships mostly through intercommunal marriages and the sociability encouraged by the similarities of the Anglican and Protestant dogmas.[49]

From quite early on, the government of the Low Countries had considered the foundation of an independent authority that would be entrusted with the management and supervision of Dutch trade and navigation in Eastern Mediterranean. In 1625, on Haga's proposal, the Directory of Levant Trade and Mediterranean Navigation (Directie van de Levantse Handel en Navigatie op de Middellandse Zee) was founded to support, supervise and control Dutch commerce and navigation in the Eastern Mediterranean.[50] In its organization, structure and jurisdiction, it greatly resembled equivalent European bodies, particularly the English Levant Company.[51] Nevertheless, a fundamental difference between the English and Dutch companies decisively affected the profile and the control of the two bodies: in order to have commercial transactions in the Ottoman Empire, an English merchant ought to be a member of the Levant Company and, at least until 1773, of an elite of wholesale merchants; on the contrary, a Dutch merchant was free to operate in the Ottoman Empire without being a member of any institution or belonging to a distinguished group of merchants. As Metrà comments, despite the fact that Dutch commerce was under the jurisdiction of an institution that applied and imposed specific regulations and controlled commercial transactions and transports, all Dutch merchants were free to participate in it.[52] This democratic and liberal approach was due partly to the absence of a powerful central government that could, as was the case in other European countries, manipulate the economy and take protective measures or privilege specific social or professional groups. In the case of the Dutch Republic, the country's government in The Hague was in the hands of the delegates of seven small independent states, which had formed a pluralistic confederation.[53]

The Directory, which had its headquarters in Amsterdam, comprised eight directors and a secretary, who were elected by the councillors of Amsterdam's local government.[54] Its responsibilities were administrative and supervisory, and the directors' main task was to implement the central government's policies and execute resolutions and laws. The Directory's principal concern was defending Dutch merchants from piracy and enemy navies.[55] It selected and appointed Dutch consuls in the Ottoman Empire and North Africa and collected consular fees and duties from merchants and shipowners. An officer was responsible for inspecting the vessels arriving at the port of Amsterdam, while a group of employees was tasked with collecting duties. The patents, all the official documents and the bills of lading carried by the vessels were examined in both Dutch and Ottoman ports.

The Directory followed the example of the English Levant Company as regards the appointment and the establishment of diplomatic representatives in the Ottoman Empire; it also devised a taxation system of sorts for commercial transaction and transports.[56] To cover the expenses of maintaining diplomatic officials in the empire, the Directory collected all the duties and consular fees paid by Dutch and foreigners.[57] A 1633 decree ordered that every Dutch or foreign vessel leaving Amsterdam's port or any other Dutch port, with or without cargo, pay 1 florin for every last of capacity.[58] The Directory collected also a duty of 2 per cent on the value of merchandise arriving in the Dutch Republic from the East – this percentage was later halved – while a series of resolutions in 1671 and 1679 imposed a duty of 5 per cent on the freights of all vessels arriving from the Levant. In 1773, another duty of ½ per cent was imposed on specific commodities imported from the Levant, such as silk, yarn, rice, sodium, saltpetre, camel wool, carpets, salt, bonnets, ribbons, various other substances for pharmaceutical use, hems, edgings and so on.[59] After 1770, the Dutch government imposed a new duty of 5 per cent on the value of all the commodities that arrived in Amsterdam from the Levant loaded on foreign and Ottoman – but not Dutch – vessels; the main reason for this decision was to halt the free entry of foreigners, Ottoman subjects in particular, into Dutch trade.[60]

Dutch trade in the East

Dutch trade in the Levant can only been interpreted as part of the broader phenomenon of the reinforcement of the European commercial relations with the Ottoman Empire since the sixteenth century.[61] The first Dutch to operate in the empire transferred their business to the traditional commercial centres, Smyrna, Cyprus, Cairo and Aleppo.[62] With Amsterdam being usually the port of departure, they sent Dutch products, English and German textiles, grains from northern Europe and industrial and manufactured commodities to the Levant. For their return trip they loaded Levantine products and raw materials, which they transferred to various European countries, mainly England. In Smyrna, the principal destination of Dutch vessels, the Dutch trafficked colonial goods, raw materials, precious metals, European and Dutch textiles and other manufactured products. They loaded Levantine goods destined for various European ports, foodstuffs, cotton, wool, leathers, yarn and threads, dyes and drugs for pharmaceutical use.[63] By the seventeenth century, their coordinated and well-organized activity allowed the Dutch to prevail over the Venetians and the French and develop into very significant competitors of the English. The Dutch managed to enter the English textile trade as carriers and distributors, having as their intermediary station Livorno and destination various Ottoman ports. Similarly, the Dutch assumed a very important intermediary role in the trade of colonial goods, mainly spices, coffee, sugar and metals, to Ottoman ports that had been transported from the East Indies via Amsterdam or Hamburg.[64] During this time the cooperation of the Dutch with Ottoman nationals – Muslims, Christians and Jews – was extended to the field of trade in bulk and luxury goods. Dutch ships arrived at Ottoman ports via intermediate stations in Hamburg, Danzig, Enkhuizen, Rotterdam, Dordrecht, Cadiz, Lisbon, Emden, Barcelona, Marseille, Genoa, Naples, Livorno, Malta and Zakynthos, and the Dutch lion dollar emerged as the currency of choice in the empire's markets.[65]

For what concerns Dutch trade in Smyrna in particular, it seems that as early as 1669, the international port had developed into a key port for the reception of ships originating in Amsterdam. Dutch ships transported large quantities of English textiles, spices from the East Indies, lead, tin, copper and foreign currency to Smyrna. At the end of the seventeenth century some Dutch companies exported fabrics made in Amsterdam, Rotterdam and Leiden, as well as German fabrics from Leipzig, to the city.[66] Returning to Europe, Dutch ships transported various goods and products from the East, mainly raw silk and mohair yarn, which were often utilized in the mohair and silk textile industries in France. It is estimated that by the end of the seventeenth century, four to five Dutch ships arrived in Smyrna each year.[67]

The gradual halt in the dynamic of Dutch trade and shipping from the end of the eighteenth century appears to have affected Dutch trade in the East as well. According to calculations by the Levant Company, which closely monitored trade in Ottoman ports, in 1702 the value of the Dutch textile trade had halved compared to twenty years before while in the 1670s only one or two Dutch traders were established in Aleppo, which did not justify the presence in the city of a Dutch consul.[68] Although weakened, the activity of the Dutch trading houses continued due to the key role of the Amsterdam commercial and financial market within the international trading system as well as the uninterrupted operation of the Dutch banking system for trading, saving and transferring capital worldwide. Meanwhile, international conflicts, the subsequent treaties and the necessary adjustments to the economic policy of European governments shaped an ever-changing environment in international transport and trade, giving nationals of individual neutral countries, in this case the Dutch, the opportunity to exploit the circumstances to their advantage.[69] Therefore, in times of crisis, the Dutch merchants and shipowners resumed the activity of intermediaries and carriers which had made great profits for them in the seventeenth century. When during the War of the Austrian Succession (1740–8) and the Seven Years' War (1756–63) French navigation in the Mediterranean was hampered by the English navy, the French allowed foreign nationals to transfer cargoes between France and the Ottoman Empire. Thus, the Dutch were integrated into the French commercial networks of the East and undertook to represent French trading houses. A similar juncture that favoured Dutch shipping in the Mediterranean in the mid-eighteenth century was England's decision in 1753 to ban the import and unloading of goods originating in the East at its ports without the presentation of a clean bill of health issued by the British consul at the ship's port of origin – unless the goods had been quarantined in Malta, Venice, Ancona, Messina,

Livorno, Genoa or Marseille. This decision, which was intended to protect the country from the spread of infectious diseases, in particular the plague that often affected the Ottoman ports, was particularly damaging to the trade carried out by the English merchants and members of the Levant Company between the Ottoman Empire, Spain, Portugal and Britain. This was because the stay of the goods in quarantine for long periods of time led to long delays in the conduct of trade. This objective difficulty was quickly exploited by Dutch traders and shipowners. According to the Dutch government resolution, Dutch consignments arriving from countries in plague were quarantined for only forty days in the Netherlands, and therefore merchants who traded goods, especially those transporting cotton from the Ottoman Empire, gained a significant time advantage over everyone else. As expected, this development was the trigger for the transport of large shipments of cotton to England by Dutch ships during the reign of George III (1760–1820); in 1792, the Netherlands arrived to supply Britain with more than half the quantity of cotton imported from the Ottoman Empire.[70] Meanwhile, after the 1760s, the trade in Dutch fabric on the Ottoman markets showed a relative increase compared to previous decades but could not surpass British and French exports.[71]

The Cardamici–De Vogel collaboration took place in the second half of the eighteenth century, a period during which there was a significant extension of the activity of the Dutch merchant fleet in the Eastern Mediterranean. Having examined this period in his recent work, Thierry Allain aptly characterizes it as interbellum between the end of the Seven Years' War and the beginning of the Fourth Anglo–Dutch War;[72] Allain also underlines the Netherlands' neutral stance in the conflicts between the French and the English, Russians and Ottomans, before and after that period. Having studied the record of ship arrivals and departures of the Dutch consulate in Smyrna, Allain argues that on average thirteen Dutch ships departed the port per year, but with significant deviations; two-thirds of these ships had Amsterdam as their destination. Between 1763 and 1780, the average value of cargo carried by Dutch ships on a direct voyage from Smyrna to Amsterdam was 130,877 florins, which is undoubtedly significant (49 florins corresponded to 100 livre tournois). According to the manifests filed with the Dutch consulate, the consignments from Smyrna to Amsterdam mainly included textile products such as cotton and cotton yarn, silk and muslin. Similarly, Dutch ships arriving in Smyrna transported iron and steel products from northern Europe, craft products and colonial goods, mainly sugar and coffee.[73] Despite a significant reduction in the number of members of the local Dutch trading community, Smyrna remained a key centre of Dutch trade and shipping in the Mediterranean,[74] and in 1750 about 100 Dutch traders lived there out of a total of 700 to 800 Europeans.

Allain's conclusion, which is based on research in the archives of the Dutch consulate in Smyrna, is that Dutch merchant ships maintained during this period a significant dynamic in the trade of the East despite the difficulties faced by the Dutch trading houses.[75] This happened because the activity of the Dutch merchant fleet was largely financed by Ottoman merchant houses which, from the mid-eighteenth century, had increasingly become involved in Dutch trade of the East.[76] The Ottoman merchants, according to Allain, used Dutch traders as intermediaries in their transactions abroad, which allowed Dutch merchants and shipowners to continue with their activity in the Levant throughout the eighteenth century.

The Cardamici–De Vogel cooperation was inextricably linked to all the above conditions which determined the evolution of Dutch trade in the Ottoman Empire; it arose out of a favourable situation of recovery for Dutch merchant shipping and trade in the Eastern Mediterranean and, finally, it was a collaboration that bore profit and opportunities for both partners. At the same time, the launching of the Cardamici enterprise in the West was part of a broader phenomenon where Ottoman trading companies established themselves in Amsterdam from the first decades of the eighteenth century.

Ottoman merchants and Dutch trade in the eighteenth century

The development of trading transactions between Dutch and Ottoman subjects in the eighteenth century had two direct and interrelated consequences. The first was the decisive entry of Ottoman merchants, mainly of Greek, Armenian and Jewish origin, into the trade and shipping businesses of Amsterdam, either through their establishment in the international port or through the representation of their businesses by on-site commercial agents.[77] The second consequence, which was the result of the first one, was the establishment in Amsterdam of one of the first and most active Greek trading communities outside the Ottoman Empire.[78] Members of the merchant community represented in the local market trading houses of Smyrna and Constantinople and, over time, they became intermediaries in the transactions of Dutch merchants with trading houses from the Ottoman Empire.

As has been already argued, the liberal, progressive and flexible legal regime in force in the economic and trade sectors in the Netherlands played a decisive role in the increased participation of Ottoman subjects in Dutch trade in the East, as well as to their free establishment on Dutch territory.[79] For many historians, the limited intervention of the Dutch state in the economy was due more to the inefficiency of the state mechanism and to a system of governance that was a permanent source of conflict between the representatives of the various provinces in the federal government of the Netherlands. However, successive governments, and in particular the representatives of the local government of Holland, were in every circumstance prepared to overlook political and ideological controversies in order to serve economic and commercial interests and protect the country's prestige and power.[80]

In particular, the arrangements concerning the expansion of Dutch trade to the Ottoman Empire opened the way for the Dutch to cooperate freely with Ottoman subjects. Firstly, traders of all professional and social provenance, irrespective of their economic situation, were able to participate freely in Dutch trading and shipping in the East. The Dutch state permitted trading transactions with foreign traders, who were not charged excessive or additional payments of taxes and duties. Those Dutch and foreign merchant entrepreneurs who wished could charter Dutch-flagged ships and trade with the Ottoman Empire for their own account or for the account of others.[81] The Dutch merchants and shipowners were thus allowed to do business with merchants of Ottoman and other foreign nationality, both on Ottoman and Dutch territory, a situation which offered them great strategic flexibility; this was the trigger for the establishment in Amsterdam of an important community of Ottoman merchants.[82]

The establishment of merchant communities by Armenian, Jewish and Greek Ottoman subjects was made possible by a climate of religious tolerance and independence. The coexistence within the Netherlands of many different religious groups – Catholics, Lutherans, Protestants and Jews – resulted in the prevalence of a climate of religious independence within society combined with the recognition of individual freedoms.[83] Amsterdam, as the operational centre of an international market economy, could only be open to all people, regardless of religion and nationality, especially as they eventually became active members of the local economy, contributed wealth and were integrated into the local community.

Ismail Hakki Kadi provides an in-depth account of how trading transactions between Dutch and Ottoman merchant houses developed during this period.[84] Having as their main activity the traffic of goods to and from the Ottoman Empire, the Dutch companies of the seventeenth century either cooperated with Dutch agents, permanently established in the Ottoman Empire, or sent on the spot their younger partners, who promoted and carried out the transactions of the company for certain periods.[85] The eighteenth century, however, saw significant change in the way Dutch merchants conducted business in Ottoman commercial centres and ports. In Smyrna, the members of the Dutch merchant community ceased to represent exclusively Dutch companies in Amsterdam or other Dutch cities. On the contrary, as independent trading companies, they received goods to and from the Netherlands on behalf of Dutch and foreign traders, receiving a commission ranging from 2 to 2.5 per cent for the sale and 2.5 to 4 per cent for the purchase of goods. These rates of commission provided them with an income of between 5 and 6 per cent of the total value of a commercial transaction. In this way, they maintained a large margin of autonomy in the organization and strategy of their businesses and were not bound by partnerships with specific companies in Amsterdam and Rotterdam; on the contrary, they were able to represent many different companies and, at the same time, trade on their behalf or on behalf of other Ottoman and foreign companies based in the Ottoman Empire.

Throughout the eighteenth century Smyrna remained a key port for the arrival and departure of ships flying the Dutch flag originating from Amsterdam and Rotterdam and a centre for the arrival and distribution of goods on behalf of Dutch companies. Despite the significant decline in its members since the previous century, the local Dutch merchant community maintained its momentum; Dutch houses established in the port developed associations and joint ventures with other European and Ottoman commercial houses in the city.[86] Elena Frangakis-Syrett confirms the increased number of arrivals of Dutch ships in the port in the mid-eighteenth century. At the same time, she reveals the integration of a significant number of Dutch merchants into the local market, who, in cooperation with Ottomans, engaged in wide-ranging activity as merchants, brokers, bankers and shipowners. Therefore, between August 1760 and August 1763, an average number of 15.3 Dutch ships arrived at Smyrna annually. Between February 1764 and August 1780 the figure fell to 10.2 ships.[87] The increased arrivals of Dutch ships in Smyrna between 1760 and 1780 are also confirmed by Allain's calculations, which also demonstrate that Dutch trading business maintained an important and stable foothold in the Eastern Mediterranean in the second half of the eighteenth century. The ships originated in Amsterdam, Rotterdam, various ports in Germany, Belgium, France, Spain, Portugal, Italy as well as other smaller Ottoman ports; on the return journey from Smyrna the ships approached various ports, Leghorn usually being one of them.[88] The consignments were transported to merchants of different nationalities and ethnicities, including Armenian, Jewish and Greek Ottoman subjects. Several ships engaged in coastal trade from one Ottoman port to another, mainly on the Smyrna–Constantinople and Smyrna–Alexandria routes, trading in British and French fabrics and other goods loaded in Marseille, Livorno, Genoa and other Italian ports.[89] Members of the Dutch merchant community in Smyrna were also actively involved in banking and monetary transactions.[90] In particular, the transfer of foreign currency by Dutch ships and its introduction in the Ottoman markets was carried out with the permission of the Dutch government.

In attempting to explore and interpret the reasons that led many Ottoman merchants to cooperate with Dutch companies from the second half of the eighteenth century, Hakki Kadi comes to a number of interesting conclusions. This development was directly related to Amsterdam's stable primacy as an international market for products, capital, freight and insurance. As mentioned above, the international financial system continued to rely on the city's well-organized and reliable banking system for several more decades, until London's emergence as an international trading and financial trading hub.[91] It is no coincidence that the bulk of bills of exchange circulating in Smyrna at that time were issued in the Dutch port.[92] The advanced institutional organization of the commercial and maritime sector of the country's economy and Amsterdam's excellent infrastructure had created an ideal environment for the promotion and management of trade, capital and maritime transactions, thus supporting the country's trading and shipping through international cooperation.[93] For the Ottomans, as for all European merchants, Amsterdam was a safe and reliable market where they could obtain all different types of merchandise, cash, credit, foreign exchange, bonds and bills. The cooperation of Ottoman merchants with Dutch commercial houses and commercial representatives had significant comparative advantages over cooperation with other Europeans. Moreover, the cooperation of Ottomans with the Dutch was free and flexible while cooperation with English and French trading houses inside Ottoman markets was carried out on an equal basis only after the end of the eighteenth century, always within specific regulatory frameworks or by violating them.[94] At the time, Ottoman subjects were not allowed to set up businesses in the London or Marseille markets, whereas Amsterdam was a friendly and safe environment for opening offices and expanding their businesses.[95]

The establishment of a Greek Ottoman merchant community in Amsterdam in the 1750s and 1760s[96] was the starting point for unprecedented involvement of Greek Ottoman merchants in Dutch trade. The Greek community comprised wholesale merchants from Smyrna, Chios, Thessaloniki and Zagora,[97] retailers, agents and commercial employees. Around them gathered members of their families and a 'moving population' of friends, employees, merchants and businessmen, sailors, loggers and priests.[98] From the personal correspondence of two members of the community, Stamatis Petrou, a merchant and employee of a well-known merchant and intellectual Adamantios Korais, and the merchant Ioannis Prigkos, we can draw interesting information about the organization and strategy of local Greek companies.[99] We can learn about the relationship of the Ottoman Greeks with members of other merchant communities, their transactions with each other as well as their autonomous participation in the Stock Exchange of goods and securities of the city.[100] As Petrou put it, most Greek merchant houses took the form of a *syntrofia* (limited partnership) with a specific number of partners investing capital and participating in profits and losses at a percentage proportional with the capital they had invested. Petrou mentions the names of some important merchants of the local Greek community, among them Ioannis Prigkos, Stefanos Isaiou and Tuffektzoglou, Rigas & Niotis, Jasegiroglou and Antonios Zingrilaras.[101] The headquarters of some of these companies were located in the Ottoman Empire, usually in Smyrna, and their representation abroad was taken over by other trading houses, in some cases by partners in the same company and in some others by appointed representatives. Most of the Greek companies that were established in the Dutch port or had secured their representation on the local market had as their main and often sole activity the traffic of goods.[102] Transit trade with the East remained for a long time the most important occupation of Ottoman traders, Hakki Kadi points out, despite the fact that Amsterdam was the ideal place from which they could promote their transactions worldwide, diversify their economic activities and join an international business network. However, as it turns out, when the Ottoman merchants decided to expand and invest capital in other sectors of the economy, they made sure that these sectors were closely linked to their commercial activity. Commercial shipping in the Mediterranean was a trade-related sector and therefore several Ottoman traders in Amsterdam and Rotterdam appear to have invested in the Dutch merchant ship market.[103]

The existence of a Greek merchant community in Amsterdam with significant interconnections within the city and activity that extended to the trading and shipping sectors was expected to change the rules of the game for all other merchant houses that traded between Amsterdam, Smyrna and Constantinople. According to the testimonies of Prigkos and Petrou, many Greek companies in Smyrna began to abandon their previous partnerships and to cooperate with Greek merchants established in Amsterdam in order to represent them in their transactions in the international port.[104] These partnerships elicited a strong reaction from local Dutch companies, which until then had undertaken, almost exclusively, the representation of Ottoman merchant houses in the Dutch market.[105] In order to protect their activity and profits, the Dutch traders and shipowners went so far as to denounce the moderate and liberal policy of their governments and called for a halt to the uncontrolled involvement of Ottoman merchants in Dutch trade with the Ottoman Empire. The positions and rights of traders and shipowners were supported in various memorandums by ambassadors and consuls, as well as members of the Dutch merchant communities established in the Ottoman Empire. This concerted effort was mainly directed towards merchants of Ottoman citizenship, mostly Greeks, Armenians and Jews, who had managed to exploit the possibilities offered to them by the outward policy of the Dutch government. The result of this general reaction was a review of this policy and the introduction of new, stricter, regulations and control mechanisms in the trade and shipping sectors. Furthermore, the Dutch authorities imposed additional duties on Eastern goods and products transported by foreign ships to Amsterdam.[106] Finally, on the initiative of the Dutch merchant community of Smyrna, an amendment to the regulation on the transport of cargo by Dutch ships was introduced so that the Dutch trading houses could reap some benefits. There was also a call to give authorization to import goods from the East only to those merchants who transported their consignments by Dutch ships or by ships from countries which respectively authorized Dutch traders to import goods from the East into their countries.[107] The intention of the Dutch merchants established in the Ottoman Empire was to control and restrict, through this arrangement, the ability of the English and French to transport goods freely in the Netherlands by interfering and influencing the country's trade and textile industry. In fact, up to that point, the English and French were authorized by the Dutch authorities to sell freely on the Dutch market Ottoman mohair yarns which they had exchanged in the market of Smyrna with large quantities of fabrics from their countries. This procedure allowed them to place their fabrics on local Ottoman markets and to increase the prices of mohair threads in Smyrna, which was eventually directed at the expense of Dutch traders as well as the Dutch textile industry. While the interventions of the Dutch government seem to have finally succeeded in curbing the uncontrolled involvement of European traders in Dutch trade, it does not appear to have achieved the same in the case of Ottoman subjects. As it seems, the Dutch authorities tried, since the mid-eighteenth century, to implement a policy of 'imperceptible protectionism', that is, by adopting a series of mild measures that restricted the trade of Greek, Jewish and Armenian Ottoman subjects. As it turned out, this strategy had no effect.[108] Each package of new restrictive measures alerted the reflexes of the Ottoman merchants who devised new methods to circumvent the prohibitions and continue their unhindered trade with the Netherlands.

Merchants and correspondents

The first letter we refer to from the letterbooks of the Dutch merchant Thomas De Vogel addressed to Bartholo Cardamici is dated 7 March 1760.[1] Both its content and the style of writing indicate that this was not the first exploratory understanding between the client merchant and the merchant acting as his commercial correspondent; on the contrary, it is clear that the cooperation between the two merchants had started earlier. In this letter, De Vogel informed Cardamici that he had taken care to procure and send him two barrels of pistols while he had put in another order, at his request, for the manufacture of a quantity of pistols and nails. In addition, De Vogel wrote that he had been unable to charter a ship to Smyrna at an advantageous price to send him the sugar he had ordered and had, therefore, been forced to postpone the purchase of the product in question. He also expressed his enthusiasm at learning Cardamici had found high-quality cotton on the Smyrna market at an advantageous price. He even urged him to buy and send him a shipment that he would make sure to sell in Amsterdam at the greatest possible profit on his behalf. In concluding the letter, De Vogel assured Cardamici that he had experience in handling cotton, as he represented other companies trading this product on the local market. Cardamici therefore had every reason to trust his judgement and intention as his main concern was to propose investments in commodities that would bring him great profits.

The letter revealed at once the basic characteristics of cooperation between the two trading houses. Thomas De Vogel & Son, as a commercial correspondent of Bartholo Cardamici & Co. in Amsterdam, bought and sold goods on its behalf, in consultation with the head of the company, Bartholo Cardamici, and his nephew Raphael, who ran a branch of the company in Constantinople. De Vogel also provided Cardamici with additional financial, insurance and maritime services, receiving from them a commission on transactions; at the same time, he provided them with information and advised them on how to move within the markets to promote their businesses.

The study of the evolution of international trade in the eighteenth century underscores the fundamental importance of representation in a broad geographical area and demonstrates the difficulties in organizing a reliable and effective international system of representatives.[2] The agency problem, or the problem of 'principal-agent' as it referred to in the social sciences, concerns the high probability that an appointed commercial correspondent, in our case De Vogel, would exploit the geographical distance separating him from his principal/client, the Cardamicis, and serve his personal interest instead of the common interest.[3] The issue of the representation of a commercial company abroad was therefore closely linked to the creation of 'personal' relationships of trust that would ensure the good cooperation of all those involved in the business. Already in the seventeenth century trade manuals referred constantly to the importance of trust between a merchant and a commercial agent/correspondent.[4] Social and historical scientists have explored the exact meaning and significance of this primordial feeling that throughout the evolution of commercial capitalism has been a cornerstone of commercial relations. Diego Gambetta's view, in the *Trust: Making and Breaking Cooperative Relations*, is that trust is an expression and act of faith based on our personal judgement; when one says that we trust someone or that someone is trustworthy, one means indirectly that the possibility that they will carry out an act that will be beneficial to them is so great that they engage in some form of cooperation with them.[5]

In exploring the concept of trust in specific historical examples, historians Sebouh Aslanian and Tijl Vanneste formulated separate definitions. The former states that trust was a person's ability to be certain that another person to whom he had 'trusted' an object or entrusted him with an act would not act in a way that would be harmful to him.[6] The latter, on the other hand, elaborates on the concept of 'commercial trust', arguing that it is a personal assessment of a trader's reputation by another and is linked to the latter's expectation of the future conduct of the former.[7]

The establishment of a trust relationship between a merchant like Cardamici and his correspondent De Vogel was of fundamental importance. If it was undermined in any way, it endangered both the capital of an enterprise and the good name of both. To expand his activity to a broad geographical area and reduce the risks of unreliable and inadequate representation, Cardamici had to choose between alternatives. He could take over the representation of his business in various distant markets himself, a choice that would nevertheless cost him time, would have an impact on the organization of the business and would make it almost impossible to manage and exploit opportunities that would arise simultaneously in different geographical locations. A second solution was to entrust the task of representing him in the same market to more than one representative. This option, however, significantly increased the company's costs and may have posed even greater risks as he would be obliged to remotely check the reliability and adequacy of more than one partner. The signing of a cooperation agreement with a commercial correspondent, as a third solution, could ensure the faithful observance of the contract from a distance; it seems, however, that this practice was not particularly widespread at the time as it was very difficult to predict and record in a written agreement all possible scenarios that would require action and cooperation in unforeseen conditions. Finally, some merchants chose the establishment of a joint venture with another merchant who acted as a distant partner and with whom they shared revenues, expenses and losses.[8]

In order to ensure access to the commercial, maritime and financial market of Amsterdam, an unknown and competitive environment, Cardamici chose the third solution and picked up a remarkable Dutch company with international connections to act as their main, if not sole, correspondent under commission in Amsterdam. Another interesting observation in relation to this appointment concerns its choice to assign to a well-known large foreign company its representation in Amsterdam and not to another Greek company established in the international port.[9] The most self-evident and secure option for a commercial company seeking to establish an effective and reliable system of international representation was to recruit members of the nearest and widest family environment, relatives and friends and to install them as partners and representatives.[10] As has emerged over the last twenty years through the study of various ethnic and religious groups engaged in the field of international trade throughout the modern era – Jews, Armenians, Greeks, Huguenots – common ethnic and religious identity, culture and language formed an environment of intimacy and trust that supported and promoted commercial partnerships.[11] However, a number of recent studies seem to question the fundamental nature of trust as a component of family and ethnic relations, arguing that close cooperation between merchants belonging to the same religious-ethnic minority or family did not automatically involve relationships of trust and creditworthiness.[12] So, despite the fact that, in general, the family, friendly and ethnic-religious environment have often been presented in the past as key pools for obtaining partners, newer investigations into personal records and commercial correspondence show that merchants were forced to work with a wealth of known and unknown partners in order to expand and diversify their businesses; it was neither possible nor feasible for all these individuals to come from a numerically limited family or ethnic-religious environment.

Returning to our original position, we will recap that the problem of representing a trading house in an international environment required cooperation from a distance with agents, intermediaries, representatives and necessarily revolved around the issue of establishing relationships of trust. But how did trust in cooperation at such a distance ultimately work and how can it be used in historical research for an interpretation of historical phenomena?[13] First, the study of the notion of trust needs to be placed within the wider spectrum of social relationships, as the collaboration between a merchant and his commercial correspondent was not bilateral but multilateral and was part of a wider network of business and social relations that formed social networks.[14] Historians have made extensive use of the theory of social networks in the analysis of international trade in the modern era. However, as Xabier Lamikiz rightly points out, the concept of a social network has been used more figuratively with an emphasis on its qualitative characteristics:[15] instead, it is also a concept which, even when used as a metaphor, effectively reflects the organization and functioning of trade as a network of people who communicate and jointly pursue an objective.[16]

In any case, the methodological use of the concept of social networks and a comparative approach requires interpretation, measurement and the placement of boundaries, which leads us to choose as an easier and more reliable solution the study of specific network cases.[17] It is obvious from the above that at the level of microhistory one can identify and interpret the way trust operated at the various levels of a long-distance commercial cooperation and the way in which cooperation developed in the form of networks within the professional and social setting.

The Cardamici business environment

Thierry Allain's investigation into the archival documents of the Dutch consulate in Smyrna, which record the arrivals and departures of Dutch ships, permits us to reconstruct the broader professional and social environment within which the Cardamicis operated – in other words the setting of their business networks, both in Smyrna and in the Netherlands.[18]

This valuable material offers an instant but profound picture of the activity of Dutch–Ottoman trade from 1760 to 1770 and, in particular, the participation of Greek trading houses in it.[19]

Comparing the data available for 1763 and 1770, which correspond approximately to the beginning and end of the period under consideration, we see a significant increase in the number of Dutch, other European and Ottoman companies transferring cargoes between Smyrna, Amsterdam and Rotterdam by Dutch ships. In particular, in 1763 thirteen companies of Dutch and other European and Ottoman interests (excluding Greek companies, which are listed separately) traded goods on their own behalf or on the behalf of others; by 1770 that had reached twenty-eight (see Tables 2 and 3).

At the same time there was an even more significant increase in the number of Greek Ottoman companies involved in Dutch trade. In particular, Greek companies based in Smyrna chartering Dutch ships for the transport of cargoes increased from twenty-four in 1763 (Table 4) to an impressive number of seventy-two in 1770 (Table 5). The comparison of these tables with Table 3 confirms the remarkable entry of Greek merchant houses into Dutch trade in the East and their overwhelming numerical superiority over Dutch, Jewish, Armenian, Italian and British companies trading goods between Smyrna, Amsterdam and Rotterdam. Tables 4 and 5 show Greek Ottoman companies chartering Dutch ships to transport cargo to and from Amsterdam and Rotterdam during the two years of reference, 1763 and 1770; they also record their commercial

Table 2 Foreign, Dutch and Ottoman Companies Trading Goods between Smyrna and the Netherlands, 1763

Jan Acherman & Co.
Jan Theodore Binman
Petronella Bobbit
Chaves & Fernandez Diaz
Jacob De Vogel
Masse & Son Di Herabeth
Fremeaux & Hopker
Maurin & Peretie
Van der Oudermueller & Sons
David Van Lennep & Enslie
Van Sanen & Clement

Source: Nationaal Archief Den Haag [NA], Consulaat Smyrna [CS], 1.02.22, Manifests series, 547 (1763) to 563 (1780).

Table 3 Foreign, Dutch and Ottoman Companies Trading Goods between Smyrna and the Netherlands, 1770

Aretun di Miriman

Giovanni Bata Bonnal

Bornman & Co.

Cauw & Co.

Caspar d'Arachiel & Co.

Clement Van Sanen & Van der Zee

Willem Crimped & Co.

Caspar De Staatner

De Vogel Bros

Eggizar Di Herabeth

Falcon & Arditti

Daniel Fremeaux & Co.

Giovanni Carlo Giera & Pedrini

Haim & Elias Hemzy

D. J. Hochepied

Humphries & Barker

Johhanes di Jesayas

Lee & Maltass

W. V. Lelyveld & Son

Johan Frederic Mann

Christian Rodermüller

C. & G. N. Schultz

J. F. Schultz

Hubsch & Timoni

David Van Lennep & Enslie

Clement, Van Sanen, Van der Zee & Co.

Source: Nationaal Archief Den Haag [NA], Consulaat Smyrna [CS], 1.02.22, Manifests series, 547 (1763) to 563 (1780).

representatives at the two ports. This information shows us the commercial networks in which each trading house participated individually and, at the same time, the way these networks sometimes coincided, sometimes were connected, sometimes contracted and sometimes expanded.

In 1763, twenty-four Greek Ottoman companies of Smyrna were listed in manifests. Some of them had as commercial correspondents in Amsterdam

Table 4 Greek Ottoman Companies Trading Goods between Smyrna and the Netherlands, 1763

	Smyrna (Company)	Amsterdam (Correspondents)	Rotterdam (Correspondents)
1	Alexis (son of Eleftheris) Hatzis	Stathis Thomas & Co.	Stathis Thomas & Co.
2	Grigorios (son of Nikolas)		Antonios Zingrilaras & Co.
3	Diamantis & Michalakis	Philip Clement & Co.	
4	Iakovos (son of Ioannis)	Various companies	
5	Raphael Cardamici & Co.	Thomas De Vogel & Son	
6	Alexandros & Leonardos Kontostavlos	Antonios Zingrilaras & Co.	
7	Ioannis Kourmousis	Antonios Zingrilaras & Co.	
8	Michail & Manolakis (sons of Iosif) Kourmousis	Antonios Mingrelias & Co. Stathis Thomas & Co.	Antonios Zingrilaras & Co.
9	Manolis (son of Panajiotis) Kiriakos & Jacob De Vogel	Willem Van Brienen & Son Geraard Staats & Son	Looy & Van Spaan Isaac De Reus, Pieter Rudolph Baelde Cornelius Van der Hoever Adam Y Sekkand & Co. Geraard Staats, Widow Jacob Craamer & Son
10	Nikolaos Mantzouranis & Bros	Various companies	
11	Stavrinos Mantzouranis	Geraard Staats & Co.	
12	Ambrosio (son of Dimitrios) Mavrogordatos	Stathis Thomas & Co.	
13	Georgios Mavrogordatos & Ioannis Anastasis	Stathis Thomas & Co.	Stathis Thomas & Co.
	Georgios Mavrogordatos & Co.	Stathis Thomas & Co.	Stathis Thomas & Co.
14	Nikolaos Mavrogordatos Bros	Stathis Thomas & Co.	
15	Pavlos Mavrogordatos, Apostolis Skouloudis & Co.	Stathis Thomas & Co. Various companies	
16	Leonardos Metaxas	Jan Acherman & Son Geraard Staats Various companies	Geraard Staats & Son
17	Michail Patrikios	Antonios Zingrilaras & Co. Stathis Thomas & Co. Daniel Craamer	Adam Craamer
18	Stratis Petrokokinos & Nikolaos Mavrogordatos	Various companies	

(Continued)

Table 4 (Continued)

	Smyrna (Company)	Amsterdam (Correspondents)	Rotterdam (Correspondents)
19	George Petritsis	Jan Acherman & Son Various companies	Jan Acherman & Son
20	Manolis Falieros & Avierinos Bros Dimitrios Fronimos	Widow Jack & Uberfeld Ioannis Prigkos	
21	Nikolaos Chrysogiannis, Kourmousis, Georgios Vitalis & Antonios Zingrilaras	Jan P. Hoffman, Rudolph Craamer, Bosch & Verrÿn, Various companies	Antonios Zingrilaras & Co.
22	Nikolaos Chrysogiannis, Kourmousis, Antonios Zingrilaras & Co.	Antonios Zingrilaras & Co.	
23	Nikolaos Chrysogiannis	Antonios Zingrilaras Antonios Zingrilaras & Co.	
24	Antonios Psathas & Sons	Geraard Staats & Son Jan Acherman & Son	

Source: Nationaal Archief Den Haag [NA], Consulaat Smyrna [CS], 1.02.22, Manifests series, 547 (1763) to 563 (1780).

Greek companies while seventeen of them cooperated with Dutch trading houses. These were Jan Acherman & Son, Widow Jack, Uberfeld & Jack, Geraard Staats & Son, Geraard Staats & Co., Rudolph Craamer, Jan P. Hoffman, Isaac De Reus, Pieter Rudolph Baelde, Cornelius Van der Hoever, Widow Jacob Craamer & Son, Thomas De Vogel & Son, Bosch & Verrÿn, Willem Van Brienen & Son, Philip Clement & Co., Daniel Craamer, Adam Craamer and Adam Y Sekkand & Co. By 1770, the overall picture of this activity had changed drastically: the number of Greek companies had increased to seventy-two. At the same time, as shown in Table 5 the number of Dutch trading companies based in Amsterdam and Rotterdam working with Greek merchants in Smyrna had increased significantly.

Between 1763 and 1770 the number of Greek companies based in Amsterdam or Rotterdam involved in Dutch–Ottoman trade also increased (Table 6). These companies formed the core of Amsterdam's Greek trading community and had an impressive network of partners and clients in Smyrna (Table 4); in addition to the transactions carried out on their behalf, they also took over the representation of Dutch, Greek and other trading houses in Dutch as well as in Ottoman ports.

The Smyrna consulate data on the arrivals and departures of Dutch ships show some qualitative characteristics as well as the strategy adopted by Greek

Table 5 Greek Ottoman Companies Trading Goods between Smyrna and the Netherlands, 1770

	Smyrna (Company)	Amsterdam (Correspondents)	Rotterdam (Correspondents)
1	Alexandros (son of Konstantis)		Various companies
2	Alexandros & Sotiris	Various companies	De Vogel & Enslie Various companies
3	Antonios Avierinos & Co.	Stathis Thomas, Isaiou & Co.	
4	Ioannis Avierinos & Co.		Stefanos Isaiou & Co.
5	Ioannis Avierinos	Niotis, Rigas & Co.	Stathis Thomas, Isaiou & Co.
6	Georgios Avierinos	Stefanos Isaiou	Stefanos Isaiou & Co.
7	Georgios Vitalis, Antonios Zingrilaras & Co.	Hendrik Momma Arent van Halmael Widow Jack, Uberfeld & Jack Widow Jack & Son Jan Pott François Lentfrink G. Hendrik Matter Otto Van Dam W. Cappenberg Bosch & Verrÿn Various companies	Jan Pott Bosch & Verrÿn Jan Pott Widow Jack & Son Widow Jack, Uberfeld & Jack François Lentfrink Otto Van Dam Jan Scheerenberg
8	Georgios Vitalis & Co.	Widow Jack & Son	
9	Georgios Vitalis, Stamatis Mourousis & Co.	Niotis, Rigas & Co.	
10	Georgios Vitalis & Co.	Various companies	
11	Ioannis Voroklas	Various companies	Various companies
12	Dimitrios (son of Mattheos) and Manolis Isaiou	Stathis Thomas, Isaiou & Co.	
13	Antonios Zingrilaras & Co.		Widow Jack, Uberfeld & Co.
14	Ioannis (son of Apostolis)	Various companies	
15	Ioannis Isaiou	Various companies	Various companies
16	Andreas & Manolis Capparis	Stathis Thomas, Isaiou & Co.	
17	Capparis Brothers (sons of Andreas)		Stefanos Isaiou & Co.
18	Georgios Capparis	Widow Jack & Son	Stefanos Isaiou & Co.

(Continued)

Table 5 (Continued)

	Smyrna (Company)	Amsterdam (Correspondents)	Rotterdam (Correspondents)
19	Capparis Georgios & Andreas Bros	Stefanos Isaiou & Co.	Stathis Thomas, Isaiou & Co. Widow Jack & Son Various companies
20	Pavlos Cardamici	Raphael Cardamici	
21	Raphael Cardamici & Co.	Ioannis Prigkos, Crull & Morré	
22	Alexandros & Leonardos Kontostavlos	Stefanos Isaiou & Co.	Stathis Thomas, Isaiou & Co.
23	Michail Kourmousis, Manolis (son of Iosif) & Co.	Stathis Thomas, Isaiou & Co. Ioannis Prigkos Crull & Morré Widow Jack, Uberfeld & Jack Bosch & Verrÿn Jan Saul Mores Stefanos Isaiou & Co. Various companies	Bosch & Verrÿn Hendrik De Bok Stathis Thomas, Isaiou & Co. Stefanos Isaiou & Co. Ioannis Prigkos, Crull & Morré Various companies
24	Kourmousis, Baltazzis & Co.	Jan Acherman & Son	
25	Kourmousis & Baltazzis		Various companies
26	Anastasis Krokodilos & Co.		Niotis, Rigas & Co. Various companies
27	Manolis (son of Panajiotis) Kiriakos & Co.	Geraard Staats & Son Jan Acherman & Son Johannes van Dirling Johannes Franciscus Delsing Various companies	Jan Acherman & Son Geraard Staats & Son Caspar Bakker & Co. Widow Jacob Craamer & Son Isaac De Reus Stefanos Isaiou & Co. Hendrik De Bok Daniel & Hendrik Hopker Looy & Van Spaan Cauw, Verlus & Co. Arent Bosch Jr Various companies
28	Manolis Isaiou	Stefanos Isaiou	
29	Manoussis Nikolaos Stamatis	Niotis, Rigas & Co.	
30	Stamatis Manoussis		Niotis, Rigas & Co.
31	Three Mantzouranis Bros	Ioannis Prigkos, Crull & Morré Stefanos Isaiou & Co.	Ioannis Prigkos, Crull & Morré Various companies

Table 5 (Continued)

	Smyrna (Company)	Amsterdam (Correspondents)	Rotterdam (Correspondents)
32	Mantzouranis Stavrianos & Konstantinos	Ioannis Prigkos, Crull & Morré	
33	Simon (son of Iosif) Mastorakis	Various companies	
34	Iosif Dimitrakis Mastorakis	Widow Jack & Son	
35	Iosif Dimitrakis Mastorakis & Co.	Widow Jack & Son	Widow Jack & Son Stathis Thomas, Isaiou & Co.
36	Georgios Mavrogordatos, Anastasis Ioannis & Co.	Bosch & Verrÿn Stathis Thomas, Isaiou & Co. Widow Jack, Uberfeld & Jack Geraard Staats & Son Reinhard & Scheerenberg Jan Acherman & Son Stefanos Isaiou & Co. Various companies	Bosch & Verrÿn Stathis Thomas, Isaiou & Co. Jannels & Son Widow Jacob Craamer & Son Stefanos Isaias & Co. Jan Acherman & Son Hendrik De Roo Jan Pott Hendrik De Bok Geraard Staats & Son Jan Willis & Son François Lentfrink Niotis, Rigas & Co. Various companies
37	Ambrosio Mavrogordatos	Niotis, Rigas & Co.	Niotis, Rigas & Co.
38	Ambrosio Mavrogordatos & Co.	Niotis, Rigas & Co. Dimitrios Niotis & Co.	Niotis, Rigas & Co. Dimitrios Niotis & Co.
39	Georgios Mavrogordatos & Bros	Stathis Thomas, Isaiou Thomas & Co.	Stefanos Isaiou & Co.
40	Dimitrios Mavrogordatos	Stathis Thomas, Isaiou & Co.	Stefanos Isaiou & Co.
41	Theodoros Mavrogordatos & Co.	Stathis Thomas, Isaiou & Co. Stefanos Isaiou & Co.	Stefanos Isaiou & Co.
42	Ioannis Mavrogordatos & Bros	Stathis Thomas, Isaiou & Co. Ioannis Prigkos, Crull & Morré	
43	Loukis Mavrogordatos	Stathis Thomas, Isaiou & Co.	
44	Pavlos Mavrogordatos & Co.		Niotis, Rigas & Co. Various companies

(Continued)

Table 5 (Continued)

Smyrna (Company)	Amsterdam (Correspondents)	Rotterdam (Correspondents)
45 Stratis Mavrogordatos & Co.		Niotis, Rigas & Co.
46 Ioannis Mavroudis	Widow Jack & Son	
47 Hatzi Konstantis Mouratoglou		Stathis Thomas, Isaiou Thomas & Co.
48 Metaxas Bros & Co.	Geraard Staats & Son	Ioannis Prigkos, Crull Morré
	Ioannis Prigkos, Crull & Morré	Geraard Staats & Son
	Various companies	Various companies
49 Metaxas Bros		Various companies
50 Ioannis Bachralis	Various companies	Various companies
51 Ioannis Xanthis	Various companies	Various companies
52 Michail Patrikios	Stathis Thomas, Isaiou & Co.	Stathis Thomas, Isaiou & Co.
	Niotis, Rigas & Co.	Widow Jack & Son
53 Georgios Petritsis & Sons	Widow Jack & Son	Stefanos Isaiou & Co.
	Stathis Thomas, Isaiou & Co.	Widow Jack & Son
	Ioannis Prigkos, Crull & Morré	Stathis Thomas, Isaiou & Co.
	Stefanos Isaiou & Co.	
	Various companies	
54 Diamandis Petritsis	Ioannis Prigkos, Crull & Morré	Stathis Thomas, Isaiou & Co.
		Ioannis Prigkos, Crull, Morré
		Cauw, Verlus & Co.
55 Stratis Petrokokinos	Dimitrios Niotis	
56 Petrokokinos Bros & Nikolaos Manoussis		Niotis, Rigas & Co.
57 Pitakos Bros	Stathis Thomas, Isaiou & Co.	Stefanos Isaias & Co.
58 Nikolaos Pitakos	Ioannis Prigkos, Crull & Morré	Ioannis Prigkos, Crull & Morré
	Widow Jack & Son	
59 Nikolaos Pitakos & Bros		Widow Jack & Son
		Ioannis Prigkos, Crull & Morré
60 Leon Prasakakis & Bros	Various companies	Stathis Thomas, Isaiou & Co.
61 Georgios Sevastopoulos & Pavlos Psychas	Widow Jack & Son	Widow Jack & Son
62 Georgios Pavlos Sgoutas		Niotis, Rigas & Co.
63 Stathis Thomas & Ioannis Bachralis	Stefanos Isaiou & Co.	
	Niotis, Rigas & Co.	
64 Stathis Thomas	Stefanos Isaiou	

Table 5 (Continued)

Smyrna (Company)	Amsterdam (Correspondents)	Rotterdam (Correspondents)
65 Manolis Falieros & Stamatis Metaxas		Stefanos Isaiou & Co. Various companies
66 Dimitrios Fronimos	Widow Jack & Son	
67 Dimitrios Psathas & Nikolaos Isaiou	Various companies	
68 Antonios Psathas		Stathis Thomas, Isaiou & Co. Various companies
69 Dimitrios Psathas		Stathis Thomas, Isaiou & Co. Various companies
70 Dimitrios Psathas & Manolis Isaiou	Stathis Thomas, Isaiou & Co. Ioannis Prigkos, Crull & Morré	Stefanos Isaiou & Co.
71 Antonios Hatzis Psathas & Luca Bastian		Various companies
72 Dimitrios Psathas & Manolis Isaiou	Stathis Thomas, Isaiou & Co. Ioannis Prigkos, Crull & Morré Stefanos Isaiou & Co.	

Source: Nationaal Archief Den Haag [NA], Consulaat Smyrna [CS], 1.02.22, Manifests series, 547 (1763) to 563 (1780).

Table 6 Greek Companies Based in Amsterdam and Rotterdam Trading with Smyrna, 1763–70

1763		1770	
Amsterdam	Rotterdam	Amsterdam	Rotterdam
Antonios Zingrilaras	Antonios	Stathis Thomas & Co.	Niotis, Rigas & Co.
Antonios Zingrilaras & Co.	Zingrilaras & Co.	Ioannis Prigkos, Crull & Morré	Stathis Thomas, Isaiou & Co.
Stathis Thomas & Co.	Stathis Thomas	Stefanos Isaiou & Co.	Stefanos Isaiou & Co.
Ioannis Prigkos	& Co.	Niotis, Rigas & Co.	Ioannis Prigkos, Crull & Morré
		Dimitrios Niotis & Co.	Dimitrios Niotis & Co.
		Raphael Cardamici	

Source: Nationaal Archief Den Haag [NA], Consulaat Smyrna [CS], 1.02.22, Manifests series, 547 (1763) to 563 (1780).

Table 7 Mavrogordatos Family Companies Involved in Trade between Smyrna–Amsterdam–Rotterdam, 1763

Smyrna	Amsterdam	Rotterdam
Ambrosio & Dimitrios Mavrogordatos	Various companies	
Ambrosio & Dimitrios Mavrogordatos	Various companies	
Georgios Mavrogordatos & Ioannis Anastasis	Stathis Thomas & Co.	Stathis Thomas & Co. (via Amsterdam)
Georgios Mavrogordatos & Co.		Stathis Thomas & Co. (via Amsterdam)
Nikolaos Mavrogordatos Bros	Stathis Thomas & Co.	
Pavlos Mavrogordatos & Apostolos Skouloudis	Stathis Thomas & Co.	
Pavlos Mavrogordatos & Co.	Various companies	
Stratis Petrokokinos, & Nikolaos Mavrogordatos	Various companies	

Source: Nationaal Archief Den Haag [NA], Consulaat Smyrna [CS], 1.02.22, Manifests series, 547 (1763) to 563 (1780).

companies in the matter of their representation. Based on the above, Ottoman Greek companies can be divided into two categories. The first is those with a wide network of contacts and a strong continuous activity, as shown by the successive charters of ships, the dispatch and receipt of large consignments on their behalf and their frequent appearance in the consulate's lists as representatives of different companies on the same freight many times. Usually, these companies participated in commercial networks that involved members of the same family and relatives.[20] Indicative is the case of the Mavrogordatos family,[21] which in 1763 engaged in the trade between Smyrna–Amsterdam–Rotterdam with the companies listed in Table 7.

In 1763 Mavrogordatos family companies cooperated almost exclusively with the company Stathis Thomas & Co., which represented them in Amsterdam and Rotterdam. A few years later, by 1770, the number of family companies involved in the trade had increased considerably. Mavrogordatos had also significantly expanded its network of representatives and associates by choosing to be represented in Dutch ports by many Greeks as well as Dutch merchant houses (Table 8).

The second category of Greek companies included those which did not appear to systematically charter Dutch ships, received one or two orders on each freight and usually cooperated permanently with the same dealers in the Dutch ports: Cardamicis belonged in this second category of companies which

Table 8 Mavrogordatos Family Companies Involved in Trade between Smyrna–Amsterdam–Rotterdam, 1770

Smyrna	Amsterdam	Rotterdam
Georgios Mavrogordatos & Anastasis & Co.	Stathis Thomas, Isaiou & Co. Bosch & Verrÿn Widow Jack, Überfeld & Jack Geraard Staats & Son Hendrik De Bok Stefanos Isaiou & Co. Reihard & Seheenenberg Jan Acherman & Son Various companies	Bosch & Verrÿn Stathis Thomas, Isaiou & Co. Jannerls & Son Widow Jacob Craamer & Son Stefanos Isaiou & Co. (via Amsterdam) Jan Acherman & Son (via Amsterdam) Hendrik De Roo (via Amsterdam) Jan Willis & Son
Ambrosio Mavrogordatos	Niotis, Rigas & Co.	Niotis, Rigas & Co.
Pavlos Mavrogordatos & Co.	Various companies	Niotis, Rigas & Co.
Ioannis Mavrogordatos & Bros	Stathis Thomas, Isaiou & Co.	
Dimitrios Mavrogordatos	Stathis Thomas, Isaiou & Co.	Stefanos Isaiou & Co.
Theodoros Mavrogordatos & Co.	Stathis Thomas, Isaiou & Co. Stefanos Isaiou & Co.	Stefanos Isaiou & Co.
Loukis Mavrogordatos	Stathis Thomas, Isaiou & Co.	Stefanos Isaiou & Co.
Ambrosio Mavrogordatos & Co.	Niotis, Rigas & Co.	Niotis, Rigas & Co.
Stratis Mavrogordatos & Co.	Dimitrios Niotis & Co.	
Georgios Mavrogordatos & Bros	Stathis Thomas, Isaiou & Co. Stefanos Isaiou & Co.	

Source: Nationaal Archief Den Haag [NA], Consulaat Smyrna [CS], 1.02.22, Manifests series, 547 (1763) to 563 (1780).

appeared to trade exclusively on its behalf, it was usually family companies and invested personal capital in the purchase and sale of goods.

The character and organization of the Cardamici enterprises is described in De Vogel's letters with sufficient clarity. Bartholo Cardamici & Co. was a Greek Ottoman trading company based in Smyrna that expanded into international commercial activity in the second half of the eighteenth century. As already mentioned, the company had as representative in Constantinople Raphael Cardamici, a nephew of Bartholo and manager of the local office. From 1760 to 1764 Thomas De Vogel & Son corresponded with Bartholo and Raphael Cardamici in Smyrna and Constantinople. The number of letters sent by De Vogel to the Cardamicis, and the content and the style of wording used in addressing each of the two merchants, reveals their place in the hierarchy of the company as well as the family.

As can be seen in Table 1, until 1763 Bartholo Cardamici was the main recipient of De Vogel's letters in the Cardamici business. Between 1763 and 1764, when Bartholo fell ill, retired to the countryside and eventually passed away, Raphael Cardamici took over the reins of the family business from his headquarters in Constantinople. This transitional period in the history of the company is reflected in Table 1: in 1760 De Vogel sent twelve letters to Bartholo Cardamici in Smyrna and seven to Raphael in Constantinople, in 1761 nineteen to Bartholo and thirteen to Raphael, and in 1762 fifteen to Bartholo and fourteen to Raphael. In 1763 the balance was overturned with the withdrawal of Bartholo due to illness and his moving to the outskirts of Smyrna. That year Raphael received fourteen letters from De Vogel in Constantinople, while the associates who replaced Bartholo at the company's headquarters received one less. In 1764, after Bartholo's death, almost all letters (twenty-one) were now addressed to Raphael, who had taken over both offices of the company and was moving between Smyrna and Constantinople. From 1765 De Vogel worked exclusively with Raphael Cardamici, and all letters were now addressed to Raphael Cardamici & Co., until 1771 when Thomas De Vogel & Son was dissolved after the death of its founder.

The letters that De Vogel sent to Bartholo Cardamici until 1764 were more confidential in nature and thorough than those he sent to his nephew, thus recognizing his primacy in information and decision-making process and confirming his authority over his partner-nephew Raphael. De Vogel received orders, directions and information from the company's headquarters and from Bartholo personally. The latter's leading role is also demonstrated by the fact that Raphael was often the recipient of short notes that occasionally were attached to the letters received by his uncle. Raphael made sure to send orders directly to De Vogel, bypassing his uncle, for the purchase of goods that he would promote on the Constantinople market. However, De Vogel systematically informed Bartholo of his nephew's requests and initiatives and made sure that he had his consent before proceeding to the purchase and shipment of goods requested by Raphael. After 1764, the content and style of De Vogel's letters to Raphael changed drastically. From the moment the nephew took over the family's business, De Vogel addressed him with respect and attention, explicitly acknowledging his authority.

Unfortunately, the De Vogel letters are not sufficient to fully understand the kind of partnership that linked the two Cardamici offices in Smyrna and

Constantinople. By 1764 all orders, shipments and remittances arrived in Amsterdam from Smyrna, while the great bulk of cargoes traded by the Greek Ottoman merchant house were received in Smyrna first and then some of them were sent to Constantinople with a new freight. The Constantinople office was the company's second operational pole, located in the heart of the Ottoman administrative, bureaucratic and military system.[22] The two offices appear to have kept different books and current purchase and sales accounts, while according to the manifests of the Dutch consulate in Smyrna, they also used a different name. It is therefore possible that the Constantinople office operated as a subsidiary of Bartholo Cardamici & Co. De Vogel's reference to an impending 'settlement of accounts' between uncle and nephew, communicated to him by Bartholo himself, could be regarded as confirmation of the independent or semi-independent form of the enterprise run by Raphael and of his contractual obligations and rights vis-à-vis his uncle. Regarding the 'settlement of accounts' to which De Vogel referred, Bartholo had taken care to inform him in due time of his decision to settle his pending affairs with his nephew. For this reason, he had taken the initiative to temporarily suspend his dealings with the Dutch trader and asked him to temporarily halt shipments to him and his nephew Raphael.

After Bartholo's death, circumstances changed radically, and De Vogel continued to work with Raphael Cardamici & Co. on the basis of a new agreement. For a short transitional period, until the final settlement of the accounts with the old company, Bartholo Cardamici & Co., the transactions carried out were recorded in two different accounts, one held by Bartholo's old partners and associates in Smyrna and another that the staff of Raphael Cardamici in Constantinople maintained. At this time, Markos Koroneos was mentioned as Raphael's proxy in Smyrna, while the merchants Nikolaos Chrysogiannis and Michail Masganas, probably partners or 'friends' of Bartholo Cardamici in Smyrna, were tasked with settling his company's accounts.

The dissolution of Bartholo Cardamici & Co. and the transfer of the powers of the family business to Raphael was followed by the entry into the business arena of Pavlos Cardamici, Bartholo's son. In 1767, Raphael Cardamici Nephew & Son, in which Pavlos Cardamici appears to have participated as the nephew, received a transfer of 1,000 florins from Raphael Cardamici & Co.

Raphael Cardamici & Co. retained Pavlos Cardamici and the David Van Lennep & William Enslie as key partners and collaborators in Smyrna. However, at the same time, the company cooperated with other Greek Ottoman companies, as is apparent from the receipt, in 1770, of large quantities of goods in Constantinople via Smyrna with the company of Ioannis Mavrogordatos &

Ioannis Anastasis being intermediary and guarantor. The goods had arrived in Smyrna from Amsterdam aboard the *St. Gregory* of Capt. Andries Andriessen. In Smyrna the cargo was loaded onto the ship *Constantinople*, which was under the Ragusan flag, and sent to the Ottoman capital on behalf of Raphael Cardamici. The *St. Gregory* cargo, with a total value of 40,950 florins, had paid the Dutch consulate in Smyrna a total duty of 819 florins, or 2 per cent of its total value. Out of a total of fifteen merchant recipients, the part of the cargo received by Cardamici represented a fifth in value, with Dimitris Fronimos, Hubsch & Timoni, Bornman & Co., Bongard, Panchaud & Series leading the way. This demonstrates that, almost five years after the death of Bartholo Cardamici, Raphael had expanded the family's business and developed its business network (Table 9).

In addition to Raphael Cardamici & Co. and Raphael Cardamici Nephew & Son, another company called Raphael Cardamici & Son engaged in commercial transactions through Amsterdam until the late 1780s. The company's representative in Smyrna was Pavlos Cardamici, who allegedly traded goods on Raphael's behalf on Dutch ships. The goods were received in Amsterdam and promoted to the international market by a Dutch commercial agent.[23]

The subsequent development of the Cardamici enterprises is unknown. The available nineteenth-century Ottoman sources contain only vague, scattered

Table 9 Cargo of the *St. Gregory*, 1770

Company Receiving the Goods	Value of Cargo (in Florins)	Type of Cargo
Dimitrios Fronimos	10,789	Textiles, nails, tin, velvets, handkerchiefs, spices
Hubsch & Timoni	7,589	Pistols, textiles, velvets
Bornman & Co.	4,770	Textiles, velvets
Bongard, Panchaud & Series	4,649	Textiles, porcelain
Raphael Cardamici & Co.	4,294	Textiles, tobacco, pistols
Salomon Haim Camondo	1,900	Textiles
Josef & Salomon Camondo	1,633	Borax, dyes, steel, arsenic
G. Reisner & Co.	1,583	Pistols
Dunan Bros	1,287	Textiles, leathers, furs
Van der Schroeff & Co.	886	Camphor, drugs
J. P. Siron	535	Borax, shellac
Pietro di Sacaria	400	Various trifles
Konstantinos Platis	380	Muslins, coffee, edgings
Marco Drago	255	Arsenic, camphor
Total value	40,950	

Source: Nationaal Archief Den Haag [NA], Consulaat Smyrna [CS], 1.02.22, Manifests series, 547 (1763) to 563 (1780).

and unconfirmed references to merchants with the same name but who may have belonged to another family: Stratis and Thanasis Cardamici, as well as a Stratis Cardamici, a merchant from Kydonies (Aivali), who had gone bankrupt and owed significant sums to French merchants. Stratis was perhaps a French protégé, as the French consul in Mytilene had intervened with the local authorities for his release from a Constantinople prison.[24]

It is almost impossible to determine the economic size of the Cardamici enterprise and to define its precise position within the wider business environment. The De Vogel letters are circumstantial and unclear regarding the value of specific transactions, thus preventing us from estimating the overall amount of capital that the Cardamicis invested in the purchase and sale of goods. The family nature of the company, the relatively limited circle of associates and contacts surrounding it and its rare presence on the lists of the Dutch consulate in Smyrna confirm the initial impression that the company was one of the many medium-sized Greek Ottoman commercial enterprises that, by taking advantage of the positive conditions, attempted to open up to international markets.

Compared to the largest Greek commercial houses of the time, the Cardamicis did not develop as an extended family business that formed a network of branches and subsidiaries that was run by blood and marriage relatives.[25] Instead, they pursued a serious and conservative strategy of careful management of their funds and the unusual tactic, given the size and business characteristics of the company, of appointing foreign commercial correspondents and representatives. Unlike other Greek companies that combined trade with other maritime and financial activities, participated in numerous partnerships and offered their services as intermediaries and agents on the behalf of other Greek and foreign trading houses, the Cardamicis followed a more introvert strategy and did not appear to have expanded their activity in other sectors or participated in joint ventures.

It is, therefore, not paradoxical that there are few references to Cardamici business in the literature on Greek Ottoman trade and Ottoman–Dutch trade relations in the eighteenth century. Ismail Hakki Kadi and Elena Frangakis-Syrett occasionally mention the company, mainly in the context of De Vogel's activity in Smyrna.[26] Also, the Cardamicis are not included in J. G. Nanninga's list of non-Muslim Ottoman merchants who traded with Dutch ships from February to August 1762 and August 1786 to February 1787.[27] However, we know with certainty that in 1762 the company conducted trade in Amsterdam, via Smyrna and Constantinople.[28] One possible explanation for the company's absence from the lists could be their representation by David Van Lennep's company,

Thomas De Vogel's partner in Smyrna, which systematically took on the role of intermediary of the De Vogel companies in the Smyrna market. The complete absence of Bartholo Cardamici & Co. from the consulate's lists of merchants receiving and/or dispatching cargoes carried by Dutch ships raises reasonable questions. In contrast, Raphael Cardamici & Co. appears a single time, in August 1763, to have dispatched a cargo to Thomas De Vogel & Son in Amsterdam on the ship *Marie & Dorothea Galley* under Capt. Jacob Hilkes. Raphael Cardamici & Co. received a cargo from Amsterdam in October 1763 on the ship *Saint Spyridon* under Capt. Paulus Blandauw.[29] And in this case, the insignificant presence of the Cardamicis in the manifests of the Dutch consulate may have been the result of their frequent representation by David Van Lennep & Enslie in dealings with De Vogel. The Dutch–British company in Smyrna operated as a middleman and front company for many other companies, receiving and transmitting shipments on their behalf.

At the level of business strategy, there can be no doubt about the reasons that led Cardamici, a family company without a highly developed network of partners or a large turnover, to choose Thomas De Vogel as a commercial correspondent abroad. Cardamici commissioned De Vogel to direct and coordinate its opening up to the international markets. It was expected from him to represent it in the appropriate business and trading circles; take advantage of the best market opportunities; achieve the most advantageous prices for selling and purchase commodities on its behalf; convince brokers, ship captains and insurers to sign advantageous agreements; and, in general, make available to it all his experience, knowledge and intuition. Amsterdam's international market was not, according to the descriptions of the Greek merchant Stamatis Petrou, a place where an inexperienced, timid and unwise trader could build a solid and profitable career. This was mainly because he would have to deal with the Dutch traders and brokers who were worthy and dangerous opponents: 'I told him [his principal Korais],' Petrou said, 'to keep his eyes open for the Hollanders, because they have no faith.'[30] By choosing to be represented by a Dutch company inside its natural professional environment, the Greek Ottoman merchants took the first appropriate move towards achieving their goal. There is no doubt that the Cardamicis could have entrusted the company's opening to Western trade to a Greek Ottoman representative, possibly one established in the Netherlands. However, De Vogel's correspondence reveals that even in Rotterdam, Holland's second largest port, Cardamici had appointed De Vogel's rival, Hendrik De Bok, who was efficient, flexible and popular among Ottoman companies, to represent them.

Cardamici was not in fact the only Greek Ottoman company that had made similar choices. In 1763 Michalakis Diamantis was collaborating with Philip Clement & Co. of Amsterdam, Stavrinos Mantzouranis with Geraard Staats & Co. and Leonardos Metaxas & Georgios Petritsis with Jan Acherman & Son, also of Amsterdam. Larger companies such as the Chrysogiannis, Kourmousis, Zingrilaras & Co., which had business transactions with more than one company in Amsterdam, in 1763 cooperated with Jan P. Hoffman, Rudolph Craamer and Bosch & Verrÿn. Another interesting observation is that the Greek Ottoman companies that chose Dutch and other foreign trading houses to represent them in Amsterdam and Rotterdam engaged with companies that had already cooperated with other Greek merchants. This strategic choice was typical inside a professional environment of people of common ethnic origin who exchanged information, participated in common trading networks and maintained professional and social relations.[31] Therefore, between 1763 and 1770, seventeen Greek companies cooperated with the Widow Jack, Uberfeld & Jack, Widow Jack, Uberfeld & Co. and Widow Jack & Son based in Amsterdam.[32]

How did the Cardamicis establish contact with Thomas De Vogel & Son in the first place? Was this important business link established through the Dutch–British company David Van Lennep & Enslie of Smyrna? The Cardamicis also appeared to have dealings with the Armenian Alexander De Masse in Amsterdam and Jean Henry Stametz in Vienna; both merchants and financiers collaborated with De Vogel and could therefore had made the recommendations. Finally, it is possible that the Cardamicis had been introduced to De Vogel by another Greek Ottoman company. However, De Vogel's business mailing lists did not include many Greek Ottoman companies; with the exception of Cardamici, De Vogel exchanged letters systematically between 1760 and 1771 with only another Greek merchant in Smyrna, Ambrosio Mavrogordatos; the reference to Mavrogordatos had probably been given to De Vogel by another Greek, Apostolos Demestikas, a Smyrna representative of Antonios Zingrilaras, the famous and well-off member of the Greek Ottoman merchant community in Amsterdam.

The Dutch merchant and commercial correspondent Thomas De Vogel

The Amsterdam-based Thomas De Vogel & Son maintained a wide network of collaborators and partners in various countries. De Vogel's business network spread to different continents and comprised several professional contacts, particularly in the wider region of France and present-day Belgium, as well as present-day Germany up to the border with Poland. As early as the seventeenth century Dutch merchants had settled in cities and ports of Germany, France and Flanders, from where they conducted international business transactions. As typically stated at that time, there was not a port along the entire length of the coastline between Flanders and Bayonne where the business with Dutch ships was not increasing steadily.[33] De Vogel had taken care to expand his trading network in these cities, many of which were situated along rivers. At the same time, he cooperated with commercial houses in the most important ports of the Iberian Peninsula (Seville, Cadiz, Bilbao, Lisbon), where one could purchase raw materials, food and industrial goods from northern Europe, colonial items, precious metals and coins. The Dutch trader was in contact with merchants who had businesses in the West Indies, as colonial products were supplied from the Caribbean.

According to Ismail Hakki Kadi, De Vogel imported leather from Havana, Buenos Aires and Brazil; flower, cochineal, saffron, mimosa and gold from Cadiz; sugar from America; coffee from Martinique, Suriname and Marseille; wood from Danzig; fabrics from Ghent; and large quantities of wool and oil from Seville. The company also bought large quantities of pepper at the auctions of the Dutch East India Company. As far as the exports of products are concerned, De Vogel exported arms to Lisbon, mohair yarn and cotton to Brussels, textiles to Cadiz and wire to Seville. In the Ottoman Empire the company had established a wide business network. De Vogel imported goods from the Ottoman Empire for his own account, which he sold in Amsterdam as well as in other commercial and manufacture centres in the Netherlands. More specifically, he imported from Smyrna mohair yarn, silk, dried figs and raisins and galls and exported woollen fabrics, pepper, nails, tin, lead, gunpowder, pistols and porcelain tableware for tea and coffee.[34] Hakki Kadi describes in detail the company's particular involvement in trading mohair yarn in the Leiden market as well as the Dutch trader's obsession with importing to and marketing on the Dutch markets first-class red yarn from the East.[35]

During the 1760s, when it was cooperating with the Cardamicis, the Dutch company communicated with trading houses and merchants in many European cities, in the West Indies and North Africa (Table 10). In Europe, De Vogel had correspondence with, among others, F. F. Baraux in Antwerp, Splitgerber & Daum in Berlin, Jean Gottlieb Benada in Breslau, Prasca, Arbori & Co. and Miguel Isquerds in Cadiz, Hirosme Capalti in Civitavecchia, Dominique Morel in Dunkirk, George Bernard Artope in Frankfurt, Guillaume Clamer Junior &

Table 10 Cities with Which Thomas De Vogel & Son traded, 1760s

Country/Area	Cities
Austria	Vienna
Belgium	Antwerp, Bruges, Brussels, Liège Maastricht, Malines-Mechelen, Malmedy, Olne, Ostend, Stavelot, Ypres
Britain	Birmingham, Brentford, London
Caribbean, West Indies	St. Eustace, St. Lucia
France	Armentieres, Bayonne, Bordeaux, Dunkirk, Lille, Marseille, Paris, Port St. Marie, Rouen, St. Amand, Toulouse
Germany	Berlin, Breslau, Brunswick, Emmerich, Frankfurt, Hamburg, Herzberg, Leipzig, Nuremberg
Ireland	Dublin
Italy	Civitavecchia, Livorno
Libya	Zintan
Luxembourg	Luxembourg
Malaysia	Labuan
Netherlands	Rotterdam
Poland	Danzig
Portugal	Lisbon
Spain	Bilbao, Cadiz, Madrid, Malaga, Seville, St. Sebastian
Spain	St. Sebastian

Source: Stadsarchief Amsterdam [StdAm], 332, Thomas De Vogel, Kopieboek, vol. 44–52, 1760–71.

Co. in Hamburg and Johan Carl Estell in Leipzig, Steinbach Frères in Liège, Ratton Bonefas & Co. and Perochon, Firth & Perochon in Lisbon, Walter Quin in London, Joseph Bengue in Madrid and Thomas Quilty in Malaga. De Vogel also collaborated with Jean Christ Schweyerd in Nuremberg, Legrand Père et Fils, Lambert & Kornman & Co. in Paris, Pierre Domine and Pierre Basco in Seville, Pelissier & Co. in Toulouse and Jean Henry Stametz in Vienna.

In the Ottoman Empire De Vogel traded with a plethora of Ottoman, Dutch and other foreign merchant houses established in Smyrna, Constantinople, Aleppo and Ankara (Table 11).

De Vogel's letterbooks for the period 1760–71 contain letters addressed to a number of companies in the Ottoman Empire (Table 12).

It is clear that Thomas De Vogel had an extensive international business network, which comprised a significant number of Ottoman enterprises or foreign commercial houses operating on Ottoman territory. His association

Table 11 Thomas De Vogel's Associates and Correspondents in the Ottoman Empire, 1760–71

	Smyrna	Constantinople	Ankara	Aleppo
1	Abraham de Jacob Arditti	Andrea Magrini & Co.	Leytstar & Santi[36]	Jan van Kerchem Willem
2	Abraham de Mozeh	Asmund Palm	Francois Mayastre	Liebergen & Heirmans
3	Adarui & De Botton	Belcamp, Meyer & Van Kerchem		Jan Heemskerk
4	Adarui Hemzy & Co.	Bongard & Panchaud		Maseyck & Co.
5	Ambrosio Mavrogordatos	Bongard, Panchaud & Series		Jan van Kerchem & Heemskerk
6	Apostolos Demestikas[37]	Bornman & Co.		
7	Bartholo Cardamici & Co.	Chasseaud & Co.		
8	Belcamp, Clement & Van Sanen	Cornelis van der Oudermueller		
9	Caszadour & Jasegiroglou	Magrini, Bornman & Co.		
10	Christiaan Hebbe Junior	Meyer & Van der Oudermueller		
11	Palm & Hibbe	Moise Sonsino & Co.		
12	Clement & Van Sanen	Panchaud & Series		
13	Daniel Fremaux	Raphael Cardamici & Co.		
13	Cassaing & Hopker	David Maynard & Son & Co.		
15	Jean Fornezy	Estieu & Boustain		
16	Joseph Magula	Frederik Hubsch & Co.		
17	Joseph Coen Hemzy	Gad Conigliano & Co.		
18	Joseph Isaac & Jacob	Hubsch & Timoni		
19	Kicer (son of Carabeth) Magaroglou[38]	Isaac & Moise de Samuel Angel		
20	Louis Stechman	Isaac de Samuel Angel		
21	Manuel (son of Panaiotis) Carabeth & Co.	Jan Rysner		
22	Missir di Eghia	Jan Hendrik Meyer & Co.		
23	Moise (Moses) Cariglio & Carillo	Jean Baptiste Chasseaud		
24	Moses S'Forno & Co.	Jean Careldes Bordes & Co.		
25	Muracht di Parisch	Jean Daniel Schaber		
26	Muyssard & De la Fontaine	Tommaso Di Serpos		
27	Ploegstert & Van Lennep	Vassalo Foresti		
28	Moses S'Forno & Isaac Angel			
29	David & Jacob Mordoh			
30	David Barchi & Son			
31	David (son of Jacob) Fernandez Diaz			
32	David Van Lennep			

Table 11 (Continued)

	Smyrna	Constantinople	Ankara	Aleppo
33	David Van Lennep & Enslie			
34	David Van Lennep & Knipping & Enslie			
35	David Van Lennep & Co.			
36	Falcon & Arditti			
37	Flechon Frères & Majastre			
38	Fratelli Abulaffia			
39	Gabriel Fernandez Diaz			
40	Gasiadour di Petros			
41	De Vogel Bros			
42	Abraham Gerzon & Co.			
43	Saul Gerzon & Co.			
44	Giacomo & Daniel Fremaux			
45	Guerin & Co.			
46	Haim & Elias Coen Hemzy			
47	Haim Coen Hemzy			
48	Haim Coen Hemzy & Co.			
49	Isaac Haim & Joseph Aravas			
50	Israel Benbeniste			
51	Israel Benbeniste & Co.			
52	Isaac & Jacob Calomiti			
53	Isaac Arditti & Haim Coen Hemzy			
54	Isaac Calomiti			
55	Jacob Isaac Salinas			
56	Salomon Ardarie			
57	Samuel Fernandez Diaz & Co.			
58	Samuel Fernandez Diaz			
59	Selomoh Saul & Bros			
60	Selomoh Saul Hermano			
61	Abulaffia Sonsino			
62	Stephano Abro & Resdages de Aharon & Co.			
63	Thomas De Vogel Junior			
64	Tricon Frères & Co.			

Source: Ismail Hakki Kadi, *Ottoman and Dutch Merchants in the Eighteenth Century: Competition and Cooperation in Ankara, Izmir and Amsterdam* (Leiden: Brill 2012), 184–5.

with a medium-sized Greek Ottoman company wishing to expand its business to the West raises some questions regarding his real motives. If Cardamici saw in him the ideal commercial correspondent and an experienced representative in Amsterdam's international market, what exactly drove him to offer his valuable services for an uncertain commission?

Table 12 Thomas De Vogel's Letters Addressed to Commercial Houses in the Ottoman Empire, 1760–71

Name	City	Correspondence Duration
Ambrosio Mavrogordatos	Smyrna	1764–8
Apostolos Demestikas	Smyrna	1764–5
Chasseaud & Co.	Constantinople	1764–5
Bartholo Cardamici	Smyrna	1760–71
Raphael Cardamici	Constantinople	1760–71
Chaves Fernandez Diaz	Smyrna	1760–5
David & Jacob Mordoh	Smyrna	1768–9
Falcon & Arditti	Smyrna	1766–70
Flechon Frères & Majastre	Smyrna	1764–70
Abulaffia Fratelli	Smyrna	1766–8
Frederik Hubsch & Co.	Constantinople	1762–3, 1765–6
Abraham Gerzon & Co.	Smyrna	1766–70
Haim & Elias Coen Hemzy	Smyrna	1766–70
Haim Coen Hemzy	Smyrna	1760–9
Hubsch & Timoni	Constantinople	1766–8
Jean Baptiste Chasseaud	Constantinople	1762–4
Jacob (son of Isaac) Salinas	Smyrna	1765–6, 1768–9
Jean Fornezy	Smyrna	1761–2
Joseph Coen Hemzy	Smyrna	1765–8
Joseph Magula	Smyrna	1766–8
Kikor son of Carabeth Magaroglou	Smyrna	1760–2
Leytstar & Santi	Ankara	1763–8
Magrini, Bornman & Co.	Constantinople	1763–4
Missir di Eghia	Smyrna	1760–1
Salomon Saul & Bros	Smyrna	1760–6
Sonsino & Abulaffia	Smyrna	1766–9
Tommaso Di Serpos	Constantinople	1770
Tricon Frères & Co.	Smyrna	1770

Source: Stadsarchief Amsterdam [StdAm], 332, Thomas De Vogel, Kopieboek, vol. 44–52, 1760–71.

Apparently, De Vogel's partnerships with Ottoman companies differed markedly from his undertakings for Dutch trading houses. Transactions with Dutch traders were conducted through partnerships which either took the form of a joint venture or were an independent, individual project. In the case of a joint venture, different companies shared responsibilities, profits and losses, depending on their shareholding in the company's total capital. A typical example of such an enterprise in which De Vogel participated with personal capital was the one he ran together with Leytstar & Santi of Ankara to trade mohair yarn on the Amsterdam market. De Vogel's correspondence with his principal representative in Smyrna, David Van Lennep, reveals that in such joint venture partnerships, De Vogel and Van Lennep held an additional 2–2.5 per cent as a commission on their account in order to offer various additional services. There were also those cases of partnerships in which the one side contributed personal capital and the other received only a commission, calculated as a percentage of the transactions it had completed.[39]

We do not know for how long De Vogel participated in joint ventures in the Ottoman Empire. However, as is apparent from his correspondence with relatives and close associates, he was sceptical about the prospect of investments in Ottoman markets, as he believed that they left him exposed financially to a high-risk business environment and required him to participate in uncontrolled and uncertain transactions.[40] Therefore, on 19 July 1765 he announced to his partner in Smyrna, Van Lennep, his intention to change strategy and now conduct business exclusively as a commercial agent, offering his services to trading houses of the Ottoman Empire with a commission of 2 per cent. As Hakki Kadi points out, De Vogel implied that he was no longer interested in participating equally in commodity trading companies to and from the Ottoman Empire in cooperation with Ottoman or other foreign trading houses. On the contrary, he wished to profit in the form of a commission calculated on the value of transactions on the Amsterdam market on behalf of other trading houses. Referring to the cooperation with Leytstar & Santi, De Vogel indicated that he had no intention of abandoning his network of acquaintances inside the Ottoman markets but, quite the opposite, he wanted to exploit it by undertaking to represent the interests of former partners and associates. In order to successfully fulfil his plan and reach new mediation and service agreements, De Vogel had instructed his son Thomas De Vogel Junior to go to Smyrna and explore the possibilities of working with local trading houses.[41] The Dutch merchant's business manoeuvre is verified in his correspondence with his son. In his letters, Thomas De Vogel expressed doubts about the credibility and honesty of the Ottoman merchants he undertook to represent. For this reason, he called on his son to devise methods that would protect the reputation and capital of the company from embezzlement and abusive clients. By undertaking to carry out specific transactions in which he managed his clients' goods and capital, De Vogel overcame his concerns and insecurities. In any case his concerns were justified given the conditions of uncertainty and risk prevailing on the Ottoman markets. His reticence towards long-term and grandiose commitments also reflected his concern at a difficult economic juncture, during which serious liquidity problems in the Amsterdam market had led many commercial companies to go bankrupt.[42] Moreover, fierce competition for dominance in the Eastern markets between Dutch companies and between Dutch and Ottoman merchants, mostly Greek, Armenian and

Jews, had resulted in market fragmentation and a sharp decline in the profits of all companies. De Vogel himself had repeatedly criticized the Dutch merchants who maintained Ottoman companies as representatives in Smyrna and the Dutch merchants of Smyrna who cooperated with Armenian and Greek trading houses in Amsterdam.[43] Cooperation with the Cardamicis should therefore be seen as an early manifestation of De Vogel's strategic choice to gradually limit the direct placement of funds in transactions with Ottomans and to undertake exclusively the representation and provision of services to trading houses in the East. The Cardamicis were not the only Ottoman merchants who entrusted De Vogel to act as their Amsterdam correspondent: the Armenian Kikor son of Carabeth Magaroglou, the Greek Ambrosio Mavrogordatos and many Ottomans Jews followed their example. However, it seems that, despite his statements, De Vogel continued to participate autonomously in Eastern trade by collaborating with various European trading companies operating in the Ottoman Empire.[44] In these partnerships Ottoman merchants in Smyrna and Constantinople sometimes acted as local representatives: when Bongard, Panchaud & Series went bankrupt, De Vogel used a well-known Armenian merchant of Constantinople, Tommaso Di Serpos, as intermediary to recover money owed to him.

Through the services and intermediation offered by De Vogel, the Cardamicis and other Ottoman merchants gained access to the commercial, maritime and financial centre of Europe. De Vogel had taken care to form a system of cooperation that required Ottoman and other clients in the Ottoman Empire to subject themselves to on-the-spot checks of their intentions and credibility. This control was carried out by his Smyrna associate, David Van Lennep & Enslie, and by his subsidiary, Thomas De Vogel Son & Brother,[45] which operated both in Smyrna and Constantinople.[46] David Van Lennep & Enslie was a partnership of the Dutch David Van Lennep and the English William Enslie.[47] Van Lennep represented other Dutch companies, as well as British houses in Constantinople and Smyrna, acting as an intermediary for the shipment of cargoes on their behalf to Amsterdam and Rotterdam.[48] His many years in business, and his social and family relations with members of the European and Ottoman trading community, made him the ideal intermediary for De Vogel's operations. Van Lennep & Enslie acted as De Vogel's agents and brokers and were also part owners with him of the ship *De Vrouwe Catharina*. Despite his close and long relationship with De Vogel, the great trust that connected them and the considerable responsibilities that Van Lennep & Enslie had assumed on his behalf, Van Lennep did not always meet De Vogel's expectations. As revealed in De Vogel's later correspondence with Raphael Cardamici, by the late 1760s the

Dutch merchant's relationship with Van Lennep had soured. De Vogel accused his compatriot and a close associate of manipulative behaviour and called on the Cardamicis to exclude him from their transactions.

The Cardamici–De Vogel cooperation was achieved during a favourable time for Dutch trade and merchant shipping in the Eastern Mediterranean. The Cardamicis, like other Ottoman merchants of the time, turned to Amsterdam to gain access to goods, information and services and to trade Eastern products in the most profitable and effective way. Participating in an international business network, relying on trust and a professional ethos to find their way in an unknown environment and using their credibility and good name as an asset, they plunged into the arena of international trade. How did this venture work in practice and what kind of transactions did it involve? The following chapters attempt to decode its specific characteristics.

3

Threads and diamonds

The Cardamicis' main activity was the import and export of goods between Europe and the Ottoman Empire at a time when international trade was flourishing. As already mentioned, by the eighteenth century, several circumstances had contributed to an increase in the volume and value of trade worldwide, making merchants key to each country's national economy. Significant population growth in most European countries had contributed to this development. Demographic progress had fuelled a process of urbanization and a sharp increase in the population of major European cities. The establishment of population groups in urban centres led to an upward trend in demand for food and essentials, leading to the further development of trade. Significant progress in agriculture through the introduction of new techniques and crops, the development of manufacturing and raw material processing sectors – in particular the textile industries – and colonial trade all contributed to an increase in the number and variety of goods that met an increasingly wide range of preferences and needs, forming a new consumption culture in the eighteenth century.[1]

Trade between Europe and the Ottoman Empire had developed rapidly since the sixteenth century and reached a tipping point during this period. Some historians linked this development to the Europeanization of Ottoman society, the Ottoman economy's integration into the world economy and its gradual decline.[2] An alternative view is that of Fernand Braudel, with whom many later historians seem to agree, that until the beginning of the nineteenth century the Ottoman economy remained dynamic and the entry of European trade into the markets of the East did not affect it greatly. The products consumed in Ottoman cities, Braudel argued, came mainly from local producers, Ottoman manufacture was rudimentary but largely covered the needs of the local population while strict controls on the exports of specific basic and food products ensured food adequacy, despite the great boom in smuggling.[3] In much the same direction, Frangakis-Syrett claims that the economic resources and needs of Europe and the Ottoman Empire were largely complementary, which also justifies the creation of wide networks of imports and exports linking the Ottoman markets with the centres of international trade in the largest European countries.[4] Western artisanal and industrial products, together with a large variety of colonial products, were exchanged for foodstuffs, plant and pharmaceutical substances, crafts and especially raw materials of the East which, for the most part, supplied European textile industries. In addition to European companies, many Ottoman companies engaged in this trade.[5]

The Cardamici company, comprising a medium-sized commercial enterprise in Smyrna and a branch office in Constantinople, traded in the Ottoman markets industrial products, raw materials, foodstuffs and everyday use objects obtained on the Amsterdam market, where a wide variety of items arrived from all parts of the world. As mentioned above, for the Cardamicis the question of finding a reliable and effective partner to take over as a representative of the company in the Dutch city was fundamental. Their options were limited since they did not have a subsidiary established in Amsterdam or a representative employee of their business there: they had to trust one or more of the local businesses in a role of a commercial correspondent. The appointment to this position of a Greek established in the city would possibly enable the Cardamicis to move more comfortably and control more effectively their Amsterdam partner's activity and trustworthiness. Some Greek companies in Smyrna and Constantinople also seem to have followed this practice, as revealed by the correspondence of merchant Dimitrios Kourmoulis. Kourmoulis was based in Venice, where he represented the partner trading houses of Lukas Kalvokoresis & Co. of Constantinople and Ioannis Avierinos & Co. of Smyrna. He was also responsible for the management and supervision of the transactions of these companies in Amsterdam. According to his correspondence with Kalvokoresis and Avierinos, the two partners had instructed two different Greek companies to represent them on the Amsterdam market, the companies of Stefanos Isaiou and Adamantios Korais. Both Isaiou and Korais were under the constant supervision of Kourmoulis, who systematically corresponded with them. Both Greek companies took pains to supply their customers, Kalvokoresis and Avierinos, with the best goods at the best prices – unaware, however, that they both represented the same customer. The orders of Kalvokoresis and Avierinos to Kourmoulis were clear: Isaiou and Korais had to perform as much as possible, but not knowing who participated in the interests they represented. Kourmoulis had also received permission from his superiors to address other London trading houses to act as an intermediary for the shipment of goods that the Greek representatives in Amsterdam were unable to obtain.[6]

Cardamici, a company with a more limited range of transactions than Kalvokoresis and Avierinos, could not bear the cost of hiring two dealers on commission (even though it seems to have appointed Hendrik De Bok as its correspondent in Rotterdam). Moreover, it does not appear to have formed a large circle of contacts with Greek companies in Smyrna, Constantinople and Amsterdam. The services that were therefore necessary for it to develop its business abroad through the Dutch port could be offered by a well-known and reliable Dutch trading house, such as Thomas De Vogel & Son. At that time many Dutch companies assumed the representation of foreign companies in Amsterdam. As Metrà mentioned in his guide, by the end of the eighteenth century, major Dutch commercial enterprises were involved in extensive intermediary trade, mainly in Amsterdam and also in Rotterdam.[7] Acting as agents and representatives, local trading houses received goods and products of all types at the two ports on behalf of trading companies from all over the world, selling them directly to the local market or storing them in port facilities until they were able to move them on to the trader who offered the best price. As Metrà noted, the business skills of Dutch merchants and the organization of the market allowed them to achieve significant economies of scale and attract foreign traders by offering them goods at prices much lower than those on the markets of their countries of origin. This special treatment, access to many opportunities, mediation in a well-organized services sector and the dynamism of the financial sector were among the reasons why foreign traders switched to Amsterdam and hired Dutch dealers to supply goods, money and services, even when the type of trade they conducted did not make it compulsory to pass through the Dutch port.[8]

Dutch companies operating as commercial correspondents retained a commission of between 1.5 and 2 per cent of the value of the transaction or 3–4 per cent of the sales value as a guarantee. At the same time, since they undertook to place orders for their customers abroad by purchasing goods on their behalf, they retained a percentage of the purchases, ranging from 1.5 to 2 per cent of the capital that the customers invested.[9] The commission trade had taken on a wide-ranging dimension on the Amsterdam market. It could therefore traditionally concern a merchant's order to his correspondent to buy and sell goods on his behalf or store them and arrange for them to be sent to other destinations; the mandate could, however, relate to the management of all types of banking and financial affairs, including the drawing, acceptance and payment of bills of exchange, the promotion of remittances in order to be accepted and repaid by third parties and the withdrawal of cash from banks and individuals – or in the maritime sector, the chartering of ships, the negotiation and signing of insurance contracts. As mentioned by contemporaries, with some exaggeration, in Amsterdam a merchant could buy, sell, insure and even order the building of a ship or its repair.[10]

The Cardamicis were looking for this kind of extended cooperation with a Dutch commercial correspondent when they selected a large and reputable Dutch company to represent them on the Dutch market. Thomas De Vogel's company was able to manage all these cases in an environment that was unknown to them and to carry out complex negotiations in an honest and efficient manner.

The difficulties faced by Greek Ottoman companies in adapting to the Dutch market environment and promoting their businesses on Dutch territory, as described by a Greek merchant, Stamatis Petrou, vindicate the Cardamicis' choices. In his letters to his principal in the Stathis Thomas & Co. of Smyrna, Petrou described, through the surprised gaze of a newcomer in Amsterdam, the behaviour, mentality and practices of Dutch merchants and brokers. Goods that arrived in Amsterdam on behalf of Stathis Thomas and other Ottoman merchants were stored in the warehouses of their correspondents and representatives, where they were inspected by Dutch merchants/brokers, who might choose to make an offer for them. The whole process involved the so-called 'resellers', traders who bought the products at a very low price and sold them to gain within the same market the difference in the price. Through his descriptions, Petrou implied that the Dutch were comfortable and cunning in negotiating prices, in a trading game where time, reliable information and the psychology of sellers and buyers played a decisive role.[11]

Thomas De Vogel & Son was tasked with representing the Cardamicis in these demanding circumstances. De Vogel placed the goods he received from the Cardamicis on the Amsterdam market while carrying out the orders of the Smyrna company, buying and sending it the goods that it had requested for the best quality and price he could secure. Deeply familiar with the trade and production sector, De Vogel approached various industries in the Amsterdam and Liège areas and ordered the manufacture of nails, pistols and various types of firearms ordered by the Cardamicis.

His primary concern was to act in an efficient manner for his principals, while ensuring his funds and reputation; for this reason, he adopted specific techniques that provided him with safeguards in the transactions he carried out on their behalf. Thus, in the purchase and sale of goods for the Cardamicis, he entrusted the receipt and the dispatch of the cargoes to David Van Lennep & William Enslie. The important and central role played by the Dutch–English company in the Cardamici–De Vogel partnership became more significant after 1764, when Raphael Cardamici took over the reins of the family business. The process was simple and effective. The Cardamicis delivered goods and remittances to the Dutch–English company in Smyrna, and Van Lennep made sure to complete the work of its mission with De Vogel in Amsterdam. De Vogel followed a similar procedure, by sending orders through Van Lennep to the Cardamicis; Van Lennep first received the goods and then delivered them to the Greek Ottoman merchants. Some goods were transported through the Smyrna market; others were transported by boat to Constantinople. In addition to Van Lennep & Enslie, the role of mediator in the transactions between the Cardamicis and their commercial correspondent De Vogel was occasionally assumed by the De Vogel Son & Brother company, with De Vogel's son, Thomas Junior, and his brother.[12] The mediation of a third company in the process of sending and receiving goods to and from the Cardamicis offered Thomas De Vogel a considerable amount of time which he could use to his advantage to ensure that Van Lennep checked the consignments and remittances on the spot. He therefore utilized his close partner and fellow national to enforce the observance of certain rules in the dealings of the Cardamicis, to know their movements and to verify the truth of their claims. The expansion of the company's activity with the involvement of new members of the family created new conditions for cooperation between De Vogel and the company: the Raphael Cardamici Nephew & Son and Pavlos, son of Bartholo Cardamici, joined the family business network not only as partners but also as independent traders, enhancing the Cardamicis' presence in the business game between Smyrna, Constantinople and Amsterdam and multiplying the business opportunities for the two companies.[13]

What, however, was De Vogel's contribution to the Cardamici business and how was the relationship between them formed? From the moment De Vogel received in Amsterdam the goods sent to him from Smyrna by the Cardamicis, he was obliged to promote them for sale on the local market, making sure to sell them at the best possible price to obtain the highest profit. The selling of goods in an international market where goods from all parts of the world arrived was neither short nor easy. As modern observers say, in bustling Amsterdam, everything seemed to be 'cramped', the ships in the port, the traders who packed into the Stock Exchange and the goods in the warehouses. As soon as the merchant ships arrived at the port, the city's agents and correspondents made sure to sell the merchandise at the next meeting of the Stock Exchange, then the ships unloaded within four to five days and were ready to set sail on a new voyage.[14] Locating and attracting direct buyers could prove time-consuming. However, large quantities of goods were stored in Amsterdam warehouses at any time for short or long periods until they were sold. As has been argued, the storage of goods was the cornerstone of the successful Dutch trade strategy as it played the game of demand and supply and consequently that of the pricing of goods.[15]

The variety, quality and quantity of goods received by De Vogel from the Cardamicis depended on the timing and the international demand, the conditions prevailing in the Ottoman markets, the opportunities that the Greek Ottoman merchants were able to exploit and the general strategy of the Cardamici company. It also depended on the conditions of supply and demand of products on the Amsterdam market. The frequent oversupply of goods of the same category and quality lowered their price and reduced demand, forcing traders to store them in anticipation of changing conditions. By keeping certain goods in the storage facilities of the international port, traders were able to react immediately to any opening up of the market and increase in demand. And if, in the end, the Amsterdam market appeared to have a decisive influence on European commodity prices, this was because of the volume of stock in its warehouses which, at any time, could be sent to the various markets or taken off the market and stored for long periods.[16]

The storage of goods was, in another sense, a direct consequence of delays in transport and, in general, the irregular pace of the arrival and departure of ships. It was also caused by delays in the arrival of traders' orders to commercial correspondents and, finally, the general uncertainty caused by the uncontrolled movement of news within the markets. To maximize their profit, traders and their agents/correspondents engaged in a race to be the first to sell a particular good; to achieve this, they had to, first, pick up the cargoes that arrived by boat at the port. Therefore, the timely arrival of ships from the East was crucial. Cargoes were timed to arrive at the most opportune time for their sale on the market in the early phase of high demand; the second, decisive factor determining the course and completion of transactions was the quality and quantity of goods. When the goods received by De Vogel were of secondary quality or defective, they remained in the warehouses for some time and then went to auction, a process that could eventually lead to their sale at a price lower than anticipated and yield a lower return for the Cardamicis. In general, the position of De Vogel, which he often expressed in his letters, was for his principals/clients to make sure that they sent him high-quality goods; De Vogel consistently advocated a well-thought-out and coordinated promotion of very good-quality and high-demand products on the international commodity market at the right time. To win the Cardamicis over to his view and to successfully carry out the transactions entrusted to him, he systematically informed them of the types and qualities of the goods most in demand in Amsterdam, encouraging them to invest in the purchase and dispatch of specific items.

Another factor that had a decisive influence on the cooperation of the two companies was the nature of the Amsterdam market, where Dutch and Greek, Armenian and other Ottoman trading houses competed for the primacy in the trade in Eastern goods. In his letters De Vogel often referred to the strategy of many Greek companies in Amsterdam, which, he argued, had a very negative impact on the functioning of the Dutch market and harmed the circle of Dutch traders trading with the Ottoman Empire. In his letters to the Cardamicis, he did not shy from criticizing the practices of a particular Greek trader, whom he did not name, claiming that he was adopting various tricks to manipulate the demand and prices of goods to achieve the greatest possible profit. He may have been referring to Antonios Zingrilaras, whose activity – and those of others – De Vogel closely monitored.[17] De Vogel appeared to resent the often obscure and, in this sense, unfair practices that Greek trading houses used to gain access to and exploit the best market opportunities. It is not coincidental that his letters made limited reference to collaborations with Greek companies. On the contrary, with constant, deliberate or random references to persons and events, De Vogel captured the environment in which the Cardamicis' operations were unfolding. He mentioned persons who participated in the various transactions or who could be potential partners, trading houses whose strategy was an example to be emulated or, more rarely, to avoid, and also their action plans, methods and techniques. Table 13 shows this universe of associates, acquaintances, 'friends', traders and trading houses, whose names De Vogel often referred to; the references were linked to relationships, transactions, thoughts and ideas and formed the real or mental universe of the two cooperating companies.

In his letters De Vogel gives the impression of being permanently involved in the purchase and sale of goods; a continuous negotiation on qualities, quantities and prices; and a confrontation with climate and time. At a time when markets were being squeezed by new goods, products and raw materials that met the increased needs of European industry and in particular the textile industry, the correspondent of the Cardamicis attempted through his letters to influence their decisions on which goods they should trade in.

Two documents of the period offer an idea of the goods flowing between Smyrna and Amsterdam at this time: Metrà's *Guide* and a standard bill of

Table 13 References to Commercial Houses from Thomas De Vogel's Correspondence with the Cardamicis

Name	City	Year
Jan Ackerman	–	1765
Bongard	Constantinople	1767
Christoforos Boni	Livorno	1764
Bornman	Constantinople	1767
Bornman & Van der Schroeff	–	1765
Camondo	–	1765
Pavlos Cardamici	Smyrna	1763, 1765
Pierre Cardamici & Co	Smyrna	1769
Raphael Cardamici Nephew & Son	–	1767
Chasseaud & Co	Livorno	1764
Chasseaud & Panchaud	–	1766
J. H & E. Coen Hemzy	–	1769
Markos Coroneos	Constantinople	1763
Nikolaos Chrysogiannis	Smyrna	1763
Hendrik De Bok	Rotterdam	1765
Johannes De Cologne	Liège	1769
Alexander De Masse	–	1760–2, 1765–6, 1768
Apostolos Demestikas	Smyrna	1763–4
Densel	–	1768
Isaac De Reus	Rotterdam	1764
De Vogel & Enslie	Smyrna	1769, 1771
De Vogel Son & Brother	Smyrna	1764, 1766, 1768
Thomas Jr De Vogel	–	1771
James Enslie	–	1768
Falcon	Smyrna	1769
Antoine & Francisco Filigoni	Livorno	1764
Fremeaux	Smyrna	1764, 1767
Gautier & Puzos	–	1767
Hendrik & Daniel Hopker	Amsterdam	1769
Hubsch & Timoni	Constantinople	1765, 1767
Samuel Himenes	–	1764
Sechir Jasegiroglou	–	1761
Antonios Zingrilaras & Co.	–	1761
Juda de Abraam Nunes	Livorno	1764
Jacob Le Clercq	–	1764
Jacob Le Clercq & Son	Amsterdam	1765
Series	Constantinople	1767
Series & Van der Schroeff	–	1770
Michail Masganas	Smyrna	1763
Nunes	Livorno	1764
Antonio Nunes	Livorno	1762
Ch. Dieder Oldembergh	Livorno	1764
Asmund Palm	–	1765, 1767
Panchaud & Van der Schroeff	–	1768
Panchaud	Constantinople	1767

Table 13 (Continued)

Name	City	Year
Konstantinos Platis	–	1766
Jacob Pauw	–	1767
Widow Pauw & Son	–	1768
Rigas, Niotis & Co.	Amsterdam	1769
Jean Henry Stametz	Vienna	1760, 1763–4, 1767
Stathis Thomas, Isaiou & Co.	–	1768
Stathis Thomas & Co.	–	1768
Ioannis Theocharis & Co.	Livorno	1764–6
Tidirepos	–	1764
David Van Lennep	Smyrna	1768–70
David Van Lennep & William Enslie	Smyrna	1764, 1766–71
F. & H. Van Sanen	–	1766
Van der Dudermuller & Son	Amsterdam	1764
Van der Santhuevel	–	1764
Van der Schroeff	Constantinople	1767
Octavio Watson	Livorno	1763

Source: Stadsarchief Amsterdam [StdAm], 332, Thomas De Vogel, Kopieboek, vol. 44–52, 1760–71.

lading, issued in Greek and which circulated among the Greek merchants in the Dutch port.[18] According to Metrà, in the mid-eighteenth century, Dutch exports to Smyrna included fabrics of various colours and qualities, pepper, cinnamon, cloves, nutmeg, cochineal flower, sulphuric acid, silver, bronze reels, copper and iron wire, turquoise, sugar, red lead, Danzig steel, English tin and lead, terracotta, Japanese campeachy wood, Fernambourg (Pernambuco) wood, raw amber, French cream of tartar, metal plates and cylinders, ginger and various kinds of coins.[19] The same goods exported to Smyrna were also shipped to Constantinople, Aleppo, Alexandria and Cairo. In particular, the Constantinople market absorbed a wide variety of goods and luxury products, including fine fabrics in various colours. From the Ottoman Empire different qualities of threads and yarn were introduced to Amsterdam, mohair yarn, senna leaves, opium, mastic, saffron, gum, wax, yellow wax, coffee, alunite, potash, palm tree wood, anise, wool and cotton thin fabrics, camel wool and camel wool fabrics, white ribbons from Mytilene, yellow, turquoise, and red ribbons, carpets of various sizes, buffalo skins, mattresses, Bursa silk, goat wool and angora wool. At the same time, the bill of lading circulating among the Greek companies in Amsterdam, in the category of goods of European and colonial origin sent to Smyrna, listed, among others: 'lead, shots, white and black ginger, amomum (yeni bahar), Fernambourg, campeachy, Santa Martha and Brazilian wood, indigo, red dye, camphor, coffee, cinnamon, pepper, sugar, tin, powder'.

The category of Eastern goods imported into Amsterdam included: 'galls from Smyrna and Aleppo, incense, ginger, Corinth black currants and red raisins, figs, vitriol of Cyprus, alum, rhubarb, scammony, Bursa silk, silk cocoon, opium, gum adragant, mastic, cotton, yarn, fringes, carpets'. According to the bill of lading, all these goods were transported to and from Amsterdam by ships that made a station not only in Livorno but also in other important Adriatic ports where they probably filled their cargoes or unloaded part of them.[20]

The De Vogel letters contain a wealth of information relating to the type, quantity and qualities of the goods traded by the Cardamicis. Table 14 presents this information in tabular format. Thus, the following information was gathered in parallel columns: the types of goods received by De Vogel in Amsterdam; the goods which De Vogel proposed to the Cardamicis to send to him; the Cardamicis' orders to De Vogel; De Vogel's shipments to Smyrna and Constantinople; and, finally, the goods which De Vogel himself proposed to the Cardamicis to send to Smyrna and Constantinople. By comparing this information by year, the type of trade carried out by the Cardamicis and their development over a ten-year period become clearer. At the same time, the decisive role played by De Vogel in the commerce of the Greek Ottoman traders emerges through his critical or positive responses to their choices. In terms of his approach and choices, he often disagreed with the Cardamicis. Finally, the information shows the extent to which he responded to the Cardamicis' requests; in this way we can evaluate the quality of their communication and investigate the presence, content and function of trust in their relationship.

Set up as a family business with personal funds, but without a wide network of partners, the Cardamicis relied for the promotion of their transactions abroad on De Vogel's acquaintances and associates as well. The Cardamicis launched their international trading activity following the dominant trend of the time, that is, importing iron and steel products, manufactured products and colonial goods and exporting raw materials mostly intended for the European textile industry. They were thus systematically exported cotton, silk and their by-products such as cotton fabrics, cotton yarns, silk and angora yarns. The particular involvement of many other Greek merchants in the trade of cotton and cotton yarn at a time of high demand in western European markets was one of the main parameters of their success in international trade.[21] The Cardamicis maintained a personal circle of suppliers not only in the hinterland of Smyrna but also in various regions for the production of cotton and silk, which is not surprising as it has been argued that the specialization of Greek traders in these areas of foreign trade was the result of the activity they traditionally carried

Table 14 Thomas De Vogel's Involvement in the Cardamici Business

	Goods De Vogel Received in Amsterdam	Goods De Vogel Proposed Cardamicis Send to Amsterdam	Cardamicis' Orders to De Vogel	De Vogel's Consignments to Cardamicis	De Vogel's Proposals on What to Send to Smyrna
1760	Fine-thread textiles wide and narrow fringes, Corinth and Zakynthos raisins	First-quality Kirkağac[22] cotton, Hebron wool, new crop cotton, Corinth and Zakynthos raisins, gum adragant	Sugar, coffee, lead, diamonds, velvet	Pistols, nails, lead, white iron, gunpowder	
1761	Fine-thread textiles wide and narrow fringes, raisins, red cotton yarn, cotton, silk	Galls, angora yarn, first-quality Kirkağac white cotton, raw silk, dry fruit, Hebron wool, new crop cotton, Corinth and Zakynthos raisins, gum	Handkerchiefs embroidered with the initial J	Diamond samples, Suriname and Martinique coffee, lead, weapons, gunpowder, white lead, nails, pistols	Suriname and Martinique coffee, diamonds
1762		Black raisins, new harvest lemons, wax, thin cotton thread		Santa Martha wood, Fernambourg wood, sax blue paint	
1763	Sponges, red and white cotton yarn, dried fruit	Cotton yarn, cotton, angora yarn		Nails, lead, tin, porcelain sets, Santa Martha wood, Fernambourg wood, blue sax paint, red lead, wire, swords, tartar	Textiles of his own production
1764	Cotton, white and red cotton yarn, fringes, silk, ten bales of angora yarn, fine-thread cloth, goat wool yarn	Cotton, first-quality cotton yarn, goat wool yarn, silk, red cotton yarn, dry fruit	Indigo, pistols, tin, pepper, nails, campeachy wood, porcelain sets	Santa Martha wood, mirrors, porcelain sets, timber, tortoiseshell, pistols, Canadian ermine, tin, nails	

(Continued)

Table 14 (Continued)

	Goods De Vogel Received in Amsterdam	Goods De Vogel Proposed Cardamicis Send to Amsterdam	Cardamicis' Orders to De Vogel	De Vogel's Consignments to Cardamicis	De Vogel's Proposals on What to Send to Smyrna
1765	Dry fruit and figs, red cotton yarn		Slippers, lead, porcelain sets, cambric textile	Nails, pistols, pistols the English or the Venetian style, sugar, St Vincent tobacco, Santa Martha wood, porcelain sets	
1766	Dry figs, currants, dry fruit, white and red cotton yarn, silk, cotton from Kirkağac, Bursa silk	First-quality Kirkağac cotton, Bursa silk	Ermine, foxskin, tortoiseshell, porcelain, cochineal	Nails, tobacco, Santa Martha wood, indigo, porcelain and porcelain sets, flower bowls, pistols, tortoiseshell, lapis lazuli, St Vincent tobacco, sugar, pepper, furs, foxskin, woollen textiles	Textiles of his own production
1767	Currants and dry figs	Cotton	Tortoiseshell, tobacco	Santa Martha wood, pistols, porcelain sets, foxskin, lead, violet tobacco, slippers, gunpowder, Fernambourg wood	
1768	Currants, dry figs	Bursa silk		Firearms, various types of pistols, gun barrels, gun boxes, nails, gunpowder, Fernambourg wood, lead, tin, slippers, purple tobacco	Delivery of information on the commerce of beauty products, silk textiles, canvases and toile, dry fruit and currants, various types of leathers

Year			
1769	Fringes, incense, cotton yarn, dry fruit	Porcelain sets with cups for hot chocolate and coffee, slippers, nails, gunpowder, pistols, various kinds of cheese, cloves, tortoiseshell, three types of canvas, faience and porcelain sets with cups	Canvases, sail cloths, various cheese and semolina flour, porcelain sets with cups for hot chocolate, faience plates, gunpowder for canons, Santa Martha, Fernambourg and campeachy wood, cloves, tobacco, nails, candle snuffers, pistols, guns, purple tobacco, porcelain sets, nails
1770	Red and white cotton yarn, cotton yarn, cotton wool, dry fruit, currants, incense, silk, boxwood		Nails, tobacco, porcelain sets, pistols, semolina flour

Source: Stadsarchief Amsterdam [StdAm], 332, Thomas De Vogel, Kopieboek, vol. 44–52, 1760–71.

out within the local economies of north-west Anatolia.[23] The decisive presence of Greek Ottoman companies in the Amsterdam cotton market is confirmed by the trader Stamatis Petrou through the description of specific incidents in his letters to Stathis Thomas, his principal in Smyrna. The incidents involved dealings between Greek traders and Dutch dealers concerning the purchase of cotton and yarn from the Ottoman Empire and revealed their competition and the tricks adopted by both sides to ensure a better price or to promote and sell even defective loads.[24]

As far as the import of goods into the Ottoman Empire was concerned, the Cardamicis received regular instructions from their Dutch correspondent to purchase certain goods and responded positively to them. De Vogel sought to keep them informed about demand and prices in Amsterdam and Smyrna, channelling to Smyrna information he received from his circle of personal acquaintances. Knowing that De Vogel had long conducted trade on his behalf through various partnerships in Smyrna and other Ottoman markets, and in fact continued to do so to a certain degree, it is not surprising that he was aware of price, demand and supply fluctuations in these markets; perhaps he was seeking to push the Cardamicis' operations in the direction that served him. In any case his recommendations for the purchase and dispatch of the best-quality Kirkağac cotton, thin cotton threads, soft angora yarn and excellent-quality Bursa silk were continuous.[25] As he pointed out at every opportunity, the Cardamicis never lost out in buying and reselling high-quality products in Western markets. Apparently, the dispatches of the Greek Ottoman merchants did not always meet his demanding requirements. Often, the quality of the cotton and especially the thread he received from Smyrna was much lower than his expectations. Also, occasionally, both Bartholo and Raphael Cardamici appeared to have their own agenda for the trade of specific products, promoting textiles of a certain low quality and value for sale on the international market in Amsterdam. De Vogel received fringes, piping and red cotton yarn and was obliged to sell them in a market of competitive, high standards and refined taste, where the demand for products of similar quality was minimal.[26] He was often left with little choice but to sell or auction off the goods off at a low price, much to his annoyance.[27] In 1769 he returned to Raphael in Smyrna the red cotton thread, telling him to sell it on the local market as in Amsterdam such low-quality products would only cause him reputational damage.[28] On this occasion, in a sarcastic tone and with the arrogance of a distinguished merchant, he suggested that Raphael should send a friend to Amsterdam to verify his claims.[29] Monitoring closely the market demand for Eastern goods, De Vogel encouraged the Cardamicis to send new products to Amsterdam, such as dried fruit, particularly Corinth and Zakynthos black raisins and figs, which were in very high demand.[30] Occasionally, he also advised them to send him galls,[31] fresh lemons[32] and wax.[33]

As regards imports of goods and products from Amsterdam into the Ottoman Empire, the study of De Vogel's letters and the data shown in the above tables reveal that from 1760 to 1763, when Bartholo ran the Cardamici business, the company imported to Smyrna almost exclusively nails and pistols. Until 1771 these items, and various types of weapons, swords, shotguns, canes and cases, lead and gunpowder, remained the company's main import goods in Smyrna and Constantinople.[34] It is obvious that the Cardamicis supplied military material to the Ottoman Empire, which also explains the operation of an office in Constantinople, the imperial political, administrative and military centre; it appears that it was their intention to participate in the trade of goods, products and raw materials to the administration, the army, the fleet as well as the upper classes of the empire.[35]

In the early 1760s, De Vogel attempted to persuade the prudent and conventional Bartholo Cardamici to engage in the trade of a wider variety of goods, such as manufactures, luxury and colonial products.[36] He also suggested that he get into textiles, buying at a special, very low price and promoting on the Ottoman markets fabrics that De Vogel himself would produce.[37] Apparently, De Vogel's efforts were not well-received. When later Raphael Cardamici took over the reins of the company, De Vogel made him the same proposal, urging him to cooperate with him in a woollen textile business, buying and promoting in the Ottoman markets fabrics whose production De Vogel would finance. De Vogel made a similar proposal to another Greek Ottoman merchant with whom he had established a similar association, Ambrosio Mavrogordatos. In a 5 March 1767 letter to Mavrogordatos, De Vogel referred to the dispatch of samples of fabrics of his own production to Mavrogordatos on the ship of Capt. De Leeuw. According to a later letter, Mavrogordatos found the fabrics to be of a very good standard and particularly refined due to the fine quality of the wool used in their manufacture.[38] However, he informed De Vogel that to invest capital in the business and promote them in the Ottoman markets, he would like these fabrics to be made of thicker wool so that they would be 'more solid and better looking' (*e che sola la vogliono forte e di buona veduta*). De Vogel replied that he was prepared to take over the production of the fabrics desired by Mavrogordatos and send him a shipment of two bales for approval. If Mavrogordatos also wished to obtain fine cotton fabrics produced by De Vogel, he would also send these to him. De Vogel proposed also to Raphael Cardamici to send him samples and a small quantity of fabrics of his own production. But these proposals were made fleetingly without the intention for a broader cooperation that would include the manufacture of fabrics on demand, as was the case with Ambrosio Mavrogordatos's company.[39]

Unlike his uncle, Raphael Cardamici had already been willing, since the early 1760s, to expand the company's trading scope by introducing luxury goods to the order list dispatched to De Vogel. Initially, he attempted to import expensive fabrics and jewellery into the Constantinople market. So, in 1760 he asked De Vogel to send him diamonds and velvets worth a total of 1,200 florins.[40] These goods were to be transported to the Ottoman capital, the seat of the political and administrative leadership, the upper classes, foreign diplomatic missions and generally wealthy professional and social groups that consumed refined, luxurious and valuable items of Western production and origin.[41] De Vogel responded to Raphael's demand, making sure to send him samples of velvets, while he also informed him about the various types of gems and their cuts. At the same time, however, he did not fail to inform Bartholo of his nephew's bold initiative and tried to buy time until he was instructed on how to handle this order.[42] These kinds of initiatives of Raphael Cardamici conflicted with the perceptions of the firm's founder of the selling and buying strategy that they had to follow. So, the diamond and velvet business did not proceed due to Bartholo's strong resistance and, at least until 1764, the list of goods Bartholo Cardamici & Co. ordered from De Vogel continued to include a limited, specific, number of items.

The situation changed dramatically after 1764, when De Vogel began receiving orders exclusively and directly from Raphael. The orders of the new manager included a wide variety of products and merchandise, which in the following years expanded even further at an impressive rate. Along with the pistols, nails and lead that continued to be the company's main imports, from now on Raphael ordered porcelain crockery; mirrors; Santa Martha, campeachy and Fernambourg wood; azul Saxe blue paint; red lead; wire; tortoiseshell; needles and swords;[43] Canadian ermine;[44] indigo; tin; pepper;[45] St Vincent sugar and tobacco; English and Venetian pistols;[46] foxskin; various types of fur; woollen fabrics;[47] and even flower pots.[48] In 1766 Raphael expressed his desire to import cochineal and asked De Vogel for information on the different qualities and prices of this item on the Amsterdam market.[49] In 1767 his interest in the diamond trade was rekindled[50] and, a year later, he considered expanding his operations to Russia. He therefore asked his Dutch correspondent for information on commodity prices, the cost of freights and commissions and the duties charged on the St Petersburg market.[51] In 1769 Raphael further enriched the list of items he ordered in Amsterdam with porcelain sets for coffee, tea and chocolate consumption, flour, cheese, cloves, candlesticks and various kinds of canvases.[52]

As can be seen from Table 14, De Vogel's attempts to manipulate the Cardamicis concerned more the shipments of goods to Amsterdam and less the orders sent to him from Smyrna. Indeed, De Vogel systematically attempted to direct the Cardamicis to the market for a specific quality and quantity of Kirkağac cotton, excellent white and red cotton yarn and high-quality Bursa silk, goods for which there was demand. The Cardamicis took his recommendations seriously, to the greatest possible extent, given the funds the company had and contacts in the local Ottoman markets. On the other hand, De Vogel did not express the same interest in some of the goods suggested by the Cardamicis, limiting himself, in some rare cases, to sending them information on goods of interest to them. His letters, however, were usually accompanied by lists of goods and prices traded on the Amsterdam market. Through the catalogues, the Cardamicis were informed of the conditions prevailing on the Dutch market at a given time. They then chose which goods to order, having previously considered the demand and needs of the Smyrna and Constantinople markets, the preferences of their own customers, the capital they had and, finally, their instinct. Without a doubt, the commodity/cost lists acted as a lever to push the Cardamicis to deal with or trade in a greater variety of goods. However, De Vogel himself took a rather neutral stance on their final choices and did not encourage them to buy certain items. He also often stated an inability to either locate or buy at a favourable price the goods requested and postponed their purchase and shipment.

From the above one can conclude that the visible change in the import strategy of the Cardamici company after 1763 did not result from De Vogel's encouragement but was a conscious choice of the new company director at a time when the conditions prevailing in international trade favoured it. At the same time, Raphael Cardamici's orders from 1764 onwards captured the evolution of consumer habits within European society and their reflection in the societies of the two largest urban centres of the Ottoman Empire.[53] A list of customs duties imposed by the Ottoman customs authorities on various goods and products imported into Constantinople proves that after 1738, the variety and origin of goods had expanded in the imperial capital, where more goods from countries of Europe and the New World were being consumed.[54]

The import by Raphael Cardamici of not only porcelain crockery and objects made from faience,[55] special dinnerware for the consumption of coffee and chocolate,[56] flower pots, coffee, pepper, various types of cheese and flour but also luxury clothing such as ermine and foxskin and linen handkerchiefs with monograms confirms the well-known assumption that in the eighteenth century in Europe a consumer revolution was taking place as an endless series of new goods and products created a new global 'economy of quality and enjoyment'.[57] In the West these commodities appeared more and more often in the houses of the bourgeoisie and did not concern exclusively the daily life and habits of the aristocracy or the members of the royal courts. On the contrary, they reflected the expansion of aesthetic horizons, taste and everyday needs of an up-and-coming middle class and turned material culture in a new direction. The new consumer goods – many of them of British manufacture, which revealed modernity, kindness, style and independence – were also acquired by people who belonged to the lower levels of the social and professional hierarchy. They were accessible in an endless variety of designs, qualities and prices – what counted was appearance, elegance and price.[58] The Cardamicis did not specialize in the trade of European fabrics on the Ottoman market, a trade that more than any other revealed society's need for a particular lifestyle and habits that emphasized appearance.[59] However, diamonds, velvets, cosmetics and toiletries, mirrors and furs,[60] even precious pistols and swords, met the needs for a certain refined lifestyle of an increasingly augmenting group of people within the empire, which included members of the upper and middle classes, as well as the lower social classes.[61] As McKendrick, Brewer and Plumb state, internationally a spirit of emulation developed that encouraged people of different social origins to buy these goods.[62] The new consumer attitudes did indeed seem to affect the everyday life and behaviour of all classes of Ottoman society at this time.[63] Through the study of hereditary registers, Fatma Müge Göçek proves that the replication of Western models of social behaviour affected both the elites of the empire, the middle classes and the lower strata of society.[64] The consumption of Western luxury goods and products first developed in major ports and urban centres in the eighteenth century.[65] The Ottoman archives confirm the large concentration of luxury goods by the social groups that had the greatest purchasing power, by the members of an up-and-coming bourgeoisie as well as by the class that had the least resources at its disposal: the ordinary people.[66] The sudden change in strategy of the Cardamicis, a middle-sized Ottoman trading company, reflected precisely the desire of the new director to exploit these new trends within the Constantinople and Smyrna markets.

Trading goods between East and West was the Cardamici company's main activity. Thomas De Vogel acted as a catalyst in the transfer and establishment of this activity within an international business environment. De Vogel's extensive network of business contacts, the direct and reliable information he obtained from it and his acute business instinct that was based on experience and knowledge offered the Cardamicis a specific action plan. For the Greek Ottoman merchants, however, the opening to Western markets and the entry into the world of international trade also required a long and arduous journey through the Mediterranean. In practice this meant the completion of another demanding process which also required a network of contacts and personal acquaintances, information, experience, judgement and determination – in this process the weather was an independent and immeasurable variable. On this occasion too, the Cardamicis trusted De Vogel to undertake the task of organizing the transfer of the merchandise, in other words, of drawing up a strategy, identifying priorities and implementing the necessary actions.

4

Ships, freights and insurance

As a commercial correspondent for the Cardamicis, Thomas De Vogel chartered ships to transport goods between Amsterdam, Smyrna and Constantinople. He was also responsible for the cargoes' insurance, a requirement which was seen to at the same time as the appropriate freight was found and signed. De Vogel would have been aware of the regulations in force in both the Netherlands and the Ottoman Empire and would have then performed all the requirements necessary to secure the most advantageous business agreements. An interesting detail which seems to have had a decisive influence on the way he handled his activities in these two areas was his parallel endeavour as the owner and co-owner of vessels which were often chartered to Ottoman merchants for transporting cargoes on the Amsterdam–Smyrna route.[1]

The chartering of a ship required a lengthy negotiation process, and this was true for Dutch ships chartered either in the Netherlands or in Ottoman ports.[2] The charter agreements bore the signatures of the two contracting parties – the charterer and the owner or captain of a vessel – and did not differ widely, no matter if the negotiations took place in Amsterdam, Hamburg or Smyrna. These texts describing the obligations and rights of the captain and the charterer had remained essentially the same since the end of the sixteenth century.[3] Amsterdam's freight and insurance market offered a multitude of opportunities to secure the most profitable agreement following research and consultation with interested parties. In this circumstance, the successful completion of a commercial enterprise depended to a large extent on a merchant's ability to properly assess the prevailing conditions on the free market – in this case on the freight and insurance market. A worthy commercial correspondent had to take advantage of opportunities and avoid risks that threatened the property of those he represented.[4]

Within this dynamic business world, Thomas De Vogel had a contractual obligation to his Greek Ottoman principals to choose vessels, captains and freights and to sign insurance policies that covered their needs as much as possible.

Captains and charterers for Ottoman clients

De Vogel's correspondence clearly shows that the Cardamicis exclusively chose Dutch-owned ships manned by Dutch captains in their transactions with him. The freight procedures entrusted to De Vogel were long and laborious, and as will be seen, this justifies the Cardamicis' choice in entrusting them to a Dutch trading company in Amsterdam.

Since the sixteenth century shipping had been one of the most advanced and profitable sectors of the Dutch economy. This development was directly linked to the progress of Dutch shipbuilding and the superior technical specifications of their vessels, the experience of Dutch mariners and the international network present in the major Dutch ports.[5] The development of the maritime sector ultimately led the Dutch authorities to promote major structural reforms and develop a highly sophisticated and progressive regulatory-institutional framework for matters relating to the brokerage, chartering and insurance of ships and goods. Legal institutions and procedures that controlled illicit speculation emerged that protected private commercial enterprises from the charge of treason.[6] The establishment of control mechanisms operating under the supervision of administrative courts and audit committees ensured legitimacy in these sectors of the economy and shaped the institutional environment in which a merchant entrepreneur had to operate. To defend commercial and maritime property from unforeseen misfortunes and obstacles, the Insurance Council was created to supervise the insurance of goods, ships and individuals. This was a decisive contribution to the rationalization of transactions and the sharing of business responsibility.[7]

In the eighteenth century, Amsterdam's shipping and insurance market was one of the most important and prosperous worldwide. As far as charters of vessels for voyages to the Ottoman Empire were concerned, the procedure was as follows: the captain had to contact various charterers of the port, who in turn informed the public concerned and the market of the ship's departure by printing circulars to be posted on the Amsterdam Stock Exchange and in various public buildings. The circulars contained information relating to the vessel and the voyage: reference was made to the price of the freight, its destination, the vessel's equipment, including cannons, the firman obtained by the captain from the Ottoman Porte and where the boat was docked to receive the cargo – river, port or natural port. The circulars also included the name of the charterer to whom any interested party should apply. A ship could be chartered in whole or in part, and cargo – the weight of which was calculated in *last*[8] – could be transported in barrels, packages and bags. The freight usually covered one or two trips or a specific period calculated in months. The charterer, or *nollegiatore*, sealed the agreement after negotiations with the captain or with the ship's owner. The transaction involved the commercial correspondent on commission (in this case De Vogel) who received from his merchant client (in this case Cardamici) an order for the transport of goods. Finally, the *sensale*, or broker, occasionally mediated between the correspondent and the charterer to find an appropriate ship that could best serve the interests of the merchant client. When the right ship was found, De Vogel signed a contract with the charterer recording the terms of the agreement, the amounts of freight and the commission to be paid. The contract detailed the type and quantity of goods as well as the prices of the *avaria* (average paid for damages) and the *coppa* (money sometimes paid to the captain as an additional fee).[9] Reference was also made to travel arrangements – the departure date, duration, arrival date and stations to be visited, among other details. By the end of the eighteenth century, it was common practice for freights entering to the Netherlands from foreign ports and vice versa to be paid in Dutch florins.[10]

The charter contract was signed in two or three copies and approved and validated by a notary. The captain or another official issued a receipt recording all packages loaded on board on behalf of a merchant. To anticipate and address the risk that the document of proof could be lost during the journey, the bill of lading, or *conoscimento*, was drawn up.[11] The bill of lading was a document issued by a carrier, often a ship's captain, which acknowledged the receipt of cargo for shipment. In it a captain would state that he had received packages on board his ship on behalf of a merchant, had collected a freight, *avaria* and *coppa*, and was obliged to transport and deliver them safely to the agreed destination, indicated on the bill.[12] Sometimes the shipment of the bill of lading was prior to the arrival of the goods. In 1762, De Vogel declared to the Cardamicis: 'We have the bill of lading . . . on the ship of Capt. E. Hellesen [and when] we know the happy arrival of this ship we will secure the mooring and sell at the biggest profit for you.'[13] Usually the bill of lading was attached to a copy of the insurance policy received by the merchant: 'Here attached together . . . the bill of lading of 100 pieces of bullets and the barrels with pistols loaded on board *La Johanna Lambert & Kristina* of Capt. Adriaanse Mallaga and also a copy of the receipt of 900 florins . . . insurance for the barrels with pistols.'[14] The captain was obliged to announce his arrival at the ship's destination – either directly himself or through a charterer, broker or agent – to the merchants and correspondents registered as the cargo's recipients. The interested parties, having already received the bill of lading from Amsterdam, sent small boats to the ship and, after presenting the captain with the bill, received the goods.

Captains and ships in the service of the Cardamicis

As a commercial correspondent of the Cardamici company, it was Thomas De Vogel's job to organize and attend to the above procedures. The timely, safe and economically advantageous transport of goods between Amsterdam, Smyrna and Constantinople was a fundamental phase of the trading cycle conducted jointly by De Vogel's company and that of the Cardamicis, always through the mediation of Van Lennep & Enslie in Smyrna. This phase of business was risky and required De Vogel to maintain a large web of contacts, have up-to-date market knowledge and the ability to negotiate, make bold choices and take risks. A relationship of trust between merchant and correspondent was also essential, as the Dutchman would have had to secure the Cardamicis' consent before any attempt to promote agreements and sign contracts. We do not know with certainty whether negotiations conducted by De Vogel involved third parties as charterers and *sensali*, as this is not mentioned in his letters. However, either he or a representative of his company in Amsterdam was in direct contact with captains and shipowners. In negotiations, personal acquaintances and access to reliable information played a key role.

The process of chartering a ship and sending off a vessel to the East is often presented as a captivating story in De Vogel's letters. The closing of negotiations and signing agreements were time-consuming and complex procedures that could be affected by uncontrollable, and even unforeseen, factors. De Vogel had to deal with delays in the production and delivery of goods from local manufactures, while also awaiting the delivery into Amsterdam of colonial products from distant markets, such as coffee and sugar. As soon as he was able to collect the goods detailed in a Cardamici order, he then had to source a suitable vessel and begin arduous negotiations for the freight with the vessel's captain or owner. After reaching the most economical agreement and the various organizational and technical issues had been arranged, the merchandise was loaded on board. Following that, departure was delayed until the remaining orders from other merchants were loaded on board and there were favourable weather conditions. As

De Vogel characteristically stated, unexpected weather changes could significantly delay a ship's departure, especially when rain and frost prevented the transport of goods from port warehouses to ships by boat through the canals.

De Vogel's substantial experience, as well as his extensive network of local and international contacts, ensured he always possessed a comprehensive and reliable picture of the local freight market, which allowed him to conduct negotiations with relative comfort. He had direct contact with captains, through whom he obtained route information, departure and arrival schedules and freights prices. With this information De Vogel could swiftly create business strategies and seek out the best – and most lucrative – market opportunities. His access meant he could organize and book freights not only on the Amsterdam–Smyrna route but also on the Amsterdam–Constantinople and Smyrna–Constantinople routes. His familiarity with commercial ship charters was also related to his direct involvement with the commercial shipping sector because De Vogel, as mentioned previously, had invested part of his capital in the commercial vessels market that often operated in the East.[15]

De Vogel's letters contain frequent references to the names, personalities strategies, behaviours and abilities of the captains, owners and co-owners of vessels chartered to carry cargoes ordered by the Cardamicis.[16] His descriptions allow us to recreate the maritime trade environment within which the Cardamicis had to navigate. They paint a vivid picture of the negotiations necessary to charter a vessel for travel between Amsterdam, Smyrna and Constantinople. They also highlight the contribution made to commercial enterprises of a most important figure: the captain, the maritime professional and 'businessman of the sea', who played a decisive role in facilitating international trade.[17] The Dutch captains appeared, in fact, to be the protagonists in the discussions and decisions surrounding freight prices, the settlement of bureaucratic and practical issues, route setting and specifying departure dates; they dealt with the weather conditions and any unforeseen events at sea, they bore responsibility for the safety of the goods they were transporting and they were asked for explanations in the case of their damage or destruction.[18] Apparently, Thomas De Vogel collected information about the international freights market through partners and friends who were established in ports overseas. However, it was his direct contact with captains in Amsterdam and his familiarity with this sector that gave him access to information on developments related to the interconnection with Ottoman ports.[19] De Vogel often named the captains with whom he was negotiating. These names, together with the names of their vessels, when mentioned, are presented in Table 15.

Table 15 Ships and Captains in Thomas De Vogel's Correspondence, 1760–71

Name of Captain	Name of Ship
Andoni Andonis	*La Fortune*
Andries Andriessen	*St. George*
Albert Jean Bakker	*De Jonge Michiel*
Paulus Blandauw	*St. Spiridion*
Willem Blom	*De Gysbert Jan*
Ernst Boermaster	*De Vrouw Catherina*
Arnoldus Brons	
Bruyn	
Albert Connenhove	*De Vrouwe Margaretha*
Couvret	*De Hester*
De Groot	
Pieter de Leeuw	*De Vrouw Catharina*
De Vries	
Deffauer	
Auke Disma	*De Snelle Galley*
Henry Douwesz	*De Hester Galeij, Helvoit*
Ernst Dowes	
Johannes Evererd	
Ryndert Everts	*De Dolphyn*
Rander Foresee	
Forti	
Dirk Frost	
Claus Gerritz	
Pietersen Hendriks	
Jacob Hilkes	
Hraneux	
Andries Jurrians	
Kectel	*De Vreede (La Paix)*
Jacob Kersies	
Klip	
Krimpe	
Kert Langendyk	
Abraham Macrielsen	
Adriaanse Mallaga	
Ab. Matthy	*St. Spiridion*
Matteo Mattierik	*N.S. Madonna del Rosario*
M. Mettiernich	
Hendrik Miren	*De Meer en Amstelzicht*
Misela	
Marten Pante	*De Hellespontus*
Primke	
Hans Rave	
Cornelius Ruyter	*De Euphrates*
Ring	
Schaap	

Table 15 (Continued)

Name of Captain	Name of Ship
S. P. Schreuder	
Mente Schryver	
Pierre Vailhart	
Pierre Vanson	
Visser	
Vlaming	

Source: Stadsarchief Amsterdam [StdAm], 332, Thomas De Vogel, Kopieboek, vol. 44–52, 1760–71.

In his letters, De Vogel informed the Cardamicis of incidents that had occurred during negotiations for ship chartering. In most incidents, the captain was crucial to the successful conclusion of an international trade transaction.[20] It is for this reason that all the major European trading houses, trade agents and commercial correspondents of the period paid particular attention to a captain's skills and experience when choosing a ship. Like De Vogel, they formed personal networks of trusted sea professionals with whom they had previously worked with and to whom they turned when tasked with a new job.[21]

The Dutch captains involved in the Cardamici trade operations between Smyrna, Constantinople and Amsterdam emerge, therefore, as experienced and competent seafarers, responsible for the safety of the vessel, crew and cargo and also those who handled all negotiations and freight agreements.[22] Negotiations that took place on behalf of the Cardamicis suggest that captains could veto the choice of items to be transported and set limits on the maximum weight and volume of goods they would load, the number of passengers they would accept on board and the crew they would hire. They had, in other words, the right and obligation to protect the ship and prevent overloading. It was also at the captain's discretion to determine the ship's departure date – he decided whether to accelerate or delay procedures to complete a charter, loading times and departure dates. The captain, who was sometimes also the owner of the ship, had the power to impose his terms on merchants, commercial correspondents and charterers and to carry out various business manoeuvres in order to maximize profits.[23] By assessing current conditions in the freight market and the opportunities offered to it by the merchants and agents who approached him, he negotiated freights, offered storage facilities, modified a voyage's schedule and, ultimately, behaved like an experienced businessman.[24]

All these conditions and interventions contributed to the fact that the negotiation of a freight remained a long and arduous process, even in the most optimal circumstances. De Vogel's style, when describing various cases of ineffective negotiation to his Greek Ottoman principals, makes apparent the prevailing tension in the weeks that led up to the final signing of the fare, the loading of the ship and its departure. In September 1760, he informed Bartholo Cardamici that he had been obliged to load the pistols he had ordered for him on the *La Paix* of Capt. Kectel, who had ultimately refused to include them in his cargo for a price of less than 27 florins per *last*, as he had already loaded a lot of goods and was about to set sail.[25] De Vogel often referred to the uncertainty caused by the unpredictable and arrogant behaviour of some captains and expressed concern when he was unable to influence or reverse their decisions. In this way he allowed the Cardamicis a glimpse of the difficulties he faced in order to carry out the assignments he had undertaken for them. 'We are very upset,' he noted in 1766, 'as Capt. Disma couldn't load twenty cotton bundles despite the help and appeals of our Son & Brother [the company De Vogel Son and Brother of Smyrna] that brought no results. We're very unhappy to see that Capt. Andriessen loaded only eight bundles.'[26] And when referring to the same captain a few months later he mentioned sarcastically that with the high freights he was charging, 'he thinks already that he is doing a favour'.[27] Negotiating a ship's charter agreement became even more complicated when the captains themselves were engaged in trade, even occasionally investing their capital in goods which they loaded together with the rest of the vessel's cargo in order to sell them at one of the destination ports.[28] In 1763, De Vogel informed the Cardamicis that Capt. Blandauw had loaded, on his own behalf, a large quantity of tin and lead and so, as the ship had gained significant weight, he had refused to load the nails intended for them.[29] After Blandauw's refusal, the Dutch merchant had attempted to load the goods onto whichever ship offered him the lowest freight and the most favourable terms.[30]

Ships sailing to ports in the East crossed the Atlantic, passed through the Strait of Gibraltar and entered the Mediterranean Sea where, after numerous stops in ports in the western Mediterranean and Italy, they arrived in the Ottoman Empire. There they unloaded their cargo and loaded goods which they then transported to the Netherlands, either directly or by following a route with successive stations at the ports of Livorno, Genoa, Trieste, Malta and Marseille. According to the series of manifests held in the archive of the Dutch consulate, there was a significant increase in the number of arrivals and departures of Dutch ships in Smyrna between 1763 and 1770.[31]

As Table 16 shows, the number of arrivals and departures of Dutch ships increased gradually but decisively between 1763 and 1768 and returned to an

Table 16 Arrival and Departure of Dutch Ships at/from the Port of Smyrna, 1763–71

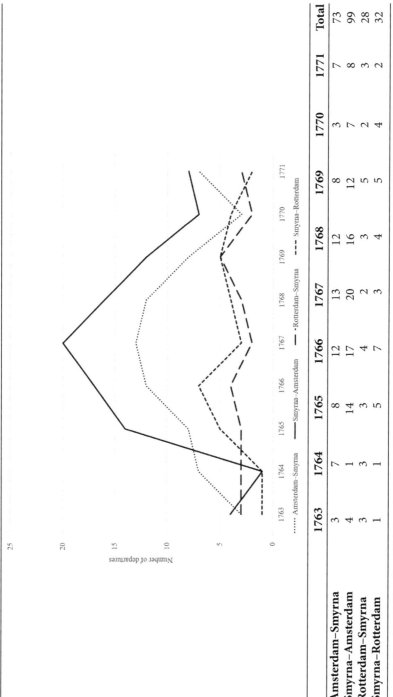

	1763	1764	1765	1766	1767	1768	1769	1770	1771	Total
Amsterdam–Smyrna	3	7	8	12	13	12	8	3	7	73
Smyrna–Amsterdam	4	1	14	17	20	16	12	7	8	99
Rotterdam–Smyrna	3	3	3	4	2	3	5	2	3	28
Smyrna–Rotterdam	1	1	5	7	3	4	5	4	2	32

Source: Nationaal Archief Den Haag [NA], Consulaat Smyrna [CS], 1.02.22, Manifests series, 547 (1763)–563 (1780).

earlier rate after 1768. The period 1766–9 saw traffic reach its highest levels. The ports of Amsterdam and Rotterdam were the most common ports of departure for ships that arrived at the Ottoman port, and all Dutch ships originating in Smyrna returned there. Amsterdam had significantly higher numbers of arrivals and departures than Rotterdam, which was often a forced choice for merchants who were unable to find suitable freights to their first port of choice. Between 1764 and 1769 the number of arrivals and departures to and from Rotterdam also increased, although in absolute numbers they remained lower than those relating to Amsterdam. The routes followed by the ships often included stations in other Mediterranean ports such as Genoa, Trieste, Marseille, Malta and especially Livorno, which, at this time, represented, an intermediate, operational hub in the movement of goods between the Netherlands and the Ottoman Empire.[32]

Table 17 shows instead that a specific fleet of Dutch vessels travelled systematically to and from the major Ottoman ports at the time, in particular on the Amsterdam–Smyrna–Amsterdam route. Some vessels even made more than one voyage a year (such as the *Saint Spyridon* of Capt. Ab. Matthy or the *De Vrouw Catharina*, captained by Pieter De Leeuw) while others appeared to have made fewer journeys or, occasionally, a single one on a particular route.

Thus, the *De Cornelia Petronella* made a journey on the Amsterdam–Smyrna route in 1765 and a return journey in 1766. It made another trip on the Smyrna–Amsterdam route in 1767 and again on the Smyrna–Amsterdam route and one to Amsterdam–Smyrna in 1768. It sailed from Amsterdam to Smyrna and from Smyrna to Amsterdam in 1769, a journey on the Amsterdam–Smyrna route in 1770 and one on the Smyrna–Amsterdam route in 1771. By contrast, the *De Vrouw Susanna* appears to have made one return trip on the Amsterdam–Smyrna route in 1771. As Tables 16 and 17 suggest, there was a wide enough range of freight options for the transfer of the Cardamicis' cargoes. Apparently, in certain years, a relatively large number of Dutch ships serviced the Amsterdam–Smyrna–Amsterdam route. Thus, in 1763, eight ships departed from Amsterdam for the Ottoman port. In 1766 and 1767 that number was twelve and thirteen, respectively. Similarly, in 1765, thirteen Dutch ships departed from Smyrna for Amsterdam, in 1766 seventeen, in 1767 twenty and in 1768 sixteen.[33]

News of ship arrivals and departures was transmitted very quickly, by word of mouth, from one port to another: As De Vogel wrote to Raphael Cardamici in 1770:

> We haven't had a chance to load the nails here as we can't find ships but we have the feeling that we will be able to load them on the ship of Capt. Claus Gerritz,

Table 17 Amsterdam–Smyrna and Smyrna–Amsterdam Trips of Dutch Ships, 1763–71

Name of Ship	1763	1764	1765	1766	1767	1768	1769	1770	1771	▲	▼
St. Spiridon	▲▼		▲▼	▲▼	▲▼	▲▼	▲▼	▲▼	▲	7	8
De Vigilantie	▲▼	▲	▲▼	▲▼						3	2
De Vrouw Maria	▲		▲							0	1
De Nieuwe Hoop	▲	▲								1	1
De Vrouw Catharina	▲	▲	▲▼	▲	▲		▲▼			5	3
De Vreede	▲	▲	▲	▲						2	3
De Juffrouw Suzanna	▲	▲				▲				2	2
De Reijsende Son	▲	▲								2	0
De Vrouw Margaretha	▲	▲	▲	▲	▲▼	▲				2	4
St. Gregorii	▲		▲	▲	▲▼					1	3
De Margaretha en Catharina			▲							0	1
Constantinopolen			▲▼	▲	▲		▲			2	2
De Vriendschap			▲▼		▲▼			▲	▲	3	3
De Juffrouw Anna Elisabet			▲▼	▲	▲▼					1	2
Meer en Amstelzicht			▲▼	▲	▲▼					2	3
Azia			▲	▲	▲		▲▼		▲▲▼	4	3
De Cornelia Petronella			▲	▲	▲	▲▼	▲▼	▲	▼	4	5
Middelloo			▲	▲	▲					2	1
Unie			▲							1	0
St. George				▲▼	▲▼	▲▼	▲	▼	▲	5	4
De Hellespont				▲	▲▼	▲▼				1	3
De Jonge Michiel				▲	▲▼	▲				1	3
De Jonge Juffrouw Anna Maria				▲▼	▲▼		▼			3	3
Oosterleek				▲▼						1	0
De Dolphyn				▲▼	▼		▼			1	3
De Jonge Juffrouw Maria				▼						0	1

(Continued)

Table 17 (Continued)

Name of Ship	1763	1764	1765	1766	1767	1768	1769	1770	1771	◄	►
De Jonge Cornelis				►						0	1
De Vrouw Helena				►	◄►					1	2
Oosterhout				►						0	1
De Snelle Galeij				►						0	1
De Smirniotta				◄►		◄				2	0
Sniringshoek				►						0	1
De Zeeridder					◄	◄				1	1
De Zwaan					◄►	►	◄►	►	◄►	3	4
De Vrouwe Elisabeth					◄	►	◄►			1	2
Belus					►		►			1	2
De Hester Galeij					►					1	1
Geertruv										0	1
De Gysbert Jan						►		►	◄	1	2
De St. Antonio						►				0	1
De Vliegende Mercurius						▼◄				1	1
De Kryters							►◄			1	1
De Smirna							►			0	0
De Spierenthoek								►		0	1
De Vrouw Helena Maria								►		0	1
De Hamsteede								►		0	1
De Zeeport										0	1
Ouwerkerk aan den Amstel									►	0	1
De Vrouw Susanna									◄►	1	1

Source: Nationaal Archief Den Haag [NA], Consulaat Smyrna [CS], 1.02.22, Manifests series, 547 (1763)–563 (1780). The symbol ◄ denotes an Amsterdam–Smyrna trip and the symbol ► a Smyrna–Amsterdam trip.

who is now in Rotterdam and loading; you will learn about it when you receive the bill of lading with our first letter.[34]

De Vogel, like other merchants, usually had time to weigh the various factors that could affect a ship's departure date and to anticipate developments to amend his strategy. In 1768, he conveyed to his clients his thoughts on what he had to do:

> The ship remains in front of the city, and it is very uncertain whether it will be able to depart this year or not and also requires a very high freight and so we will make sure that all the goods are passed on to the ship of Capt. Boermaster who charges very low freights.[35]

Unforeseen events could often occur and impact business because the conclusion of a shipping operation was ultimately subject to the captain's mood and his assessment of the prevailing conditions. In 1768, De Vogel wrote:

> Capt. Hendriks, who was loading his ship to come to your places, as he has done many times, will remain here and will not depart this period and so he unloaded – we thought this would happen and so we did not load goods on his ship; the outrageous prices he was asking for caused us many doubts.[36]

Knowing from experience how a vessel's technical specifications and a captain's personality and abilities could affect a job, De Vogel generally avoided chartering vessels he did not know from experience. The same was true regarding the cooperation with captains who were unknown to him. Insurers were similarly hesitant to insure vessels and cargoes when the identity of the owner, the skills of the captain and the qualities of the vessel were not known to them. De Vogel made sure to keep his principals informed of these delicate balances that defined operations within the Amsterdam insurance market and which they had to consider when selecting a freight. He made certain to maintain these balances and to choose captains and vessels he knew from previous voyages; personal relationships, in this case too, ensured better and safer trading conditions. In November 1764, De Vogel wrote to Raphael Cardamici: 'As far as the orders you have placed with us are concerned, we will send them all to you on the first ship to depart, which will happily be the ship of Capt. Kectel.'[37] As revealed in the letter's follow-up, Capt. Kectel was bound for Constantinople and De Vogel intended to negotiate with him on the price of the freight, 'otherwise we will look for other opportunities', he concluded.[38] Some years later he assured Raphael Cardamici that he would send him the goods he had ordered but was not yet able to inform him about the price of the freight because he did not know which ship would depart on time, 'except the ship of Capt. Boermaster which is located in Texel already and will definitely depart'.[39] The trusting relationships De Vogel maintained with his captain contacts often developed into relationships of mutual concessions. In 1766, he referred to his 'special relationship' with Capt. Brons, who made sure to always offer him lower prices: 'We will send the above mentioned goods to Rotterdam to be loaded on the ship of Capt. Brons for Smyrna as on this ship we are charged with a very low fare'.[40] A relationship of trust and mutual service with a ship's captain could be highly beneficial as it often gave De Vogel additional – and sometimes necessary – time to complete the process of collecting the goods ordered by the Cardamicis, which included receiving the necessary remittances in exchange for cash in due time, paying off debts to traders and suppliers, purchasing new goods and receiving products from local industries.

In his letters, De Vogel returned frequently to the matter of correct timing, which encompassed the coordination of all logistical operations, in the right sequence, that brought goods onto the market at the right moment. He consistently wrote that business actions must be sequential and required timings that could hardly be calculated in advance due to the possibility of unexpected market and maritime transport conditions. Under these circumstances an operation's success required readiness, organization, patience and understanding from all those involved. Particularly complex here was the synchronization between product production, timely transport to the port and loading on board. The case of previously mentioned nails, manufactured in Liège on behalf of the Cardamicis, is indicative of this need for logistical harmony: De Vogel had to wait for the manufacturer to complete production before finding appropriate transportation to the port, where the ship he had arranged to charter with the lowest market freight he had found was anchored; the ship was about to depart for Smyrna. The coordination of these steps was not always successful. Between March and April 1761, De Vogel commissioned a shipment of thirty barrels of nails to a Capt. Vlaming, but due to production delays ('we have hired Capt. Vlaming to load on his ship the thirty barrels of nails you ordered'[41]) and despite the fact that he had paid the freight on behalf of his Greek Ottoman principals, the transaction was cancelled – 'we intended to send you the nails you ordered this winter in Constantinople on the vessel of Capt. Vlaming but we were not yet ready'. De Vogel was then forced to turn to Capt. De Leeuw who, in addition to being an old acquaintance, also owned his own ship. De Leeuw accepted the barrels and eventually transported them to Smyrna and delivered them to Bartholo Cardamici.[42] Unlike Capt. Vlaming, who had left Amsterdam in 1761 without loading the Cardamicis' nails, Capt. Mente Schryver waited patiently in 1769 for a shipment of nails to be produced before loading them and setting sail with the first favourable wind:

> You see from our last letter that the nails are ready and delivered here and we went yesterday to the ship of Mente Schryver who will have to depart with the first favourable wind after April 1st from Texel to Smyrna and gave us a very good and cheap freight, almost under half the [usual] freight.[43]

Here it is clear that Schryver – in addition to other captains – collaborated with De Vogel to better organize the dispatch of merchandise. In December 1763, De Vogel informed Raphael Cardamici that Capt. Kectel 'did not put pressure on us to load your orders, as the nails will be ready in spring'.[44] In 1765, he stated in another letter that he was able to influence and accelerate the charter and departure process of the *Snelle Galley* by 'persuading' the captain to not wait unnecessarily for the decision of 'one person' who was said to have promised him a 'very good load'.[45] Sometimes, when faced with a long delay and when all other ships had departed from Amsterdam for the East, De Vogel was forced to turn to Rotterdam's freight market: 'The forty barrels of nails we expect . . . they'll be loaded in Rotterdam on the ship of Capt. Visser with the lowest freight and on this we will refer to a subsequent letter.'[46]

The sudden complications and various obstacles that could arise during the negotiation of a freight were dealt with by the Dutch merchant with fresh plans and strong organization. The Cardamicis learned about all his manoeuvres after they had taken place. De Vogel felt that he had their prior consent, and therefore when confronted with unexpected schedule changes on the part of the captains or the imposition of exorbitant prices on freights, De Vogel did not hesitate to cancel the agreement, receive a refund of the freight and choose another vessel. This happened in 1764, when the Dutch merchant chose to load St Martha wood on Capt. De Leeuw's ship, which was due to depart soon because Capt. Bruyn, his first choice, had loaded his Smyrna-bound ship but did not want to commit to an exact departure date. After being informed that the captain's behaviour was due to his uncertainty as to whether he would eventually make the journey, De Vogel cancelled the freight and withdrew the cargo from the ship. In his report to the Cardamicis, he noted that Bruyn had started loading his boat many months before and De Vogel had chosen him from the outset by paying the required freight and signing the insurance policy. However, the pervasive uncertainty surrounding the departure date forced a change of plan, so when the insurance was returned to De Vogel, he proceeded to sign a new agreement to transport the goods on De Leeuw's boat.[47] Occasionally, in 'special circumstances', the Dutch merchant was obliged to take a risk by chartering a ship that was unknown to him for a single journey. A miscalculation of the time limits available to him to collect an order's goods, a delay in the delivery of goods by manufacturers and producers, a change in a ship's itinerary or the severe weather conditions that could delay departures and keep ships anchored in port required De Vogel to find emergency solutions. As he wrote to Raphael Cardamici in April 1765: 'Bad weather, storms and rains, prevented the transport of most of the cargoes, we hope that soon we will have good news, and everything will be loaded on the ship of Capt. Auke Disma.'[48] In December 1768, he described in detail the adventures of Capts. Boermaster and Mallaga:

> Capt. Boermaster went out to sea in good conditions on 15 December and, as the wind was favourable for four days, we believe he went away . . . Capt. Boermaster did not want to load so as not to be kept here by the frost, and Mallaga stayed a little longer and loaded the goods and gunpowder you ordered . . . And when the frost passed, Capt. Mallaga also set sail, leaving behind a few goods, but there was a headwind the next day and so did not go very far.[49]

The process of transporting goods between Amsterdam and the Ottoman Empire became even more complicated and demanding when merchandise arriving in Smyrna had to then be transferred to Constantinople, where Raphael Cardamici would receive them. The transport of goods between these two Ottoman ports required a separate chartering of ships and insurance of goods. Freight and insurance on this route cost exorbitant amounts that often far exceeded the prices charged for travelling from Amsterdam to the Ottoman ports.[50] In particular, the freights for trips to the imperial capital were very expensive, something which troubled De Vogel every time the Cardamicis wanted to receive orders in Constantinople.[51] Seeking to take advantage of the lower prices that their correspondent could achieve through his acquaintances in Amsterdam, the Cardamicis had charged him with managing the Smyrna–Constantinople–Smyrna route. Thus, in 1764 Raphael Cardamici sent ten bales of goat yarn from Constantinople to Smyrna on the tartane of Capt. Vailhart, which were to be loaded on Capt. De Leeuw's Amsterdam-bound ship and addressed to De Vogel.[52]

In addition to the exorbitant amounts the Cardamicis had to pay for freights, they also dealt with some unexpected adversity which could complicate smooth business operations. Some captains stubbornly refused to load 'special type' goods such as fruit – both fresh and dried – apparently because of its sensitive nature.

Their position remained firm even when the Cardamicis tried persuading them otherwise by paying particularly high amounts for freights.[53] De Vogel himself referred to this problem in 1762. In a letter, he said several captains had refused to carry dried fruit on behalf of the Cardamicis: 'We see that Capt. Bakker did not wish to load fruit and we hope with your next letter to find out that you managed to load some fruit on board Capt. Bakker's ship.'[54] De Vogel carefully monitored the way the Cardamicis handled the issue of chartering ships in Smyrna to send goods to Amsterdam and offered them his opinions and advice. In 1765, he expressed his dissatisfaction that they had loaded only six bales of merchandise onto Capt. Andriessen's ship: 'We are not very happy with you as you have only been able to load six bales onto the ship of Capt. Andriessen.'[55] A year earlier, he assured Raphael Cardamici that he was very satisfied with their attempt to send him goods that could be easily distributed on the Dutch market, calling them 'worthy' consignments; at the same time he expressed to Raphael his hope that Cardamicis would hire Capt. De Leeuw to transport their merchandise because, according to the information he had, De Leeuw's ship would be the first to depart from Smyrna for Amsterdam.[56] A few months later, the Cardamicis' decision to send a cargo of fruit to Rotterdam on the ship of Capt. Gerritz, having not found a suitable freight for Amsterdam, annoyed De Vogel. He emphasized that dispatching the fruit to Rotterdam was unnecessary because there was a well-known captain, Auke Disma, who would have loaded the fruit 'very gladly' and was bound for Amsterdam. If, however, they had chosen 'another route . . . we wish you good luck with the fruit . . . This means that we are forced by order of our friends in Rotterdam not to work on this project.'[57] It is obvious that the Cardamicis' free choices could harm De Vogel's interests, offend his pride and damage confidence in their relationship.

As is evident, De Vogel had clear and strong opinions regarding the choice of vessel that would transport his clients' merchandise to Amsterdam, and he often attempted to influence the Cardamicis' choices. An obvious explanation for the persistence with which he occasionally proposed cooperation with certain vessels and captains could be the fact that some of these vessels had ties to his company, either because he was their owner or because he had shares in them. As he claimed, his 'own' ships were often loaded with the goods of his 'friends', clients and associates, as he was able to intervene in the organization of journeys and the price of freights – 'keeping prices low', he wrote. According to De Vogel, the ships he offered to his friends and associates had the additional advantage of departing from Amsterdam much earlier than others and arriving on time in the Ottoman Empire so that the merchants who received the goods could be the first to channel them into local Ottoman markets. In a letter to Raphael Cardamici in 1766, De Vogel listed the benefits that the Greek merchant could derive from the fact that he, in addition to being his commercial correspondent, also owned ships travelling to the East:

> You can reflect on whether you will send us some quantities of cotton with the ship of Capt. De Leeuw. We are talking to you about this ship because we are waiting for more goods with it and in this case, we will receive them all together. We are also able to keep prices low and get good prices, so [please] give preference this ship with your missions, much more because it is our ship.[58]

The captains of the vessels to which De Vogel referred were connected with him in an employer–employee relationship, which enabled him to negotiate with them in relative comfort and to provide the merchants he represented as commercial correspondent with the most up-to-date information, favourable conditions and special prices. Capts. Kectel and De Leeuw captained ships owned, or partly owned, by De Vogel: 'Capt. Kectel who will depart next month, can load the items you have ordered and we can agree with him on the freight as he is bound for Constantinople . . . otherwise we will look for other opportunities.'[59] When Kectel passed away that same year and his death delayed the departure of his ship, De Vogel informed the Cardamicis that his company had proceeded to replace him with another captain so that the ship could depart as soon as possible.[60] De Vogel's separate relationship with Capt. Pieter De Leeuw was revealed in his letters as he systematically recommended the captain and his vessel to the Cardamicis; he also invited them to introduce him to their merchant friends, so they might choose him for the shipment of their goods to the Netherlands.[61] Indeed, in some cases De Vogel managed to send the Cardamici cargo via De Leeuw by paying half the freight. In 1761, in a letter to Bartholo Cardamici, he justified his choice of De Leeuw's ship instead of Capt. Klip's, which was to depart from Amsterdam sooner:

> Let us tell you that you have no right to complain . . . as you received the lead free of charge freight [something] which we cannot guarantee to everyone and in addition we loaded all the goods at a very reasonable price and Capt. De Leeuw will arrive much earlier than Capt. Klip, who departed before him but should stop in Thessaloniki.[62]

And in April of that year he repeated: 'From Capt. De Leeuw you will also receive 150 pieces of lead free of charge.'[63] In 1770, he introduced the Cardamicis to Willem Blom, as captain of 'our' vessel *Gysbert Jan*.[64] On this occasion De Vogel asked Raphael to charter this ship in order to send him first-class Kirkağac cotton.[65] The close association between De Vogel and some captains developed into a relationship of trust. It was not therefore strange that the Dutch trader received cheques and cash sent to him by the Cardamicis and delivered by various captains. In 1760, Capt. De Leeuw handed De Vogel a remittance of 10,000 florins he had received from Bartholo Cardamici.[66] De Vogel himself encouraged Bartholo to continue sending him, through De Leeuw, remittances that he wished to receive safely and on time – 'it is kind of you to have asked Mr Raphael to send us remittances and Capt. De Leeuw . . . will load everything.'[67]

Each time an agreement was signed, the freight and insurance policy had been paid and the ship had departed the port in favourable weather conditions, De Vogel sent the Cardamicis copies of the receipts with the amounts paid, together with the additional costs that accompanied the payment of the freight and calculations of the commission they were due to pay him for his services.[68] In addition to the personal interests which led the Dutch merchant to favour the chartering of certain ships, his attitude also expressed his firm belief that the transport of goods should be carried out without delay and with absolute security in order for transactions to take place quickly and efficiently. His wish was to take advantage of market supply and demand conditions swiftly and to profit from price movement. On 16 December 1766, he conveyed to Raphael Cardamici his troubled thoughts regarding the chartering of a ship with Capt. Ryndert. According to De Vogel, Ryndert had chosen a route that would have delayed the arrival of the Cardamicis' cargoes in Amsterdam, thus damaging business. It was already too late, De Vogel maintained, to attempt to send the goods on another vessel as all the other ships that had long since departed from ports in the Ottoman Empire would arrive in the Dutch capital well in advance, loaded with goods similar to those traded by the Cardamicis; these goods would flood the market, prices would fall significantly and De Vogel would be unable to react because Capt. Ryndert's ship would not have yet arrived at the port.[69]

The Cardamicis were generally persuaded by their Dutch correspondent's arguments; they trusted him and made sure to charter the ships he proposed. At times, however, they expressed dissatisfaction and surprise at De Vogel's insistence on selecting and recommending the same ships and captains. Perhaps they sensed that De Vogel had an ulterior motive in recommending certain associates. In reply to such concerns, De Vogel provided explanations that the Cardamicis were unable to verify. Thus, in 1765, he insisted that he was right to reject Capt. Bruyn and to load their order, yet again, on Capt. De Leeuw's ship. From the outset, De Vogel insisted that Bruyn had been unable to provide a reliable answer as to when he intended to depart from Amsterdam. That uncertainty saw him once again turning to De Leeuw, on whose timely departure he was certain. And so, despite having already paid insurance for Bruyn for the goods of all his 'friends' and clients, he took care to cancel them on time and sign new insurance agreements, this time for De Leeuw.[70] Two years later, De Vogel found himself once again in the difficult position of having to defend his choices in this matter. On this occasion, he assured the Cardamicis that they had no reason to complain about the choice of De Leeuw as, at the time, no other ship in the port of Amsterdam was ready for departure. De Leeuw's vessel would follow a relatively short route by making a single stop in Livorno, where it was scheduled to remain for ten days. Additionally, De Leeuw had managed to provide them with a very low freight and premium. In concluding his argument, De Vogel advised the Cardamicis to consider that Capt. Mallaga's ship, the first that had departed after Capt. De Leeuw's, had been subjected to a twenty-day quarantine and had not yet reached its destination.[71]

These exchanges show that there was a constant game of power and prestige being played out between the Cardamicis and De Vogel. In this game, their relationship altered between one of trust and one of suspicion. However, De Vogel was often able to impose his terms and opinions on his Greek principals. He knew in advance the departure schedules of several vessels through information forwarded to him by their captains or notices circulating the port and the market. He was trying to organize and coordinate, as far as possible, cargo shipments for his customers. However, at times, it seems that the issue of the timely chartering of a ship and the dispatch of goods that the Cardamicis anxiously expected in Smyrna was used by him as a means to put pressure on the Cardamicis to send him remittances, so he would not have to invest his own resources in the business – something that greatly displeased him. In 1769, he wrote:

> Capt. Andriessen will be leaving town shortly, we'll see if you'll allow us to do consignments for you as we wait until the last minute to receive your remittance . . . as his ship will stay [here] until the end of the month, we will see what we will be able to receive from you and how we will manage to do the shipments of the goods you have ordered from us.[72]

Over time, the Cardamicis may have acquired a stronger position, imposing their own rules and occasionally defying the insinuations of their Dutch associate. In 1766, Raphael Cardamici chartered Capt. Rander Foresee's ship to send a consignment of dried fruit to Amsterdam. This ship was unknown to De Vogel, which displeased him.[73] A year later, Cardamici promised to charter a ship that De Vogel had indicated to him in exchange for a special favour from his Dutch correspondent: 'We will assess the favour you want to have so that you will charter our ship *Dame Catherine* as a priority', De Vogel wrote to Cardamici.[74]

Thomas De Vogel was responsible for insuring goods transported between Amsterdam, Smyrna and Constantinople on the behalf of the Cardamicis. The insurance sector for ships, goods and persons was one of the most dynamic and lucrative sectors of Amsterdam's economy, as it was directly and compulsorily linked to the international trade and shipping sectors.[75] According to the regulations in force in all European states, all vessels moving cargoes to and from Europe had to be insured.[76] As is well known, until around the mid-eighteenth century, merchants themselves negotiated and signed insurance policies on behalf of their own enterprises or those of their friends and associates. Mediation in transactions of this kind brought them significant profits as the negotiation and signing of insurance contracts provided commercial companies with additional income, usually calculated as a percentage of the premium paid by the merchant concerned. Additionally, the payment of insurance by joint ventures of commercial houses allowed for the division of liability and risks that were involved in undertaking a business venture, as well as the division of losses and profits between participating merchants. Since the beginning of the eighteenth century, the insurance process was modernized with the establishment of specialist insurance companies. This development affected the income of many private traders and trading companies, which until then had benefitted from the additional income of this sideline activity. However, some of them chose to participate as shareholder-partners in the new insurance companies by investing significant amounts of capital in them.[77]

Amsterdam, as an international trading and maritime hub, remained the centre of international insurance trade throughout the eighteenth century. One could buy all manner of insurance in its port, as it was widely known that ships, goods, money and people from all over the world were insured in the city's market at highly competitive prices and on preferential terms. The scope and value of insurance transactions carried out in the city was so great that the cost of insurance premiums was much lower than in other commercial and maritime centres. Furthermore, the professionals involved in the insurance trade were extremely competent and experienced, and compensation was carried out smoothly and without delay.[78]

The insurance sector produced significant profits for individuals, local businesses and the Dutch state, and so it was inevitable that the sector would eventually be organized under a single industry body. Thus in 1598 the Insurance Council was established in Amsterdam. The council, which comprised three directors (which increased to four in 1765), was a chamber responsible for ensuring the legality of transactions. The legislation underpinning its work was adopted and ratified on 17 July 1612. The Dutch state enacted a series of laws defining an insurer's role by setting out the rights and obligations of insurers and policyholders. The laws were reformulated in 1744, and then in 1756 the entire legal framework for insurance was improved and developed to include new provisions. Those involved in the insurance market – insurers, traders, captains and brokers – were obliged to comply strictly with these regulations, and in the event of disagreements or conflicts of interest the Insurance Council intervened as arbitrator.

By the eighteenth century, Amsterdam's insurance market was the most reliable and active in the world, but the insurance process could be rather time-consuming. The *polizza*, or insurance policy, was an act through which insurers declared that they were taking on the risk to which the policyholder was exposed, either personally himself or through the transportation of his goods during a journey. Danger could be in the form of bad weather, a pirate attack or some other unpredictable factor. In Amsterdam, the *polizze* were printed at the expense of the Insurance Council and then signed and sealed by its secretary to prevent the illegal publication and trafficking of counterfeit copies. On the policies, the contracting parties included details of the ship, the captain and the insured persons, followed by a description of the ship's route, with reference to the final destination and the stations where goods would be loaded.[79] Of particular interest is the regulation which allowed a ship and its cargo to be insured even after leaving a port and heading to its destination. This regulation reveals the authorities' concern and desire to ensure the rapid and uninterrupted conclusion of a ship's chartering and its departure from a port, even if it meant that some necessary procedures would have to be postponed.[80]

As a representative of the Cardamicis, Thomas De Vogel had the knowledge and experience to successfully sign reliable insurance policies by guaranteeing very low prices and favourable conditions for his clients. He was well aware of the institutions and procedures governing the Dutch insurance market; he had extensive experience of concluding such contracts and knew the current premium prices as they were formed in a free and competitive environment. As was the case with the chartering of ships, the Dutch merchant was also authorized by the Cardamicis to negotiate and sign insurance policies concerning the transport of goods inside the Ottoman Empire, on the Smyrna–Constantinople route;

from Amsterdam he was able to achieve prices far lower than those that the Cardamicis could obtain in Ottoman ports. De Vogel had a very clear strategy on how to achieve this. His main objective was to finalize negotiations and sign insurance policies as soon as possible, and in any case within the charter period of a ship. He argued that time was a crucial factor in the pricing of premiums and therefore in the overall burden on a merchant: 'We have already started to do the insurance to take advantage of the low premiums so that we do not have to pay a larger amount [later]', he used to say.[81]

The early conclusion and signing of a security for sending a cargo on a particular ship could very easily become void if an unforeseen impediment to the charter agreement's completion or a change in the schedule of a ship's departure required the finding of a new freight and commencing negotiations anew elsewhere. Such circumstances required the merchant or his representative to show readiness, maturity and determination:

> We'll load the St. Martha wood on board the Capt. De Leeuw's ship set to leave shortly as Capt. Bruyn who was loading up to come to your places didn't want to commit from this month or next and as a result we were informed that he is still very unsure if his voyage to your place will take place – as he had started loading [the ship] since last July . . . we started to reckon that we would load certain commodities on it and we did the insurance – now the insurance [premium] has been returned and done on the [ship of] Capt. De Leeuw.[82]

As mentioned above, the regulations generally safeguarded the interests of policyholders, so as not to burden commercial capital or stop their activity – therefore in such cases the premiums were reimbursed immediately. The premium was also refunded to a merchant when the insured goods did not reach their destination and when the insured ships did not complete their scheduled voyage. Insurers were entitled to keep 0.5 per cent of the premium paid if the goods, despite the cancellation of a trip, had meanwhile been transferred from shore to ship on small boats and a 1 per cent rate if the goods had been loaded onto the ship.

De Vogel's second objective was to identify the lowest and most reliable premiums on the market. However, in accordance with his consistent position that the low cost of a commodity, transaction or service should never undermine their quality, he made sure to seal agreements which, although they sometimes weighed on his clients' funds, he felt was in their interest: 'The premium of 5 per cent on the Capt. Kersies is definitely high . . . but we didn't want to sign [an agreement paying] less . . . on the contrary we would pay even more.'[83]

As far as his personal contribution to the handling of the issues that emerged during negotiations was concerned, De Vogel never missed an opportunity to praise the great services he offered to his clients. To sign an agreement, it was necessary to convince insurers that they were securing competent pilots and solid vessels and therefore the money invested was not at serious risk. Through his involvement in the shipping sector, De Vogel had a personal circle of insurers who trusted him and on whom he systematically relied. His familiarity with this milieu allowed him to negotiate with conviction while advising the Cardamicis in order to protect them from errors and oversights: 'It was impossible for us to carry out the insurance of the 630 florins on board the ship *N.S. Madonna del Rosario* from Ragusa . . . as none of our insurers agreed to do it.'[84] Negotiating and signing an agreement required experience and knowledge of how the insurance market operated, but De Vogel's personal connections with insurers, captains and agents also played a decisive role. De Vogel often pointed out to the Cardamicis that signing insurance contracts from Amsterdam for the transport of goods on the Smyrna–Amsterdam route or smaller ferry routes on the Smyrna–Constantinople–Smyrna route was a particularly demanding and difficult process but one he was experienced in seeing through: 'You should know that no one can offer you an insurance from here to Smyrna directly and also for small ships from Smyrna to Constantinople with [a premium of] 2 per cent.' [85]

When the time came to claim and collect insurance for goods damaged en route, it was De Vogel who informed the Cardamicis about ongoing developments and guided them on how to deal with the various bureaucratic issues. In Amsterdam's insurance market, the appropriate authorities carefully assessed claims from insured persons for compensation for damaged goods or ships; the procedure lasted one and a half years for incidents that occurred in Europe and three years for incidents outside Europe. In the event of the complete destruction of a ship, or the loss or confiscation of the goods without any hope of recovery or repair, the insured person submitted a written declaration to the insurers through the Insurance Council. Insurers were then obliged to pay compensation within three months. The loss was calculated using the consignment's gross value at its place of arrival. For damage, the beneficiaries received compensation where it concerned more than 3 per cent of the value of goods and more than 10 per cent of the value of a special category of goods such as jewellery. When a captain was the owner of a ship, they were responsible for any damage caused to the cargo by storms and unexpected disasters: 'With regard to the declaration on damaged nails, we submitted it to your insurers, who asked us to give them a statement or protest from the Capt. Disma so they know if the weather was bad and there were waves which destroyed the merchandise.'[86] Of course, insurers were not obliged to compensate for damage that was the fault of the insured. The usual procedure first required a prior affidavit from the ship's captain to the Insurance Council and a presentation of evidence proving his innocence. The council decided whether the damage ultimately weighed on the captain or was due to other factors – a decision that ultimately determined the outcome of the procedure and the amount of compensation. The council also delivered an opinion on *avaria grossa*, that is, those cases where the damage had been caused by deficient governance of the vessel and the captain's failure to take necessary safety measures. In these cases, their decision required a complex and demanding investigation into all the different factors that had caused, or contributed to, the damage. On similar occasions De Vogel followed the process closely and described it in lengthy letters to the Cardamicis:

> In the end you will need a proof that the damage was caused by seawater and then you will need to get a statement from Capt. Frost that the seawater was up on the deck of the ship and a copy of his protest against the seawater, if the damage caused to the nails is visible . . . as insurers could imagine that the damage to the nails was not actually caused by seawater, assuming that moisture could in fact have damaged them which could be reasonable, so in order to avoid such assumptions everything would have to be presented in the clearest and most obvious way.[87]

In 1764, De Vogel informed the Cardamicis that they would receive in instalments a large amount of insurance for the destruction of cotton carried by Capt. Kersies: 'Capt. Kersies, who carried forty bales of cotton, brought the documentation of the great damage done before the directors who settled the matter and will continue to pay us until his debt is cleared.'[88]

Apparently, De Vogel received – whether on a one-off basis or in instalments is unknown – the compensation paid by the insurers on behalf of the Cardamicis, and he then added those sums to their current account. Copies of the insurance contracts he signed on behalf of his clients, as well as receipts for compensation, were sent attached to his letters, often together with the bill of lading accompanying the goods: 'Here attached together . . . the bill of lading of 100 pieces of bullets and the barrels with pistols loaded on board *La Johanna Lambert & Kristina* of Capt. Adriaanse Mallaga and also a copy of the receipt for 900 florins [paid] insurance for the barrels with pistols.'[89] And in another example: 'The other letter, concerning the settlement of the damage to the nails by Capt. Disma, you will find it here attached.'[90]

The money trade

Amsterdam's position within the eighteenth-century international trade system was based on two main axes: the city's commodity and services market and its financial sector.[1] As early as 1609, with the establishment of the city's first foreign exchange bank, Amsterdam became the largest European centre for Stock Exchange and credit transactions. The Wisselbank accepted and exchanged securities, supervised and imposed the divestment of those circulating on the local market and managed all foreign exchange of over 300 guilders in value.[2]

On the international market in Amsterdam, a merchant's credit rating was vital. Free and secure access to credit was essential, particularly for merchants trading within a market that functioned as Europe's entrepôt, where large quantities of goods were stored for months, ready to be moved at the right time. As early as the seventeenth century, in Amsterdam many payments were made with advances in order to ensure favourable conditions for the purchase and sale of goods and services: this model of transaction made money, in all its forms, the 'hidden weapon' of Dutch traders' supremacy over their foreign competitors. The cheap credit that Dutch companies and major Dutch traders were able to provide with great ease to traders throughout Europe was transmitted to their recipients through various communication channels and even financed high-risk speculative activities. It is therefore no coincidence that this sector of the Dutch economy had developed into a key and lasting factor of its prosperity.

Trade in goods and money and the provision of services were inextricably linked and served by various professionals, traders, trade correspondents, agents, brokers and intermediaries, who were involved in various forms of cooperation. At that time, as mentioned above, trade on commission was a very widespread method of representing foreign interests in a market. It was a kind of association which, however, automatically represented a relationship of inequality between the parties. The contemporary author Accarias de Sérionne described how this uneven relationship evolved: Dutch merchants granted daily credit to foreign merchants who had hired them to buy goods on commission on their behalf. To obtain the goods listed on the orders they received from abroad, the Dutch correspondents would pay for them and the principal traders would repay them two to three months after they received the goods. In other words, the merchant's principal/client received from their Dutch representative four months' credit; in this way the whole transaction was based on the Dutch correspondent, and he gained a basic advantage over the merchants he served, an advantage which allowed him to retain control of their cooperation. In the case of the sale of goods, that advantage was further guaranteed, according to de Sérionne: when a merchant sent a consignment of goods to a correspondent on commission in the Netherlands with the order to sell it at a specific price, the dealer made sure to advance one quarter, half or even three quarters of the agreed price. The advance was made at an interest rate charged to the merchant principal. This way, the Dutch representative in Amsterdam indirectly financed his operations.[3]

This was not exactly the case with the De Vogel–Cardamici association. This was a partnership that deviated from the well-known standard of trade on commission in a peculiar and characteristic way that reflected the personality, principles and habits of the Dutch trader. De Vogel, who acted as a commercial correspondent/agent on commission to promote the international transactions of another, obtained through his access to the Amsterdam international credit market control of his partner's commercial cooperation. He had direct access to the city's international market, institutions and information and therefore gained a comparative advantage over the Ottoman trading company that wished to be represented in that market; this advantage allowed him to influence decision-making and take the lead in trade transactions.[4]

In order to finance himself through advances on the purchase of goods and services in Amsterdam and to cover all the additional costs required, De Vogel had to participate in a circular process. The Dutch merchant expected, first, the arrival of goods sent by the Cardamicis. He then made sure to promote them for sale on the Amsterdam market. The sale yielded cash and credit that De Vogel then used to purchase goods ordered by the Cardamicis, freights and insurance, as well as to pay off previous debts. The sale on the Ottoman markets of the goods received from Amsterdam gave the Cardamicis capital, part of which they invested in the purchase of new goods they sent to Amsterdam for sale by De Vogel and so on.

This circular movement, which was a simple and practical form in its conception, could not function in real market economy conditions unless the relationship between demand and supply, price fluctuations, the timing of departures and arrivals and the choices-actions of merchants and correspondents combined and operated in perfect coordination. However, this ideal and perfectly synchronized transfer was not possible, especially in unpredictable and unstable conditions. In the case of the Cardamici–De Vogel cooperation, there was the factor of instability and asymmetry, the origin of which we referred above. In fact, De Vogel maintained in Amsterdam a current account where he imported the income and expenses from the various commercial and other financial transactions he carried out on behalf of the Cardamicis.[5] He kept Bartholo and Raphael Cardamici regularly informed about their current balance of account and capital movements. However, the consistent deficit in this account was an issue that continuously worried him. The European and colonial goods ordered by the Cardamicis and purchased by De Vogel always cost more than the proceeds of the sale on the local market of Eastern goods received from Smyrna and Constantinople. In addition, the goods sent by the Cardamicis to be sold in Amsterdam either did not arrive on time or were not sold at the right time and price to provide him with the capital required to proceed with other transactions. In order not to interrupt the flow of business, De Vogel was forced to use his own funds, paying advances which he then reimbursed from the account of the Greek merchants when that account was in the black; but he was not happy with this approach. As Chapter 2 shows, De Vogel had repeatedly expressed in letters to associates and relatives his distrust of Ottoman merchants in general and had stated unequivocally his refusal to invest in joint capital with Ottoman companies. The lack of liquidity was therefore an issue that he resented, as he made clear in every letter. By informing the Cardamicis that he was not prepared to use his own capital to finance transactions concerning them, he underlined that they needed to send remittances in the form of goods, foreign exchange and gold to be able to serve them in a timely manner.[6] In fact, he often went so far as to threaten to cease his cooperation with them if they did not meet this demand.

De Vogel's strong and persistent stance on the financing of Cardamici enterprises largely defined both the organization and development of their collaboration. As he was solely responsible for a multitude of financial transactions, De Vogel had to manage the capital of the Ottoman Greek merchants wisely and seriously but, at the same time, remain alert and move with determination, often without prior information, as communication between them was infrequent and developments within the markets were stormy. He therefore often put serious obstacles on the continuous flow of transactions by stating in a rather bold manner that he would not purchase goods for them unless he had received the necessary cash from them in advance.

The Dutch trader's persistence on ensuring a continuous flow of capital from the Cardamicis had another explanation.[7] The sharp increase in the volume of transactions and movement of paper money at that time in the Netherlands, Amsterdam in particular, had put traders on alert, suspended the provision of credit and had ultimately caused serious economic instability.[8] It all started when the great growth of trade and shipping encouraged many Dutch trading companies to become involved in large-scale credit transactions, which had a decisive influence on the organization and functioning of the Dutch credit market. A multitude of securities began to move in uncontrolled and unregulated conditions, with commercial enterprises enjoying unconditional freedom, accepting foreign exchange and debt securities of various kinds or transferring them to other companies through speculative and often risky agreements. At one point in the Amsterdam market securities had accumulated up to 'fifteen times' more value than the cash being traded and 'credit was everywhere'.[9] The situation began to take on dramatic proportions when various trading houses began to refuse to pay cheques and accept bills either because they did not want to or because they were not able to do so. In 1763, the Netherlands was hit by a credit crisis and another followed in 1772–3. A third crisis ran from 1780 to 1783.[10] The lack of cash led many businesses to bankruptcy and the crisis spread: from Amsterdam and Berlin, it passed to Hamburg, Altona, Bremen, Leipzig, Stockholm and finally London.[11] This was a liquidity crisis that affected the market of some cities, such as Hamburg and Rotterdam, more than others and hit the weakest companies; Amsterdam managed to find some balance after the first vibrations. The crisis of 1772–3 was similar to that of 1763.[12]

In these conditions of instability and uncertainty, a merchant entrepreneur of De Vogel's character and ideas would be expected to stubbornly reject the prospect to spend capital on companies that did not inspire confidence and to pursue a strategy of prudent management of his funds. As an observer of the time characteristically stated, 'only the reckless made great commitments'.[13] The crisis of 1763 and the foreshadowing of the crisis of 1772–3 could therefore further justify the Dutch trader's insistence on protecting his capital; De Vogel strongly supported the adoption of a system that would ensure the direct financing of Cardamici enterprises by the Greek Ottoman merchants themselves and would offer him freedom of movement and resources that he could exploit as he considered. Under pressure from De Vogel, the Cardamicis were obliged, if they wished to promote their trade in the Netherlands, to provide him with the necessary liquidity in due time. These requirements were certainly difficult to meet for a medium-sized trading house, with a limited network of contacts and activity that mainly took place inside the Ottoman markets. The frequent devaluations of currency, the lack of money in the Ottoman market and the great slowness in the production and transport of goods made it necessary for the Cardamicis to ensure an instrument that could, on the one hand, replace the hard-to-find money and, on the other, be easily and quickly transferred between different countries. As is apparent from the relevant correspondence, the Cardamicis financed their businesses through the direct shipment of cash and gold. However, the dispatch of bills of exchange and their reimbursement in De Vogel's name seems to have been the main means of financing their transactions.

Liquidity and the trade in bills of exchange

The use of checks and bills as money substitutes was a practice that had been discovered by Italian merchants as early as the fifteenth century and gradually evolved until the seventeenth century. From the eighteenth century, the increase in the volume of trade contributed to the expansion of credit transactions and the spread of the bills of exchange trade at a dizzying pace. The geographical expansion of trade contributed to this phenomenon. By this time, the very mentality of merchants seems to have adapted to the new trading reality as bills of exchange largely replaced money in all European markets; their transfer from one trading house to another had as an additional advantage the collection of interest charged on their repayment, endorsement and transfer.[14] Issues, transfers, endorsements and repayments made the bill of exchange a 'tireless traveller' from one country to another, from one market to another, from the hands of one merchant to the hands of another.[15] The unprecedented movement of bills of exchange and other forms of bills and checks between merchants resulted at certain times in their value exceeding the value of the currencies circulating in a market. These developments were reflected in the Amsterdam international market very clearly as the city emerged as a kind of international hub of capital and financial/credit transactions.

As already mentioned, the establishment in 1609 of the Wisselbank, or Exchange Bank, ensured the proper and efficient operation of foreign exchange trade. The organization of this sector of the economy was necessary as the volume of international trade carried out through Amsterdam flooded the local market with a plethora of bills, facilitating the uninterrupted flow of transactions and the easy supply of paper money. As Metrà argued, almost all cases relating to international foreign exchange and bills were handled at some point, in some way, through the city. As he noted, when an Englishman wanted to pay a Russian, he did so by using bills of exchange issued in Amsterdam, and when an Italian wanted to pay an Englishman, he used the same method. And in this way the trade of all European countries was operated either directly by the Dutch or through them.[16] Throughout the eighteenth century Amsterdam's bills of exchange market greatly resembled that of nineteenth-century London. Dutch merchants and bankers operating in Amsterdam accepted and paid off all kinds of bills drawn in their name. They also financed foreign, private and public loans.[17]

The usually negative balance in the Cardamici account in Amsterdam led De Vogel to push them to choose, other than the sale of goods, additional methods of raising capital to finance their purchases; in particular, he insisted that they dispatch to him bills that would be paid by a third trading house and would be cashed out to him. His clear preference, from a certain point in time, for this form of financing of the Cardamici trade was, as mentioned, due not only to his mentality but also to the continuing economic instability in the Netherlands in the 1760s and 1770s which had affected the commodity market – a situation to which he referred, often with particular concern, in his letters. We do not know whether De Vogel's company, apart from its involvement in the commercial shipping sector, was actively involved in foreign exchange trade and bills of exchange traffic. However, the imperative way in which De Vogel asked his Greek Ottoman principals to send various types of remittances and bills of exchange to cover the negative difference in their current account, to pay him what is due and to finance the continuation of their trade could also be interpreted as a manoeuvre of his business strategy. In his letters he made it very clear that he preferred to receive disbursements of his advances in the form of bills of exchange that would be accepted by other trading houses in the city and paid to him in cash.

It is easy to see why De Vogel asked his Greek Ottoman client-principals to send remittances in the form of bills. It is known that the bill of exchange was a binding, written promise to pay a sum of money to a particular person, in a city, on some future, approximate, date.[18] Crucial parameters that affected this process were, first, the fact that the bill usually had to be paid in a place other than the one in which it was issued and, second, in a currency – in theory – different from the currency of the place where it was issued.[19] As has been argued, the system of financing trade through bills of exchange was relatively simple and effective but also posed a number of risks. A sudden change in the currency exchange rate between two financial centres could cause serious damage to one of the two main traders, either the beneficiary or the trader who paid it off. In addition, each of the two parties involved in the transaction could discover during the proceedings that the other had gone bankrupt, was dishonest or that the money had been accidentally paid and could no longer be recovered.[20] There is no doubt that the inevitable delays in the procedure for sending and receiving the bill by post and waiting for the so-called *usanza* (the period specified in advance for the collection and payment of the amount) could cause serious problems for all players in the transaction. In addition, delays were prolonged if the recipient of the bill rejected its acceptance or payment (the so-called 'protest' of acceptance or payment) and sent it back to the person who originally issued it.[21] However, some trader-bankers welcomed the 'protest' process and the delays it entailed as the circulation of bills back and forth from one trader to another ensured some profits from commission, in other words, from participation in arbitrage and speculation on the difference in currency exchange rates.[22]

In the circumstances, this system was fast, secure and provided De Vogel with either cash or another bill of exchange that he could negotiate himself in the local market by receiving a commission. This commission (1 per cent) was added to the commission received in total on the transactions carried out on behalf of the Cardamicis. The profit margins offered by trading bills of exchange, the collection and direct conversion of currencies through the exploitation of different exchange rates and the collection of commissions received during the trading process were unlimited; in any event they exceeded the profits from commissions that De Vogel received as a middleman in the arduous purchase and sale of goods. As he argued, in an attempt to convince the Cardamicis to multiply their remittances, the profits made by this method were ultimately much greater and gave them the possibility to accumulate capital in their account in Amsterdam.

The response of the Cardamicis to the appeals of their Dutch correspondent was not immediate, however. To obtain bills of exchange, they had to go to a creditworthy trading house in Smyrna or Constantinople and 'buy' them by paying a sum of money directly or turn to a foreign trading house with which they cooperated and send them either goods for sale, gold or coins or cheques and bills that had come into their own hands. The merchants of Smyrna, Vienna or Livorno, after having calculated the monetary exchange rates and after negotiating and collecting the commission, would send De Vogel the price of the values they had received either in the form of bills or cash. If De Vogel received a bill, he would be obliged to exchange it on the Amsterdam market by collecting the price and, at the same time, a commission that usually reached 1 per cent. The whole process was essentially a simple credit transfer.[23]

At a time of economic instability, the cash traded through gold, currencies and bills enabled De Vogel to move quickly and make profits for himself and the Cardamicis, purchase their orders and deposit capital into their current account. In this way he did not depend on the sale of the goods sent to him by the Greek Ottoman merchants to secure funds; goods from the Ottoman Empire markets usually arrived late in a market saturated with similar products, or they were of lower quality than expected and their sale did not yield the expected profits.

The Cardamici business financing network

The movement of cash through the circulation of bills of exchange, currencies and gold required the existence of a secure and reliable international commercial-financial network that would support the transactions of the Cardamicis with De Vogel as their commercial correspondent. Table 18 lists the names of all merchants and merchant houses mentioned in De Vogel's letters as intermediaries in the process of transferring remittances from the Cardamicis to him. These traders belonged to De Vogel's wider circle of acquaintances involved in financial transactions through Amsterdam; they were merchants/financiers established in Amsterdam, Rotterdam, Liège, Vienna, Livorno, Smyrna and Constantinople.

The financial activity of the Cardamicis was developing in four geographical settings where there were four international commercial and financial centres. The first geographical locus was where the Cardamici headquarters were established, in the Ottoman Empire, in Smyrna and Constantinople.[24] The second area was the Netherlands, the seat of their representative, De Vogel, and comprised Amsterdam,[25] Rotterdam[26] and Liège, south, in the region of Wallonia. Vienna was the third commercial/financial centre in central Europe to which the Cardamicis turned to secure cash and bills of exchange.[27] Finally, Livorno, an international entrepôt and transit port in the Central Mediterranean, home to a very important Greek trading community, was the fourth pole of financial activity of the Cardamicis.[28]

Table 18 The Cardamici–De Vogel Financial Network

Name	City	Date
Jan Ackerman & Co.	–	1765
Bongard	Constantinople	1767
Christoforos Boni	Livorno	1764
Bornman & Co.	Constantinople	1767
Bornman & Van der Schroeff	–	1765
Camondo	–	1765
Pavlos Cardamici	Smyrna	1763, 1765
Pierre Cardamici & Co.	Smyrna	1769
Raphael Cardamici Nephew & Son	–	1767
Chasseaud & Co.	Livorno	1764
Chasseaud & Panchaud	–	1766
J. H & E. Cohen Hemzy	–	1769
Nikolaos Chrisogiannis	Smyrna	1763
Hendrik De Bok	Rotterdam	1765
Johannes De Cologne	Liège	1769
Alexander De Masse	Amsterdam	1760–2, 1765–6, 1768
Isaac De Reus	Rotterdam	1764
De Vogel & Enslie (brother of M. Enslie)	Smyrna	1769, 1771
De Vogel Son & Brother	Smyrna	1764, 1766, 1768
Thomas Jr. De Vogel	–	1771
Apostolos Demestikas	Smyrna	1763–64
Densel	–	1768
James Enslie	–	1768
Falcon	Smyrna	1769
Antoine & Francisco Filigoni	Livorno	1764
Fremaux	Smyrna	1764, 1767
Gautier & Puzos	–	1767
Samuel Himenes	–	1764
Hendrik & Daniel Hopker	Amsterdam	1769
Hubsch & Timoni	Constantinople	1765, 1767
Sechir Jasegiroglou	Amsterdam	1761
Juda de Abraam Nunes	Livorno	1764
Jacob Le Clercq	–	1764
Jacob & Son Le Clercq	Amsterdam	1765
Markos Koroneos	Constantinople	1763
Series	Constantinople	1767
Series & Van der Schroeff	–	1770
Michail Masganas	Smyrna	1763
Niotis, Rigas & Co.	Amsterdam	1769
Antonio Nunes	Livorno	1762, 1764
Ch. Dieter Oldembergh	Livorno	1764
Asmund Palm	–	1765, 1767
Panchaud & Van der Schroeff	–	1768
Panchaud	Constantinople	1767
Jacob Pauw	–	1767
Widow Pauw & Son	–	1768

(*Continued*)

Table 18 (Continued)

Name	City	Date
Konstantinos Platis	–	1766
Jean Henry Stametz	Vienna	1760, 1763–4, 1767
Stathis Thomas	Smyrna	1768
Stathis Thomas & Co.	Smyrna	1768
Stathis Thomas, Isaiou & Co.	–	1768
Ioannis Theocharis & Co.	Livorno	1764-6
Tidirepos	–	1764
Van der Dudermuller & Son	Amsterdam	1764
Van der Santhuevel	–	1764
Van der Schroeff	Constantinople	1767
David Van Lennep	Smyrna	1768–70
David Van Lennep & William Enslie	Smyrna	1764, 1766–71
F. & H. Van Sanen	–	1766
Octavio Watson	Livorno	1763
Antonios Zingrilaras & Co.	Amsterdam	1760

Source: Stadsarchief Amsterdam [StdAm], 332, Thomas De Vogel, Kopieboek, vol. 44–52, 1760–71.

Smyrna–Constantinople–Amsterdam–Vienna–Livorno

The international commercial port of Smyrna and the international market of Constantinople were the main area of business operations for the Cardamicis. The financial markets of these two cities were their first port of call to obtain bills of exchange that could be transferred abroad and paid off; the product of this transaction would be received by De Vogel, who would add it to their current account. This process could be delayed due to objective difficulties, such as the unavailability of suitable bills on the market, company bankruptcies, interruption of land and sea transport and postal connections between different countries – either because of the current exchange rates which at certain times were extremely damaging for the Ottoman Greek merchants. The Cardamicis generally agreed to the demands of their Dutch correspondent, although sometimes with considerable delay,[29] and sometimes reluctantly, especially when the difference in interest rates and exchange rates between Europe and the Ottoman Empire weighed heavily on their profit.[30] They were often forced to tell De Vogel that they were unable to obtain appropriate bills or were significantly slow to send him remittances, leading to an immediate reaction on his part. In those circumstances De Vogel himself made sure to direct them on how to do so, indicating companies to which they could turn to, promoting information from his wide circle of contacts. Sometimes by cross-checking his information, the Dutch merchant assessed the veracity of their claims and made his views known to them if necessary. Thus, in August 1765 he told Raphael Cardamici that the non-timely dispatch of remittances could not be attributed to the bad weather, as he had assured him: 'we know that this is not the case and that the exact opposite is true . . . we know that others have drawn bills of exchange onto us and that Mr Bornman & Van der Schroeff, Mr Hubsch & Timoni and also Mr Camondo have sent remittances to their friends.'[31] However, when he was able to confirm the Cardamicis' claims, De Vogel made sure to assist them and refer them to his associates and friends who could serve them. As a direct recipient of information on the operation of the financial market, the currency exchange rates and the sale of bills of exchange in Ottoman commercial centres, De Vogel proposed to the Cardamicis that they go to reputable trading houses from which he was already receiving remittances on behalf of other trading houses. Among them were Bornman & Van der Schroeff, a commercial house with which De Vogel had commercial dealings which allowed him to issue in their name bills and orders.[32] In 1765 De Vogel asked Raphael Cardamici to send him a bill drawn on Bornman & Van der Schroeff as they 'have bills of exchange on their hands constantly'.[33] De Vogel also had dealings with Fremaux & Co. in Smyrna[34] and Hubsch & Timoni, Bongard, Panchaud & Series and Bornman & Van der Schroeff in Constantinople.[35] One of these companies, David Van Lennep & William Enslie, which are already mentioned above, was a key intermediary in Cardamici–De Vogel transactions throughout the period from 1760 to 1771.[36] On this occasion too, the Dutch–British company acted as a middleman and De Vogel used it to put pressure on the Greek merchants; De Vogel often claimed that even when it seemed impossible to find bills of exchange, Van Lennep's company in Smyrna would serve them. So in December and August 1767 he wrote to Raphael Cardamici that he was wrong to complain about the high exchange rate and not send him remittances, as Van Lennep could supply him with some advantageous bills to send them in Amsterdam.[37] In another letter that year, he acknowledged that it was indeed unpleasant and 'irritating' that the exchange rate was so high and so damaging to Raphael but hoped that Van Lennep would guarantee him certain remittances for his transactions at a fairly good price. Closing that letter, he expressed his wish that the first bill that Raphael would have in his hands would make sure to send it to him.[38] In 1770 De Vogel again proposed the mediation of Van Lennep so that remittances could be sent to Amsterdam safely and on time. As he assured the Greek merchant, the amount which, in his judgement, would be collected by the sale of the goods he had sent to the Netherlands would not be sufficient to settle his account and cover his debts. Therefore, Cardamici would have to find a way to send him remittances and Van Lennep & Enslie would be able to find the best opportunity available in the market and supply him with a bill that would be paid in De Vogel's name.[39] The close link between De Vogel and Van Lennep & Enslie began to be disrupted shortly before the death of De Vogel and the dissolution of the Dutch company in Amsterdam. As early as 1768 De Vogel expressed doubts in his letters about Van Lennep's credibility and ironically commented on the negative development in their cooperation; in particular, he asked the Cardamicis to send him the necessary remittances for the continuation of their transactions through the common procedure of issuing a bill of exchange through the intermediation of the Van Lennep & Enslie, adding the ambiguous statement 'and let's confide fully in Van Lennep's honesty'.[40] A few years later, in 1771, De Vogel told Raphael Cardamici that the money paid to Van Lennep & Enslie – a sum of 1,800 piastres – to pay off his debt to him had not yet landed in his hands. As he claimed, their common 'friends' – referring to Van Lennep – had taken care to send him only a small part of the total amount due to him (365 piastres) which, as he noted, 'surprises us and we will wait to see if their next transfer will cover the rest of the amount'.[41] A few months later he appeared to complain that he had not received either cash or bills of exchange from Van Lennep, despite the fact that the Cardamicis had paid the Dutch merchant in Smyrna the corresponding cash and expected him to forward them to De Vogel.[42] Van Lennep's constant, unjustified delays had shaken the De Vogel's confidence in his partner in Smyrna and, in a subsequent letter, he asked Raphael Cardamici to start excluding him from their common transactions.

The bills of exchange sent to Amsterdam by the Cardamicis, with De Vogel as the final recipient of the amount to be redeemed, were often issued in the name of the Armenian Ottoman merchant Alexander De Masse.[43] De Masse, who was based in Amsterdam, systematically received bills of exchange from the Ottoman Empire, accepted them, paid the sum and forwarded the money to De Vogel on behalf of the Cardamicis.[44] Thus in 1760 De Vogel received from Raphael Cardamici a cheque for 1,000 florins drawn in the name of the Armenian merchant.[45] After De Masse accepted the bill of exchange and paid it off, De Vogel collected the amount and credited it to the Cardamici current account.[46] A year later the Dutch merchant received two memos enclosed in a letter sent to him by Raphael Cardamici. The two memos contained two bills of exchange for 200 piastres each, one drawn to Alexander De Masse and the other to the Greek merchant Antonios Zingrilaras.[47] This time De Vogel turned to the two Ottoman merchants of Amsterdam, forwarded to them the bills and collected the sum.[48]

In addition to De Masse and Zingrilaras, some Dutch companies accepted remittances from the Cardamicis and acted as intermediaries in the process of issuing, promoting, accepting and paying out on the bills, providing De Vogel with cash and credit.[49] These were the merchants/financiers Jacob Le Clercq,[50] Jacob Pauw,[51] Widow Pauw & Son,[52] Theodore & Jan Van Sanen, Johannes de Loover & Son,[53] B. Van der Santhuevel,[54] Jan Charles Haffelgreen,[55] the English James Enslie,[56] Isaac De Reus[57] and Hendrik De Bok in Rotterdam. Although one would expect the Cardamicis to have established in Amsterdam a network of reliable associates of Greek origin to whom they would turn to ensure the safe transfer of their money and bills, this never seems to have been the case, except occasionally; on the contrary, they trusted De Masse as the main drawee of the bills of exchange sent to the Netherlands. And they did this despite the fact that during this period several Greek Ottoman companies established in Amsterdam accepted, promoted and paid bills, such as the above-mentioned Antonios Zingrilaras & Co.[58] and also Stathis Thomas, Isaiou & Co.,[59] Rigas, Niotis & Co.[60] and Sechir Jasegiroglou.[61] These were merchant houses established in Amsterdam, but they had their headquarters in Smyrna and Constantinople or were represented in these two cities by branch offices and other Greek trading houses with which they cooperated.[62]

De Vogel did not appreciate the Cardamicis' cooperation with Hendrik De Bok in Rotterdam and expressed his displeasure without much hesitation.[63] De Bok's company, which apparently received goods and remittances from the Cardamicis, represented many Greek companies in Rotterdam. De Vogel's dissatisfaction and his negative criticism on many occasions seemed to have had a dual starting point: on the one hand, De Bok had a much greater clientele of Greek Ottoman merchants than De Vogel and, on the other, he belonged to that category of Dutch merchants that De Vogel called with repugnance the 'Greeks' favourites'. These were those Dutch trading companies that commissioned Greek trading houses in Amsterdam to represent them as their commercial correspondents in Ottoman ports and commercial centres and to undertake their trade transactions to and from the East. In fact, until then, De Vogel had himself taken on the role of the representative of De Bok and other Dutch merchants in the Ottoman ports.[64] In August 1765, when De Vogel was informed of the Cardamici–De Bok transactions, he reacted immediately and strongly: 'It is our intention,' he wrote to Raphael,

> with our method . . . to have patience in order to serve you honestly and with
> all possible efforts and if someone like Mr De Bok of Rotterdam can do it better

than us, if this is detrimental to us we will console ourselves with the idea that it is upon you to decide, but we will not continue to guarantee you advances unless we have the money in our hands.[65]

A few months later, in another letter, he returned to the same subject in a sharp tone:

We accepted your transfer of 1,000 florins to Mr De Bok; you are certainly the masters of your choices and you can appeal to anyone you think is better, [even if] we spoked to you about your transfer and that it could cover our advances and you could thus pay us back and that it would be better if you addressed it here and not in Rotterdam – finally, Gentlemen, we hope to continue [our collaboration] to the satisfaction of all parties.[66]

Although frictions between the Dutch representative and Greek Ottoman merchants were to be expected, scepticism and disapproval coexisted with a sense of trust and solidarity. Thus, when De Vogel realized that the Cardamicis, out of ignorance or haste to obtain remittances and dispatch them to Amsterdam to carry on with their transactions, defied the unfavourable exchange rates that seriously undermined their profits, he intervened. In 1764 he wrote to Raphael Cardamici:

Your dear letter arrived in which we received the second of your remittances on Mr Van der Dudermuller and saw at what an outrageous price you managed to get the money that you sent to us in return; we hope that for the new remittances you will achieve a reasonable price . . . and that we will receive them first from everyone else.[67]

Vienna, the commercial and financial centre of Austria-Hungary and central Europe, was another hub in the Cardamicis' business financing network.[68] The Ottoman Greek traders forwarded gold ingots and ducats to a banking house in Vienna which, after calculating their value, based on current exchange rates and retaining a commission, sent the return to De Vogel.[69] The Viennese merchant-banker Jean Henry Stametz, with whom De Vogel appears to have had other deals too, was the main recipient of the Cardamicis' gold and coins. Stametz received from them gold ingots and gold ducats, sold them to the Vienna precious metals market or traded them to other bankers and promoted the capital he received to De Vogel.[70] In 1764 De Vogel described the process of transferring money from Vienna to Amsterdam in one of his letters. Having once again received gold ingots from the Cardamicis, Stametz had transferred them to the Bank of Vienna, where he redeemed them for ducats.[71] Between 1760 and 1764 Stametz had redeemed gold ingots weighing 150, 163 and 237 drams and gold sequins on behalf of the Cardamicis;[72] he had sent to De Vogel 1,000 florins[73] and occasionally ducats. Stametz informed De Vogel on the selling of the gold and coins; the latter nevertheless often expressed impatience and irritation at the delays in receiving cash from Vienna. At the height of the credit crisis of 1763, when the merchant and financial community of Amsterdam was in urgent need of large amounts of cash, De Vogel became anxious and worried about any delay: 'Mr Stametz has not yet delivered to us the [amount] from the transfer you made to him on our behalf.'[74] In the end, De Vogel's suspicion of Stametz's person and practices may have been the reason why he eventually expressed his opposition to the Cardamicis' method of sending remittances via Vienna. He then advised them that the same process through Livorno was safer and could bring them greater profits. In 1763 De Vogel strongly recommended the end of the cooperation with Stametz: 'We hope that the lesson you learned . . . [transferring remittances to Stametz who apparently was liquidating his business] . . . will serve you very well', he told Raphael, implying that their cooperation had been precarious while the circuit through Livorno was more reliable.[75]

It is not entirely clear whether Raphael Cardamici's takeover of the Cardamici enterprise coincided with a modification of the company's strategy for the financing of the Amsterdam business. However, following Raphael's taking over of the reins of the family business, remittances and bills of exchange were sent to Amsterdam through Livorno more frequently.[76] In De Vogel's letters one could detect the shift of the centre of gravity of the financial transactions concerning the Cardamicis from Vienna to the Tuscan port.

From the mid-1760s the Cardamicis began sending goods and bills of exchange to Livorno to Jewish, English, Dutch, Italian and Greek trading houses: these were Antonio Nunes,[77] Juda de Abraam Nunes,[78] Octavio Watson,[79] Ch. Dieter Oldenberg,[80] Antoine & Francesco Filigoni and those of Greek origin Christoforos Boni[81] and Ioannis Theocharis and Co.[82] The bills were issued in Smyrna by local trading houses, such as Chasseaud & Co., with an order to be paid off by Livorno companies. Upon arrival and acceptance in Livorno, the bills were transferred to other companies or paid after being traded on current exchange rates. As soon as the cash-out process was completed (about which De Vogel was informed), the product was sent to him in Amsterdam; De Vogel then informed Raphael Cardamici that the transaction had been concluded.[83] Closely following the development of the process of accepting and paying off bills of exchange in Livorno, De Vogel made sure to intervene in the process where the monetary exchange rates were not favourable to the Cardamicis and recommend that they be sent and paid off to another market, in Amsterdam. In 1764 De Vogel wrote to Cardamici: 'We have in our hands your transfer of 500 piastres for Livorno at Ch. Dieter Oldenberg's charge which was accepted in Livorno.'[84] In some cases, Livorno's network of 'friend'-traders serving the Cardamicis received goods intended to be sold on the local market and to return a profit that would still be received by De Vogel in Amsterdam. In 1766 Ioannis Theocharis's company, trading as Giovanni (Ioannis) Theocharis & Co. of Livorno, informed De Vogel that he had sold the cottons he had received from the Cardamicis at a good price and that he would pass on to him the proceeds of the transaction which should be credited to the account of the Greek Ottoman merchants in Amsterdam.[85] When the sale of goods or the repayment of bills of exchange was delayed, other means and techniques were used to promote in Amsterdam the necessary capital to cover costs and purchase goods. The Greek companies with which the Cardamicis collaborated in the Tuscan port enabled De Vogel to issue payment orders in their name to proceed freely in transactions in Amsterdam; these orders would be covered when the sale of the goods in Livorno had been definitively concluded.

A similar circumstance was described in a letter from De Vogel in 1764 referring to the transaction he had carried out in cooperation with the Greek-born Livorno merchant Christoforos Boni.[86] According to De Vogel, Boni himself had sent him a letter in 1763 which had arrived very late in Amsterdam informing him that he had been instructed by the Cardamicis to forward to him in Dutch florins a transfer of 330 piastres, at a certain low rate. As Boni had not been able to obtain a bill for such a low amount on the Livorno market, he had proposed that De Vogel drew a bill in Amsterdam which the Greek trader would receive and take care to promote to other trading houses in Livorno with which De Vogel collaborated. The bill would be paid at an exchange rate that would be more favourable to the Cardamicis and then Boni would send back to De Vogel the amount that the transaction would yield. De Vogel had followed Boni's advice and had drawn a bill on the Greek trader with an eight-day deadline which he had sent him. The transaction was finally completed successfully, as the bill was paid in Livorno at an advantageous price to the Cardamicis; however, De Vogel did not miss the opportunity to disparage the Greek trader by pointing out in a letter to Raphael Cardamici his lack of knowledge and his inability to correctly write in Dutch even the name 'De Vogel'.[87]

The Cardamicis' cooperation with Theocharis, another Greek merchant established in the Tuscan port, served the financing of their businesses in Amsterdam in 1764–5.[88] During this time the Greek merchant undertook to serve the Cardamicis as their main intermediary in Livorno: Theocharis received goods, mainly cottons, from Smyrna, sold them on the local market, negotiated and exchanged bills and other cheques and was in constant communication with De Vogel.[89] In 1764 De Vogel received from Theocharis a transfer of 3,000 florins, which corresponded to the value of silver that Theocharis had received in Livorno on behalf of the Cardamicis.[90] Two years later, in 1766, Theocharis in a letter informed him that he was sending him 'the product from the sale of the cotton [received by the Cardamicis]' after he had deducted the cost of freights and some 'other expenses'. Theocharis had assured the Dutch trader that Raphael Cardamici would send him merchandise to put on sale on the Livorno market. The product of these transactions would be sent to him in Amsterdam. Until then, De Vogel could draw bills on Theocharis for the amount of the 800 piastres. This money would in future be covered by the capital that would be yielded by the sale of the new cargo that would arrive in Livorno from Smyrna.[91] As in the case of Boni, De Vogel did not hide in his letters to Raphael his distrust of the manipulations of the Greek houses with which the Greek Ottoman merchants collaborated. Particularly in the case of Theocharis & Co., he systematically expressed his reservations about the role of Theocharis as an intermediary between himself and Cardamici and criticized his failure to respect the agreed timetables which, he claimed, was detrimental to the smooth and profitable outcome of the transactions.

The expansion of the Cardamici enterprise after 1763, after the entry into the business of family members and the formation of new affiliated companies, extended their possibilities for business manoeuvres and collaborations abroad. In 1767 De Vogel received from Raphael Cardamici a transfer of 1,000 florins issued in the name of the company Raphael Cardamici Nephew & Son, which confirms that the family had established an internal system for capital circulation. This system made it easier to make payments and secure capital through the exploitation of different exchange rates and the collection of commissions within the family environment.[92]

The changes that took place in the eighteenth century in the field of the operation and organization of international trade undoubtedly marked the transition to a new era. The gradual emancipation of international trade from the protectionist and mercantilist policies of various European governments contributed to the development of a new international economic environment and to the invention of reliable, flexible and effective trading methods and payment techniques. New institutions, procedures and financial tools began to be implemented gradually in international markets, ensuring a more efficient, fast and, above all, safe conduct of transactions by private individuals. Some of these methods and practices were new and innovative; others were known and widespread from the past and had been modified to serve the new everyday life of trade.[93] The De Vogel–Cardamici collaboration confirms that the scope of these changes and the way they affected the daily life and habits of the business world, in terms of the content, speed and breadth of transactions, was ultimately a function of the personal strategy of each merchant and his relations with partners and collaborators.

6

A Dutch masterclass of trading

To the ignorant in these matters, commerce is but a game of chance, where the odds are against the player. But, to the accomplished merchant, it is a science, where skill can scarce fail of its reward; and, while the one is wandering about in a pathless ocean, without a compass, and depends on the winds and tides to carry him into his port, the other goes steadily forward, in a beaten track, which leads him directly, if no extraordinary accident intervenes, to wealth and honour.

—Malachy Postlethwayt[1]

Wholesale merchant entrepreneurs claimed and achieved an important role in eighteenth-century European society, as their means grew and their status rose. Their ascendancy in the social hierarchy had significant and lasting consequences on social organization, economy and politics while it brought into society new ideas, values and habits. As the profession of the merchant earned superior social status, it also widened to encompass other types of trade operators like retailers, commission agents and intermediaries, insurance brokers, financiers and shipowners. Together with the members of an old and distinguished elite of merchant families connected with the crown and the political establishment in many European countries, many ambitious newcomers of a lower social status attempted to pervade this business environment and pursue an international business career: some of them received a valuable training as apprentices to experienced international merchants while others combined international trade operations with their main career as retailers, factors, manufacturers, shipowners and ship commanders. As the volume, geographical range and density of commercial transactions increased, an international merchant had to assemble more skills and talents: he had to be, at the same time, a reliable *parfait négociant*, guaranteeing the 'good name' of his business, and a bold, resourceful and cunning businessman open to new methods and techniques, ready to contravene rules and speculate to achieve better profits. To run his business successfully, at home and abroad, he needed prompt and reliable information on markets, prices and deals, trusty associates and local contacts to represent him before the authorities, producers and other merchants. To get collaborators he could trust, a merchant often turned to his family, kin or to members of the ethnic/religious group he belonged. Although the international literature has emphasized the importance of family, ethnic and religious ties in the development of international trade, recent studies have underscored that international trade deals were often contracted between foreigners and strangers while business alliances and associations surpassed social, national and ethnic/religious barriers for the sake of profit. Trade transactions were carried out by individuals with no previous connection or bonding other than participation in a multinational and multi-ethnic mercantile 'community' with an inner organization, structure and conventions: in other words, a 'merchant society within society'.[2] As Margaret Jacob and Catherine Secretan note in the introduction to the volume *The Self-Perception of Early Modern Capitalists*, eighteenth-century merchants saw themselves through collective representations of the profession, a kind of 'mirror of merchants' that reflected the morals, rules and reality of the time.[3] These pictures were presented and reproduced through the plethora of trade manuals circulating since the sixteenth century in Europe, in many different languages. These manuals enhanced respect for the profession; motivated compliance with a specific etiquette, values and routines; and, most importantly, contributed to shaping a professional ethos whose strict observance automatically rendered marginal and unacceptable any behaviour and activity that could be associated with opportunism, exploitation and fraud. The standards of conduct introduced by these trade guides increased the profession's credibility and contributed to its moral legitimacy within society. They also shaped the character of traders by giving them specific instructions on how to deal with issues of behaviour and relations, strategy, the writing of business letters and even the trade of bills of exchange.[4] At the same time, the existence of a business savoir faire facilitated communication, cooperation and the establishment of relationships of trust between merchants unknown to each other, subjects of hostile countries or members of antagonistic ethnic and religious groups, operating in different countries without much chance of them ever meeting.[5] This business savoir faire was reflected in the style of the business correspondence. And yet, sometimes this sense of mutual trust and respect for one another that was reflected in the prose of business letters concealed distrust and ill feeling as within wider society economic interests, social, legal, ideological and spiritual barriers divided people and made social harmony and tolerance difficult to achieve even among partners, associates and members of the same family.

In his letters to Bartholo and Raphael Cardamici, Thomas De Vogel adopted the conventional, traditional way of expression that was customary in commercial correspondence of the time, combining it with a very personal style.[6] The polite and respectful tone of the letters was entirely consistent with the usual, prominent way of behaving within the profession.

At the same time, De Vogel's letters revealed that he invested in his relationship with his principals. The style and content of the letters was therefore not coincidental: it was all at once deliberate and spontaneous, steeped in deeply held values and principles and, at the same time, in personal opinions and ideas that echoed the perception he had of himself and the work he had undertaken to carry out. De Vogel sought to impose himself on the Cardamicis, influencing their views and actions, through his strong character that conveyed self-confidence. This sense of superiority and self-assurance, which characterized most of Amsterdam's great merchants in the eighteenth century, derived, as Clé Lesger points out, from their position in Dutch society's social hierarchy and from the way the profession was organized. In Amsterdam, the very nature of the profession and the freedom of merchants to conduct their trade outside a specific regulatory framework, which on the contrary was the case for all other professions organized in guilds, strengthened their confidence vis-à-vis other professionals; merchants dominated in their dealings with retailers, agents, notaries, chartered brokers, shipping companies, charterers, dealers, craftsmen and office employees. This fundamental imbalance between merchants and other professionals engaged in international trade, either in representing commercial houses, purchasing, selling, loading, unloading, storing or by transporting goods, was constant. This imbalance in fact affected the merchants' behaviour in all their transactions, even when they assumed the role of commercial correspondents for other companies, as was the case with De Vogel.[7] It is hard to imagine, Lesger argues, that all this power they exerted on their colleagues, partners and employees would not boost their self-confidence and would not instil in them an individualistic approach to life.[8] In addition, traders took on a large personal risk and shouldered the overall responsibility for the outcome of their actions in carrying out their operations. The failure of a business could leave them indebted while success was recognized as their personal achievement. As a result, they tended to attribute success to energy, business acumen, stubbornness and willpower, ignoring the factors of luck and misfortune.[9] Personal gifts and skills such as knowledge, intelligence and experience made them successful in their profession and, at the same time, gave them a very high opinion of themselves and the professional group to which they belonged.[10]

Based on the above, it is no coincidence that De Vogel adopted an air of superiority in his letters and sought, using various techniques, to impose his opinion on his Greek Ottoman principals. The sequence of issues he chose to share, the irony and substance of his arguments and, finally, the skill with which he switched from a friendly approach to a strict, long and sometimes counselling and paternal style represented a strategy of psychological manipulation, the ultimate aim of which was to impose specific rules and decisions on their cooperation. Thus, the Cardamicis witnessed the irritation caused to De Vogel by the fact that he had to prepay money to other merchants and craftsmen on their behalf in anticipation of the arrival of their remittances in Amsterdam. In any case, before seeking to impose his rules on the transactions between them, De Vogel wished to convey to the Cardamicis that there existed a sense of trust, common goals and aspirations between them, to convince them of his knowledge and skills, and finally to ensure their approval for his methods, techniques and choices. Trust, Lindemann writes, was a trader's best weapon against uncertainty, anxiety and inability to predict the unpredictable and the fatal, everyday conditions of life. The credibility of a trader who inspired trust and security was therefore the most important passport to successful transactions and a necessary fundamental characteristic of his image vis-à-vis others and towards himself.[11]

Establishing a relationship of trust from a distance was a prerequisite for effective cooperation. And this relationship had to be built on the basis of mutual respect, respect for professional etiquette, confidence in the skills of both partners, honesty and recognition of the financial background of each company. 'You should be sure that we treat you with all honesty and that we do everything necessary . . . in order to serve your interests', De Vogel wrote to Bartholo Cardamici in 1762.[12] In another letter to Raphael in January 1764, he referred to his professionalism and integrity, characteristics which, he stated, made him different from all other commercial correspondents and therefore the ideal partner for the Greek Ottoman merchants: 'We act with absolute sincerity without implicating you with all the situations and procedures, [something] that we know everyone else is doing.' And in September 1769, he presented him with a list of the basic characteristics of a professional relationship of mutual trust: 'we have always spoken to you sincerely and we have always acted with precision and correctness in order to keep you satisfied and you have always recognized this.'[13]

The good name of a merchant and a wide network of acquaintances guaranteed his reliability and principles, making him worthy of the trust of his associates. The ultimate decision of an entrepreneur to enter into a cooperative relationship was largely determined by the good name of his future partner and, at the same time, by his intuition, perception of reality and interest. De Vogel, having a reputation as a reliable, composed and prudent trader with a wide circle of contacts and partners in various markets, met the objective conditions in order to be hired as a commercial correspondent of a company. At the same time, his tactics to create a relationship of trust between him and his merchant principals, adopting specific behaviours, as well as advising and directing them, introduced the Cardamicis to the realities of international trade, offering them knowledge and exercising their intuitive skills.

Good faith and a sense of duty

The establishment of a professional relationship of good faith between strangers required, first, an honest, unequivocal separation of responsibilities and duties. De Vogel always took great care to separate the standing and the obligations of his company with the position and obligations of the Cardamicis. He systematically pointed out to them his duties as their commercial correspondent and made sure to always give them a convincing explanation when these were not fulfilled.[14] At the same time, he took every opportunity he had to declare his firm belief that the Cardamicis would show commitment to the agreement and undertake with honesty to meet their responsibilities to the fullest.[15]

De Vogel himself affirmed his commitment to a specific professional code of behaviour by showing his respect for the internal hierarchy of the company he was representing. Thus, he prioritized communication with Bartholo Cardamici, founder and director of the company, and declared his full support for him when some issues led Bartholo to a rupture with his nephew Raphael. De Vogel immediately informed Bartholo of any initiative that Raphael personally communicated to him and on which Bartholo may not have been informed before.[16] And when the settlement of cases and accounts between uncle and nephew was imminent in 1761, De Vogel assured Bartholo that, until the process was complete, he would temporarily suspend all transactions with Raphael.[17]

When, after Bartholo's death, Raphael took over as director of the family business, De Vogel launched a new chapter of cooperation with him in a kind letter. In the correspondence that followed, he treated the new manager with respect and recognition, assuring him that he and his company would offer him the best possible quality of service. And on this occasion too, through courteous and polite manners, the Dutch merchant managed to impose himself with his style, propagating at every opportunity his knowledge and experience. In one of the first letters he sent to Raphael in October 1763, his wording seemed restrained and precise, but he still expressed himself with superiority and self-confidence; in particular, he asked Raphael to forgive him for the lengthy letters that would follow, which he nevertheless considered necessary as his main objective was to conduct 'good business' with him and therefore understood as a fundamental obligation to inform and motivate him towards the most profitable agreements. Finally, wanting to flatter the new manager, De Vogel ended his letter by pointing out that his company would provide him with special services and services that he did not offer to other clients and associates.[18]

Throughout his collaboration with the Cardamicis, De Vogel followed a tactic of persuasion, by conveying to the Greek Ottoman merchants a detailed position about his skills and astute methods that made him worthy to represent and direct them successfully in the field of international business; at the same time, he methodically reinforced with constant references his image as an honest and meticulous professional. De Vogel's excess self-confidence came from his experience and knowledge, his long career and character. It was, however, also a product of the position of Dutch traders within Dutch society, the freedoms and recognition they enjoyed and their direct participation in administration and politics.[19]

In addition to self-confidence, De Vogel also demonstrated a strict professionalism, monitoring with consistency and care every phase of the work he had undertaken to carry out and enforcing compliance with certain basic rules: he therefore asked the Cardamicis to provide him with detailed accounts of the goods they were sending to Amsterdam, indicating their quantity and quality. He also required that he have at his disposal in due time a list of the stamps carried by each separate parcel, package or bale of goods he received. Finally, he wanted to know the names of the various merchants and suppliers from whom the Cardamicis had purchased the items they sent to Amsterdam to sell on the local market.

De Vogel's obsession with organization, order and meticulous gathering of information seemed serious and prudent. At the same time, it demonstrated the desire of most traders of the time to be recognized as 'worthy professionals', in this way drawing on the moral legitimacy of their profession.[20] And indeed according to the trend of the time, the profession of a wholesale merchant who conducted international transactions was recognized as a 'science of commerce' whose implementation required special skills, strategy, research, knowledge of techniques and methods. As Jochen Hoock maintains, the development and consolidation of various bookkeeping and accounting practices and the circulation of an increasing number of commercial guides further contributed to the introduction of trade as a 'science'.[21] De Vogel believed that through the methodical collection of information and the 'scientific' organization of each action, he would be ready to face all the risks that could arise during the transactions and to protect both his business and that of the merchant houses he represented.[22] The conditions under which international trade took place did not respect timetables and, therefore, did not facilitate the implementation of a program with absolute precision. Therefore, De Vogel's commitment to method and detail often caused him nervous outbursts, especially when the transactions did not proceed in accordance with the program he had drawn up.[23]

Wanting to project his image as an important and reliable player in international trade that served a large and international clientele, De Vogel often referred in his letters to his trusted associates and agents in various parts of the world. On 29 July 1770 he happily recalled his exemplary collaboration with a nail-making industry in Liège. On this occasion he praised his supplier for providing very low prices, good product quality and prompt delivery. He also went on to declare that the special service offered to him by the manufacturer in question was due to their direct and personal relationship – a relationship in which no agents who would receive commission at the expense of the product's final price intervened.[24] The praise of direct *en première main* transactions by De Vogel himself and the indirect criticism he appeared to exert on the appointment of intermediaries and agents could also be seen as a disapproval of the role he so often played as a trade representative of international houses. Although inexplicable, at first sight, his insinuation should not, however, be seen as fake but more as a confirmation of the multitude of different, complementary and sometimes conflicting responsibilities the merchants had undertaken to carry out in the field of international trade.

De Vogel frequently referred in his letters to general principles and regulations of international trade as well as to his personal strategy which, as mentioned above, included strict adherence to a set of rules. Having chosen De Vogel as their representative and the man responsible to guide them in doing business in Western markets, the Cardamicis approved of his methods and agreed with his instructions, thereby taking responsibility for their choices.[25] On the other hand, De Vogel's intention was to bind them to a relationship of loyalty, trust and interdependence. He often discussed his intention with Bartholo and Raphael: 'We have so much confidence in you and we are calm that you will keep your promises and send us the necessary remittances', he wrote.[26] The constant reference to the basic rules of a professional code which he applied methodically and the encouragement of the Cardamicis to participate in business projects of his own making contributed substantially to the professional maturity of the Cardamicis; there is no doubt that their cooperation with an experienced, composed and perceptive Dutch partner acted as a compass for them within an unknown, unpredictable and competitive international milieu. At the same time, the confidence with which De Vogel dealt with the Cardamicis and his belief that his clients trusted his abilities allowed him often to have the first say in their cooperation by directing, as far as possible, transactions and taking initiatives.

As he stated in a letter to Raphael Cardamici on 23 May 1766, 'we do according to what we think is most convenient for you, and we have no doubt that this will please you', thus justifying his decision to delay the dispatch of porcelain cutlery to Smyrna until demand on the market was greater for the goods in question.[27] One could argue that De Vogel's main purpose when he sought to impose himself on the Cardamicis and influence their decisions was to lead the transactions in the direction he wished so as to obtain the highest profits in commissions with the greatest possible safety. However, through this process the Dutch merchant offered to his Ottoman principals a valuable service: this was an authentic guide to organization, survival and success within the field of international commercial enterprises, a kind of eighteenth-century trade masterclass.

Through correspondence with the Cardamicis, De Vogel sought to 'educate' his Ottoman Greek principals on the rules, customs, methods, techniques and business manoeuvres that made up the 'science of commerce'. To understand the value of the guidance offered to the Cardamicis, one must consider how the uncertainty of international trade at that time could affect the career of a trading house. De Vogel sought to develop into a kind of compass for the Greek merchants by reducing the stress and distress caused to each trader by his performance and the constant adjustments in economic and financial events, even in the weather.

Uncertainty could be addressed with knowledge and tireless effort, principles that De Vogel sought to impart to his Greek clients.[28] Thus his letters were, first, tools of communication and understanding, agreement and handling of a specific plan that each side undertook to carry out separately; they also had, nevertheless, a coaching and fatherly style. Sometimes in a lateral and sometimes in a straightforward way, De Vogel developed his business philosophy by constantly returning to the four fundamental tactics that, in his opinion, ensured recognition and profits.

A trading company seeking to expand its activity to foreign markets first had to obtain timely, reliable and confidential information on the organization and functioning of the market in which it wished to be represented; it should be able to know, at all times, the evolution of the basic parameters of the local economy and to assess the relationship between them (demand versus supply, supply against prices, transaction costs, productivity and transport costs, currency exchange rates and commission rates, etc.). The second strategic option that ensured success was, according to De Vogel, the investment in quality when purchasing goods and services or choosing partners and employees. The third determining factor for a company to build a successful international career was the ability of each merchant entrepreneur to manage daily routines and unforeseen events with the same effectiveness and poise; to operate rationally and intuitively, to act proactively, to understand, analyse and deal quickly and efficiently with any situation arising within unknown, complex and constantly changing conditions. Finally, the assessment of the optimum timing for the conduct of an undertaking, the exploitation of the most favourable conditions and the utilization of profit-maximizing opportunities was the fourth necessary condition for an international business venture to become profitable.

As can be seen from the above, De Vogel's success guide identified the personality and skills of a merchant entrepreneur as a determining factor in the development of a commercial strategy; at the same time, he supported the idea that a trader had to embrace and follow a structured scheme of coordinated actions in order to succeed. This scheme was the product of the Dutch trader's experience and personal perception of the functioning of international markets; it was also the service he offered to the Greek Ottoman Cardamici. Linking these markets through the tide and ebb of international economic life allowed someone like De Vogel and other contemporaries of the trade to think theoretically about assessing the meaning of success and failure, speculation and opportunism, wisdom and recklessness.[29] It is no coincidence that at this time, as Lindemann points out, discussions on structural issues, in particular the formulation and functioning of the institutional and regulatory framework of the economy in various countries, overshadowed discussions on the ethics of the profession.[30]

Global, timely and reliable knowledge

De Vogel's letters imparted to the Cardamicis a wealth of information concerning the operation of Amsterdam's market: the traffic of the port, the organization of the local market of commodities and services, the activity of the local merchant community. This information either related to De Vogel's current activities or provided an accurate picture of the professional and social environment in which, and in relation to which, this activity was evolving. The Cardamicis were called on to process and evaluate these data and make the necessary decisions. De Vogel systematically described the different stages of a transaction, mentioned the names of all the participants, as well as those who joined occasionally, explained and analysed all the difficulties and risks he faced. The information he transmitted to the Cardamicis through his letters fell into four different categories. As a commercial correspondent of the Cardamicis on the Amsterdam market, one of his first tasks was to inform them of the prices of goods and services as well as the connection between supply and demand within the market; De Vogel informed the Greek traders about the ship charter services, the prices of freights, insurance premiums and commissions, the fluctuations in exchange rates and the circulation of bills of exchange and the happenings in the transports sector. A second category of information included in his letters concerned the production, manufacture and distribution of products, as well as the different qualities of goods circulating in Amsterdam; finally, a third category concerned issues relating to administrative, bureaucratic and legal procedures which a company should know in order to do business in an international trade and financial centre. De Vogel also often referred to the activities of other companies operating in the same or other markets, in parallel or competitive sectors of activity.

The price lists of goods which the Dutch trader attached to his letters and which unfortunately are missing from his record of letters gave the Cardamicis the opportunity to think and decide which of them they would like to include in their orders.[31] He made sure to draw their attention to those items which would be more profitable to vend in the Ottoman markets at that time.[32] Occasionally, he also provided them with information on the progress of supply, demand and prices for products such as cotton, silk, yarn and various other textile products, inside the Amsterdam market. Thus in 1760 he informed Bartholo Cardamici that the red cotton yarn he had sent him remained unsold as most buyers did not wish to pay more than 16 florins per piece. He believed they were worth more. However, in order to fulfil his duty to him, he would seek to take advantage of the best market opportunities.[33] In 1760 he pointed out that the first-quality Kirkağac cotton was sold for 20 florins but at that time sales were not going so well.[34] In 1764 he again forwarded to Raphael price lists and information on the demand for red cotton yarn and silk voile fabric.[35] Upon learning that gun prices had fallen significantly on the Smyrna market, De Vogel warned the Cardamicis not to send him orders for that particular commodity and suggested that in place of the weapons he send them 150 pieces of lead.[36] In the same year he wrote to Bartholo that the prices of first-class cotton were very high on the Amsterdam market and he did not foresee that this situation would change any time soon. But, as he noted, if the price of cotton was as high on the Ottoman markets, then by buying and selling in Amsterdam the Cardamicis would make no substantial profit. Just a month later he revised his views as the price of cotton rose again significantly.[37]

Market conditions changed faster than the time it took for the Cardamicis and their Dutch representative to communicate. However, De Vogel was consistent in conveying incidents, events and situations to them. Thus in June 1761 he assured them that he had not been able to find on the market coffee in a quality similar to that they had ordered, but as soon as he found it he would make sure to buy and send it to them.[38] In November 1762, he again advised Bartholo to abandon for a time the lucrative trade in dried fruit as its price had gone up too much on the Ottoman markets and there was already enough of it on the Amsterdam market. Instead, he recommended waiting a year as, again according to his forecasts, new, more favourable market conditions would prevail.[39] In October 1763, he confirmed to Raphael Cardamici that the demand for Bursa silk on the local market was considerable and that selling it at a high price would reap him significant profits.[40] In fact De Vogel sent Raphael, the younger partner who was generally more receptive to business openings, more detailed and frequent information on the traffic of various commodities in Amsterdam's market.

At times, the Greek Ottoman traders expressed their disbelief at the information from their correspondent as they were unable to appreciate the habits and customs in the Dutch markets. Thus in December 1766, Raphael conveyed his surprise and reservations about the very low silk prices on the Amsterdam market. In that case, De Vogel had to explain that under an old and popular city custom, every now and then silk buyers were offered a long period of discounts on the local market.[41]

De Vogel's letters also served as evidence of the agreements he had negotiated, the contracts he had signed and the amounts he had disbursed for purchases of goods and services. Cardamici also systematically received detailed accounts with the amounts disbursed for the payment of advances and commissions, the purchase of services, the exchange of currencies and gold. The successful completion of a transport was a fundamental issue and, as mentioned in Chapter 4, included a series of negotiations and procedures; De Vogel was aware of the port traffic, the availability of ships bound for the East, the costs of freights and insurance. Having created a network of personal relations in the field of merchant shipping, he drew information from the domestic circle of shipowners, captains and various naval agents. De Vogel received confidential information concerning the impulsive and intransigent behaviour of some captains, the acknowledged abilities of some and the fraudulent and hidden motives of others, finally, the contemptable demands of some third parties.[42] All this information was imparted to the Cardamicis together with specific instructions on how to choose shipowners and vessels and how to organize the transport of their goods from Smyrna to Amsterdam, with or without the help and intervention of third parties.

The accumulated knowledge, experience and capital of personal acquaintances that De Vogel offered his Ottoman principals was the best means to gradually integrate them into the international trading environment. Assessing the news they received, as well as the comments that De Vogel often made regarding persons and situations, the Cardamicis understood the fluidity of the conditions in their new business environment and the uncertainty it caused to all market players: 'We know about Capt. Disma's delay, but the reason [for this] was the bad situation [prevailing] in trade which gave him small profits when loading the ship; we hope he will arrive soon', he warned them in 1765.[43] Three years later, he informed Raphael: 'The ship remains in front of the city and it is extremely uncertain whether he will be able to depart this year; also he [the captain] is asking for a very high freight and so we will make sure to transfer all the goods to the ship of Capt. Boermaster, who is charging much lower freights.'[44] Another time, in a more personal tone, he conveyed to the Cardamicis his thoughts on the behaviour of a particular captain: 'Capt. Hendriks, who was loading [his vessel] to come to your places, as he has done many times, will remain here, will not depart this period and has unloaded – we thought this would happen and so we did not load goods on his ship, the outrageous prices he was asking for caused us much doubt.'[45] On another occasion he informed them that the only ship left in Amsterdam's port preparing to depart for the Ottoman ports was the *Le Belus*, but the owners of the vessel chose the goods they loaded according to their type and had significantly raised the price of freight.[46]

De Vogel's acquaintances at the various international ports provided reliable and timely information on the duration and development of each journey, as well as the route followed, the expected stops, arrivals and departures at the various ports. 'If your letter had arrived eighteen days earlier, we would have had the opportunity to send you the St. Martha wood with the ship of Capt. Andriessen;

but by the time we received the letter, it had departed and had gained speed.'[47] In 1760, he informed Bartholo Cardamici that the 400 pistols that he had ordered would arrive in Smyrna with Capt. Forti, who had already departed, and on Capt. Kectel's ship.[48] And that same year, knowing that Capt. Jacob Kersies's ship would be the first to depart for Smyrna at that time, he informed them that he had chartered it to send them twelve barrels of white iron.[49]

The climate was another uncontrollable factor in the development of a business. In his letters De Vogel depicted stories about how the fickle weather caused serious difficulties by putting obstacles in the way of the smooth and timely transport of cargo. Cardamici, on the other hand, received information concerning the weather conditions that affected traffic at the ports along the Amsterdam–Smyrna route: 'We hope that Capt. Pante will arrive safely and deliver the nails in good condition . . . as we learned about a tornado and very bad weather [coming]', he wrote in 1761.[50] He added:

> The ice melted and the rivers opened up to us and so we were able to see the ships of Capt. Schaap and Capt. Joachim Andriessen in front of the city with the fruit loaded. Capt. Everts with your load remains in England and we hope that soon he will arrive here and that we will find your fruit of good quality and in good condition.[51]

In 1766 he told Raphael Cardamici: 'Having very strong headwinds for ten days after his departure, Capt. Raves finally arrived in Livorno, from where he should have already departed if he had not had to go through quarantine as he had on board a man from Salento.'[52] In 1767 he declared with relief: 'Finally came the tailwind and the ships of captains Pante and Mallaga took advantage of it and went out to sea; two days later they faced a headwind and since then it became favourable again; we hope they have continued their journey.'[53] In 1769, he noted with condescension: 'Capt. Mallaga arrived. Capt. Boermaster has been forced to stay in Livorno for a month in order to repair the great damage to his ship, otherwise he would already be here, but that was God's will, and we must be patient.'[54]

De Vogel's letters comprised a variety of information on the organization and the cost of transports. In his lengthy reports De Vogel often referred to the high costs of freight that he was trying to bypass by negotiating for better prices, while exploring the possibility of reaching a profitable deal with another vessel: 'The freights in Constantinople are very expensive . . . we cannot now find an opportunity for a good price . . . And we had to pay those high freights to Capt. Kectel.'[55] In 1766 he informed Raphael Cardamici of his endless efforts: 'We try to achieve the lowest freights but we do not always know how to achieve this, as in the case of Capt. Andriessen claiming a freight of 100 florins for 20 barrels of nails.[56] And in 1767 he conveyed to him his intention to negotiate with another ship captain: 'We will talk about the lead with Capt. Marten Pante, to finally agree on the lowest freight.'[57] He also referred to vessel repairs:

> In the end Capt. Boermaster was forced to repair the door . . . in Lyon and for
> this reason and for the bad weather that continued, he was forced to stay there
> until 8 March, and after departed with a tailwind, God may bring him to safe
> harbour, and the goods loaded on his ship have no loss or damage at all.[58]

As mentioned in Chapter 5, the issue of financing the Cardamici business in Amsterdam was crucial. De Vogel, who worked for years in Europe's largest financial and banking centre, collaborated daily with merchants/financiers, bankers and brokers, closed deals, traded in currencies and bonds and was familiar with the various methods and techniques of trading with bills of exchange, precious metals and cash. His merchant and agent 'friends' in Europe and the East systematically conveyed to him news concerning the organization and operation of the financial markets in Smyrna, Livorno, Vienna, London and Marseille – also information about the economic situation of the major international trading houses and their most recent transactions, exchange rates in the various European countries and the Ottoman Empire.[59] By relaying this information to his Ottoman Greek clients, he sought to keep them informed of developments and, at the same time, to direct them on where, when and to whom they should go in order to obtain bills of exchange, precious metals and coins that afterwards they would forward it to him in Amsterdam. In November 1762 De Vogel suggested to Bartholo Cardamici to issue bills and cheques to commercial houses in Livorno and Genoa, explaining that in Amsterdam the money market was much more sensitive to the laws of supply and demand and that currency exchange rates could not be easily negotiated.[60] The final recipient of the amounts resulting from the repayment of the bills and the exchange of gold and precious metals would be De Vogel himself.

De Vogel also guided the Cardamicis on how to handle administrative, bureaucratic and financial issues that were unknown to them and related to the operation of the Dutch economy, regulations and institutions of the market and the port of Amsterdam. In December 1763, he informed Bartholo Cardamici that the Dutch customs office calculated the duties imposed on Eastern goods as a quota of their weight and/or value and did not impose a fixed price on each parcel or box imported into the Netherlands. For this reason, he explained, once arriving at the port from the East, many captains used to unwrap the parcels and wrap them in larger ones to save time and money. De Vogel warned that this practice could seriously harm the goods.[61] Having long experience of routine procedures through which a trading house obtained all the necessary documents and certificates for its transactions, De Vogel directed his Greek Ottoman clients within the unknown environment of the Dutch public administration. In October 1762 he insisted that Bartholo Cardamici should obtain a certificate from the Dutch consul in Smyrna certifying the arrival at the port of 200 pistols belonging to his company. The pistols had arrived to Smyrna from Amsterdam on Capt. Mallaga's ship. If Bartholo were to obtain the certificate within the time limit, De Vogel, who had purchased and sent the pistols to the Cardamicis, would avoid the payment of export duty on pistols and, at the same time, in accordance with the regulation in force, would be exempt from duty for any future export of this kind of goods to the Ottoman Empire.[62]

De Vogel helped the Cardamicis in those circumstances where they were confronted with the Dutch authorities and laws to support their interest vis-à-vis shipowners, captains and insurance agents. He made sure in advance to describe in detail the procedures to be followed and to advise them on how they should act. So, in 1763 he explained to Raphael Cardamici how to deal with the Dutch insurers to collect compensation for eight barrels of nails that had arrived damaged in Smyrna from Amsterdam after a long and dangerous journey.[63]

De Vogel's extensive business network provided him information on other sectors of the economy of countries with which he was trading, such as the manufacture and agricultural sectors and the production of raw materials. The Dutch trader was able to predict even the quality of a crop of Ottoman cotton, as well as the date it was harvested, and to pass the information on to his Greek Ottoman principals even before they managed to get similar information through their local contacts.[64]

One particularly important service offered to Cardamici was the confidential and reliable news on the economic situation, strategy and activity of other trading houses. De Vogel placed particular emphasis on informing the Greek merchants about bankruptcies of well-known companies and the impact they had on the operation of the various markets. This issue, in particular the debate on bankruptcy frauds, was particularly exciting in commercial circles in general but also in the light of the violation of established commercial practices and diversion from the standards of a respectable business culture.[65] De Vogel urged the Cardamicis to be vigilant when selecting their partners and adopting specific business practices that could compromise their good name and profits. At the beginning of the century the practices that caused most concern and uncertainty in business circles were uncontrolled speculation with commodities and shares, fraudulent exchange transactions and, finally, bankruptcies.[66] A series of letters from De Vogel to Raphael Cardamici in the spring and summer of 1768 referred precisely to the economic adventures and impending bankruptcy of the Armenian merchant Alexander De Masse.[67] As mentioned above, De Masse had played a central role in the transactions between the Cardamicis and De Vogel by accepting and paying off bills of exchange that the Greek merchants had drawn on him and sent to Amsterdam; the price was then transferred to De Vogel. When the ordeals of the Armenian house became known, De Vogel advised Raphael Cardamici to cease working with him and find another way to promote bills and cheques in Amsterdam. On this occasion he recommended that they pay cash to his associates David Van Lennep & William Enslie in Smyrna, who would find a way to pass it on to him. In another letter referring again to De Masse's bankruptcy, he said the large number of creditors of the Armenian company was going to cause great damage to many trading houses in a chain reaction. De Vogel pointed out to Raphael that Hemzy, De Masse's main partner in Constantinople, had made an honest and commendable deal with some of the creditors to cover 70 per cent of their claims and later all of them.[68] Hemzy, as it turned out, was an honest man, 'although Jewish', and De Vogel endorsed Raphael's cooperation with him.[69]

Quality control

One of the key principles of De Vogel's business strategy which he wished to instil in the Cardamicis was the value of investing in high-quality goods, services and partners. As far as goods were concerned, he often reiterated his firm belief that 'expensive', refined, high-quality goods and products could always be promoted on various international markets, made available at high prices and profit, even in times of economic and monetary crisis or market saturation by similar products. De Vogel often advised the Cardamicis to buy certain items at a higher price, even in smaller quantities, to offset the cost of buying them. He encouraged them to supply him with excellent-quality white cottons, Bursa silk and angora yarns.[70] In 1764 he asked Raphael to send him first-class cotton yarn in bright red colour, a commodity for which there was high demand on the Amsterdam market and could be sold at a high price.[71] De Vogel's arguments were irrefutable, and he set them out in his letters. Trading low-quality products could prove extremely dangerous for a merchant's reputation and profit and was, in any case, a counterproductive choice, he wrote. If the Greek Ottoman merchants were not able to obtain first-class goods, then it would be preferable to invest their funds in the purchase and circulation of bills and bonds, a trade that would guarantee them greater profits.[72] He also did not hesitate to warn them that all the low-quality or defective goods he would receive from Smyrna – like the red cotton yarn sent to him by Raphael Cardamici in September 1767 – would be kept in a warehouse until the right opportunity arose to sell them at a very low price. If he still could not put them on the market, he'd make sure they went to auction, and if they stayed unsold, he would send them back to Smyrna.[73] The Dutch trader understood the choice of partners and collaborators in the same way as he perceived trade: it was an option that could prove disastrous if it did not meet some basic quality guarantees. In the same way as he preferred to trade in high-quality and high-value goods, he supported the establishment of significant relationships of mutual trust and benefit with efficient and respectable suppliers, traders and representatives; these relationships were priceless and crucial for the successful development of a business. Despite the great competition in the markets, if the name of a merchant was linked to opportunistic and deceitful practices it could mean isolation within the commercial environment and reputational damage. Working with such individuals could be extremely harmful.[74] Therefore, De Vogel recommended Bartholo Cardamici to find and buy high-quality angora yarns in collaboration with *personnes de confiance* as a good acquaintance (*bonne connaissance*) inside each local market was always useful and beneficial.[75]

Selecting the most reliable, competent and renowned partners and suppliers and investing their capital for the best products and goods on the market were, according to De Vogel, two decisive actions that could ensure a safe and large profit to a successful businessman. To complete a successful transaction, the merchant and his commercial correspondent had to meet similar quality criteria in the choice of the merchant ship which would transport the cargo to a distant destination in a timely and safe manner. De Vogel insisted that for the selection of a vessel that would carry the orders of the Cardamicis to the Ottoman Empire, a necessary condition was the prior assessment of the captain's capabilities and solvency and the vessel's manufacturing, equipment and capacity. For this reason, in October 1766, he expressed his deep distrust of Raphael Cardamici's initiative to charter a ship unknown to him to send a shipment of dried fruit to Amsterdam. Raphael on this occasion had been forced to choose an emergency solution as several ship captains refused to load dried fruit due to the delicate nature of the commodity. His move to ignore, for once, the suggestions of his Dutch representative in Amsterdam caused De Vogel even more dissatisfaction.

Business intuition and sensitivity: Organization and timing

The intuition and sensitivity of a merchant, his ability to manage wisely and plan boldly, to make decisions and implement them at the right time, were necessary conditions for the success of a commercial enterprise. As early as the mid-1760s, Thomas De Vogel laid out in broad terms the basic rules for a business to be successful, fundamental conditions that several centuries later are analysed extensively in studies on the theory of modern entrepreneurship.[76]

In his letters, De Vogel called on the Cardamicis to define their strategy and objectives and to fulfil them through coordinated actions. He encouraged them to anticipate and assess potential and unforeseen risks and to seek to maximize their profit. For planning their business, they had to consider first the information they had obtained from their contacts, evaluate the data and use their intuition. They should be careful, moderate and always alert in order to protect their capital and reputation, but at the same time they should be willing to seize the opportunities offered to them and to work in new areas.

As mentioned above, De Vogel insisted that an experienced and competent entrepreneur should invest his capital in high-value goods and services, choose powerful and trustworthy 'friends' and rely on the cooperation of competent and trusted professionals. In the end, he underlined the crucial importance of 'timing' as a key factor in a business's success, that is, choosing the right time to carry out a planned action. At the time, the idea that luck in business was volatile and everything depended on the moment directed the way of thinking in business.[77] In August 1761 De Vogel explained to Bartholo Cardamici that the late arrival of a cargo ship in Amsterdam could affect the sale price of cotton. Reassuring him that the current high prices would be maintained for a period of time, he also made sure to prepare him psychologically for a future price reduction: as he wrote, the high prices of cotton were due to the late arrival of ships from the East and would return to their previous levels as soon as more ships arrived. The Cardamicis should in any case take advantage of the favourable situation and send him the same first-quality white cottons which could be made available at a fairly good price.[78] In another letter, this time to Raphael Cardamici, on 24 September 1762, De Vogel discouraged him from dealing with diamonds, which the Greek trader wished to buy in Amsterdam and sell in Constantinople. He warned him that the enterprise he was seeking to set up for trading in precious stones was doomed from the outset as he would not be able to supply him with diamonds at the low prices that Raphael wanted. He advised him to abandon his plans for a period.[79] A few weeks later, De Vogel indicated to Bartholo that he should postpone for at least a year the export of figs and raisins he planned, as their prices on the Ottoman markets were very high and large quantities had already been received by commercial houses in Amsterdam. It would therefore be more prudent, De Vogel argued, for Cardamici to wait for a while before sending new shipments, as the conditions prevailing on the Amsterdam market in terms of prices and demand of these products were expected to change to his advantage when the market was no longer saturated. Meanwhile, De Vogel suggested that his principals try to find and buy at a relatively low price a fairly large quantity of black Corinth raisins and send them to Amsterdam. This product was in high demand on the market at the time and its sale would bring to them great profits.[80] In 1766, once again, the Dutch trader advised Raphael Cardamici to buy first-class cotton as, according to the information he had collected, this quality cotton could be purchased on the Ottoman markets at a relatively low price at that time. He then advised him to send the shipment to Amsterdam where prices for this product were very high; however, he suggested that he first send a small quantity of product to see what profits the sales would bring to him and recommended that he charter the ship of Capt. De Leeuw for the dispatch, a ship in which De Vogel, as we already know, had a share.[81]

A few years later, in 1770, in another letter to Raphael, De Vogel presented him with a comprehensive business proposal on the cotton trade. He informed him of the current price of the product, which had increased to 19½ florins, which, according to his calculations, would continue to increase. He then developed his plan: Raphael would buy cotton in Smyrna at the lowest price of 26–27 piastres, which could be sold on the Amsterdam market for 20 florins, bringing him great profits. De Vogel asked the Cardamicis to let him know if he decided to follow his advice. If he did, he would charter one of his own ships on his behalf, the *Gysbert Jan* of Capt. William Blom, to transport cotton to Amsterdam by paying the lowest possible freight; De Vogel suggested to Raphael that their common 'friends', Van Lennep & Enslie, take over the whole transaction. In concluding his letter, he reiterated his belief that Raphael would have deal in the cotton trade as it was the most profitable business at the time and the demand for the product concerned was consistent; on the contrary, demand for all other products and goods in the East was very low on the Amsterdam market and would shrink even further.[82] On another occasion, in July 1766, De Vogel reassured Raphael

Cardamici that he would send him the 350 pieces of lead he had ordered, warning him, however, that the price he would have to pay for this commodity on the Amsterdam market would be particularly high. Therefore, it would be very difficult for Raphael to make any profit from the sale of the lead on the Ottoman markets – in addition, the Dutch trader provided him with the information that at the same time seven thousand pieces of lead were already on sale by another trading house on the Smyrna market.[83]

As the above shows, De Vogel's contribution to the Cardamici business was complex and invaluable. The Dutch trader, in the role of commercial correspondent, attended all the different phases of the business with confidence and determination drawn from his experience, knowledge and professional-social origins. In addition to constructive criticism and guidance to his Greek Ottoman principals, he often took the initiative to modify their orders and shift cargo shipments over time, judging for himself when the time was right to proceed with a transaction. Thus, ordering the manufacture of nails and weapons from Dutch and Belgian factories required a complex and demanding mediation process; De Vogel was obliged to negotiate first the cheap and timely construction of the goods and then their transport to the port. Once arriving at the port, the goods had to be loaded on the ship that had been chartered on the appropriate date. In the winter of 1761, De Vogel regretted the significant delay in sending the nails that the Cardamicis had ordered, attributing this unpleasant development to the high price of iron and the lack of specialized craftsmen. This situation had forced him to order the thirty barrels of nails requested by Bartholo with great delay, thus significantly delaying production. Then the transport of the barrels to Smyrna and Constantinople was postponed to a later date.[84] De Vogel took this opportunity to point out that the Cardamicis had to carefully plan the dispatch of their orders, especially when these orders concerned the manufacture and purchase of nails. This commodity had an increased delivery time from the craft industries and therefore its shipment to the Ottoman ports was very difficult to complete without a time difference. The late arrival of the nails in the port of Amsterdam, when most ships to the East had departed, resulted in the cargo remaining in the warehouses of the port and finally being delivered to the Greek merchants with a long delay.[85]

Conclusion

Merchants on the Mediterranean: Ottoman–Dutch trade in the eighteenth century

Thomas De Vogel's letters to Bartholo and Raphael Cardamici are irrefutable evidence of the early-eighteenth-century expansion of Ottoman trade to the West through the establishment of Ottoman trade networks in various European commercial and financial centres. They thus confirm that the infiltration of European merchants of Ottoman markets during the same period was by no means a one-way process; on the contrary, as the analysis of the Cardamici–De Vogel collaboration proves, Western involvement in the Ottoman trade economy was a complex and multilevel development directly connected with the concomitant access of Ottoman firms to Western markets. In fact, at the time, large- and medium-sized Ottoman companies set off business collaborations with European firms in the Ottoman Empire and Europe and were introduced into international trade networks. The Cardamicis were owners and directors of a medium-sized trading company which followed an international business strategy while Thomas De Vogel was the European merchant who guided them during their business adventure in the West.

The Cardamici–De Vogel case therefore represents an interesting deviation from the 'European merchant–Ottoman commercial agent' pattern that dominates the analysis of Levantine trade; it actually portrays a reverse model, one where the Cardamicis, Bartholo and Raphael were the principals/clients seeking to expand their business from their operational base in Smyrna and Constantinople to Amsterdam, a major Western commercial and financial market. De Vogel was employed as their local correspondent, providing on commission various market, maritime, insurance and financial services. An interesting paradox of Cardamicis' strategy to extend their business transactions in Amsterdam is that they chose to collaborate with an important Dutch firm instead of turning to a Greek merchant house established in the city and to come to a business arrangement that would serve the interests of both. By the middle of the eighteenth century a fairly important commercial community of Greeks had been established in Amsterdam and its members had business transactions with many Smyrna firms. It seems therefore that the Cardamicis' choice of De Vogel to become their key correspondent in the Netherlands diverged also from another stereotypical assumption: that ethnic solidarity in business was the pivotal factor in the success of ethnic groups involved in international trade during this period and therefore Greeks, Jews and Armenians formed business networks exclusively comprising members of their ethnic-religious milieu. As a middle-sized enterprise, the Cardamicis did not belong to an extended, ethnic or nonethnic, business network and, therefore, it is remarkable that they approached a powerful, distant, Dutch Protestant merchant and entrusted him with their representation in a foreign, sophisticated and completely unknown business environment. It seems, however, that in a similar fashion, many other Ottoman trading companies used Dutch merchant houses as intermediaries in their transactions with the West for two obvious reasons: first, because of Amsterdam's stable primacy as an international market for products, capital, freights and insurance throughout the eighteenth century and, second, because cooperation between Ottomans and Dutch and vice versa was approved and sanctioned by the Dutch authorities and was free and flexible. In contrast, collaboration between Ottoman subjects and English and French trading houses was carried out on an equal basis only after the end of the eighteenth century, always within specific regulatory frameworks or by violating them. By reconstructing the Cardamici business environment through De Vogel's letters, it becomes obvious that both Bartholo and Raphael were in contact or had some kind of transactions with Dutch and Ottoman firms, Greek, Armenian and Jewish, which incidentally belonged to De Vogel's European and Ottoman business contacts. This could be another reason why the Cardamicis turned to De Vogel, a well-known Dutch merchant from within their wider business environment, to represent them in Amsterdam. His experience and knowledge became a compass of sorts for the Ottoman-based merchants, conducting their way inside the universe of the eighteenth-century international business transactions.

Another significant but unknown aspect of this association is when exactly it was established. As it is obvious from the content of the first letter (dated 7 March 1760) found in De Vogel's archive in which he addresses Bartholo Cardamici, their collaboration had kicked off much earlier. We should therefore assume that it could have started some months or even years before, as we believe that De Vogel business career began in the 1720s. Nevertheless, it was in the 1760s that this Dutch–Ottoman relationship grew and attained a significant dynamic, a period during which incidentally, according to recent studies, the Dutch merchant marine made a significant comeback in the Levantine trade. In particular, in the period between the Seven Years' War (1756–63) and the Fourth Anglo–Dutch War (1780–4), the Dutch merchant fleet appeared to be largely financed by Ottoman merchant houses, such as Cardamici, which in the mid-eighteenth century made an impressive entrance into the Dutch Levant trade.

The Cardamici–De Vogel collaboration was determined by a number of individual and independent factors, as well as by historical events connected with the prevailing economic, political and social conditions of the period. As with all similar business ventures, geography played a pivotal role in the development of business transactions. Distance and weather imposed protocols and procedures, techniques and methods. They defined the duration and the safe conclusion of a voyage through the Atlantic and the Mediterranean, which in itself required decisive levels of communication, decision-making and strategy. At another analytical level, the account of a ten-year business relationship between a Dutch merchant entrepreneur and a Greek Ottoman family business confirms that eighteenth-century trade was, above all, an individual affair, one that required strangers, located in faraway countries, to overcome uncertainty and distrust on a daily basis, cope with day-to-day setbacks and find a common language to communicate, work together and make profits. This book is about Western trade in the Ottoman Empire and Ottomans trading with the West. The story captures moments, incidents and enduring deals from the business activity and everyday life of a multi-ethnic and multicultural mercantile community operating between Europe and the Levant in the long eighteenth century. These moments demonstrate how people of different provenance, language, culture, religion, social status and economic means carried out continuous and audacious commercial transactions between Europe and the Ottoman Empire amid fundamental changes in business, society, economy, politics and international relations. The book depicts the willingness and capacity of these merchants who emerged from the major Ottoman commercial centres to seek a career in intercontinental and transatlantic trade; it portrays their inclination to overcome insecurity and to trust distant partners and collaborators to guide them in a new business universe. As the era of merchant capitalism was drawing to an end and making way for the era of industrialization, corporate multinational enterprise and sophisticated commercial finance, the Ottoman firms that ventured into the West were called to follow new techniques and methods, learn new trends and fashions, become flexible and expeditious in coping with competition and change.

The study of the content of the De Vogel letters yields a wealth of information concerning the daily practice of trade and the operation of commercial networks. At the same time, the relationship between an Ottoman Greek trading business and a Dutch commercial correspondent unfolds before our eyes, an uneven relationship of dependency, with the decision-making centre of gravity lying with the side of the Dutch representative. De Vogel's monologues, as they emerge through his letters, reveal his strategy, tactics, manoeuvres and principles; at the same time, they reveal the position and attitude of the Cardamicis and, in this sense, often act as imaginary dialogues. The relationship between the Ottoman Greeks and the Dutch merchant ensured the Cardamicis' path to within an unfamiliar trading universe; at the same time, it was at times a manipulative relationship as De Vogel sought to impose his opinion and serve personal interests. In each letter, his rhetoric aimed to build a relationship of trust and bridge the confidence gap between strangers; at the same time a dynamical power struggle evolved between him and his clients, through his statements, innuendo and threats, flattery and praise.

Appendix

The following pages contain eighteen of the most representative letters of the dynamic relationship between Thomas De Vogel and the Cardamicis as it evolved from 1760 to 1771. For clarity, parts of the text have been expanded or modified where there are gaps or where the original French contained significant syntax and spelling errors.

1 'Hopefully you come across something that will allow you to speculate'

Thomas De Vogel to Bartholo Cardamici & Co., Smyrna

7 March 1760

On the 8th ult. we had the honour to write to you; we refer to the contents of your dear letters which we received. Capt. Pauw's ship, upon which we loaded 2 barrels with 400 pairs of pistols, is preparing to leave with the first good wind; may God guide him to a safe port. As for the sugar you ordered, we did our best to send it to you on this ship but it was not possible because she is completely packed with goods. A lot of merchandise will be left behind as we will not be able to load it. As for the price [of the sugar], it is currently quite high and [there is] very little [sugar] in town. As it is impossible for us to send any to you by this ship, we have postponed the acquisition, hoping of getting some at a more moderate price and have your instructions on this matter. By this time you will be informed of the nails and guns. They are being made and you will receive them from Capt. Pieter De Leuuw, whom you can contact. We were delighted to hear about the cotton price being around 16 to 18 [florins] . . . and that you will send us some for your account. The finest [cotton] is currently selling at 18 florins – we see that the prices are rising. Therefore, you will find here attached a list of the current prices of various commodities to which we refer; hopefully you will come across something that will allow you to speculate.

We commend ourselves to you and to God.

Stadsarchief Amsterdam, 332, 1.2.2, vol. 44, p. 6

2. 'As the only thing we desire is to see our collaboration amplify'

Thomas De Vogel to Bartholo Cardamici & Co., Smyrna

22 April 1760

On the 21st ult. we had the honour to write to you. We refer to the content of our previous letter, a copy of which you will find attached. You will also find attached the bill of lading for 2 barrels of pistols loaded onboard the ship of Capt. J. Pauw, who set sail with a good wind and may God guide him to a safe port. We have done all we could to forward you the nails and pistols with Capt. De Leeuw's ship. We have received the nails and loaded them on Capt. De Leeuw's ship as you will see from the attached bill of lading and also by the acquisition receipt amounting to 3,332.20 florins and comprising the insurance premium upon the amount of 3,200 florins, which we charge to you. Please will you be kind to put in writing a compliance letter. You will note that the insurance premium is modest and that we have considered that the merchandise will be at risk until [the arrival of the ship] at Constantinople, and we hope that you will approve this.

The pistols are on their way and we hope to receive them this month and load them onboard this ship. We are disappointed not to have received your dear letters, but we have received one from your nephew Mr Raphael in which he tells us that he hasn't received letters from you as well, and so he does not know what to forward us, and he orders us to suspend all dispatches of pistols to you and send you 100 pieces of lead. We immediately revoked the production of pistols, but we were obliged to receive and send to you those that were already on their way; we have also purchased the 100 pieces of lead and loaded them onboard Capt. De Leeuw's ship. You will find herewith attached the bill of lading and the acquisition receipt amounting 1,356.16 florins, comprising the premium insurance upon the amount of 1,300 florins which meets the same conditions as the previous one and extends to Constantinople, and we charge it to you. Please be kind to put in writing a compliance letter. You see that we are very careful to forward you the consignments you ask for and by this we find ourselves in great expenses; therefore, we ask from you new orders and abundant remittances. Regarding the freight, you will observe that we have obtained it at a good price, something that should make you happy. Please be sure that we will continue our duty with great zeal for your profit, as the only thing we desire is to see our collaboration amplify. May God give us peace and give you good business. We have sold your trimmings at 48 [florins] and the double hem at 30 [florins], which is the highest price we could get. When they are delivered, we will send you the sales receipt. The first-quality cotton, the Kirkağac kind, comes at a price of 20 [florins] and for this reason it is not selling much at the moment.

We commend ourselves to you and to your orders with great respect.

Stadsarchief Amsterdam, 332, 1.2.2, vol. 44, pp. 92–3

3. 'Gold ducats or bills of exchange or gold ingots'

Thomas De Vogel to Raphael Cardamici, Constantinople

22 April 1760

We are honoured by your dear letter of 3 April by which you urge us to send the nails ordered, and as you ask us to forward you the weapons, you order us to forward you 100 pieces of lead as well. We received the 20 barrels of nails and loaded them on board the ship of Capt. Pieter De Leeuw. As we received your letters we also purchased and loaded on board the same ship 100 pieces of lead. You will find attached a letter for your uncle in which you will see the cost of all of the commodities purchased. We have requested the pistols to be made in a finer way, so that you will see if these please you or you can send them back. We are obliged to send to you those pistols that are already on their way to us and those that will arrive to us [from the manufacturer] this week . . . the dispatch will be made on Capt. De Leeuw's ship. You will therefore receive from us a very good shipment and also our great regards and, in the same way, we hope to receive from you an abundant remittance, either in gold ducats or in bills of exchange or in gold ingots. We will let you know the exchange rate of these and we hope that it will bring you good profits and satisfy you.

We commend ourselves to your orders with honour to you and to God.

Stadsarchief Amsterdam, 332, 1.2.2, vol. 44, p. 93

4. 'He asked us to send him diamonds and velvets'

Thomas De Vogel to Bartholo Cardamici & Co., Smyrna

12 September 1760

The above is a copy of our last letter, the content of which we refer you to. With the present one we send you a bill of lading for a barrel of pistols loaded on board Capt. Kectel's ship *La Paix* . . . . He did not want to load in advance any more barrels and he sailed on 10 August; may God guide him to a safe port. Also enclosed here is the bill of lading for 20 bales of nails loaded on Capt. Marten Pante's ship *Hellespontus*, off Constantinople. You will find attached the acquisition receipt for the barrel of pistols, which amounts to 979.50 florins, and the one for the nails, which is 3,295.19 florins, comprising the insurance premium which we will charge to you. Please be kind to put in writing a compliance letter. You will notice that with our dispatches our advance payment now amounts to 12,000 florins, without counting the pistols we are obliged to send to you with Capt. Pante. And to do this please be kind to send us some remittances. As you will notice from our dispatches to you, we have great confidence in you.

We are honoured by your letter of 2 July in which we see that you have written to us to accompany the attached bill of lading for 2 bales of double hem and one of trimmings loaded on the ship of Capt. Mente Schryrer; this letter has reached us. Thank you for crediting with us the dispatch you made with Capt. De Leeuw and giving us outflow for the sale of your trimmings and fringes; we opt for that. It is kind of you to have asked Mr Raphael to send us remittances and Capt. De Leeuw, for whom we have learned that he has arrived in Smyrna, will load everything that it is possible for you, and we look forward to that; but, more than anything else, we beg you to get Mr Raphael to consider sending us from Vienna a piece of gold of 246¾ drams and please ask him to send us a significant remittance. He requested from us diamonds worth 1,200 florins and he wrote to us asking for velvets, but it is not the best time of the year to send them to him.

We commend ourselves to you with respect.

Stadsarchief Amsterdam, 332, 1.2.2, vol. 44, p. 399

5. 'Due to the Jewish holidays, we cannot obtain the necessary information'

Thomas De Vogel, to Raphael Cardamici, Constantinople

12 September 1760

Your dear letter of 4 August has reached us, together with the one sent by your uncle. Herewith enclosed, you will find our reply, describing the commodities we sent to you and you will see that our advance payments amount to 12,000 florins and therefore we need a transfer [from you] for this through Mr Stametz; we have no doubt that you will provide it. We ask you to continue providing us with these valuable remittances. For what concerns the velvets, you will find here a small sample in order to survey the quality. You will only have to mark us the colours you need, in order to have them manufactured, as we will need time to do so. As for the diamonds you mentioned, due to the Jewish holidays, we cannot obtain the necessary information for the moment. There is also not enough time to send them to you, so they will be forwarded with the next mail.

We commend ourselves to your honour and to God.

Stadsarchief Amsterdam, 332, 1.2.2, vol. 44, p. 399

6. 'A good connection could provide you with one or two bales for an assessment'

Thomas De Vogel to Bartholo Cardamici & Co., Smyrna

7 April 1761

We had the honour to write to you on the 24th ult. – you will find a copy attached – and we refer to the content of that letter. Since then, we have unpacked from Capt. De Leeuw's ship 44 barrels of Corinth raisins in very good condition. And having found their quality fairly good, we have sold them since then at the price of 10¾ florins, a very good price in the present situation, when this fruit is found in abundance here; and with this price you should be satisfied.

You will find here attached the sales receipt amounting 1,496.10 florins, a sum which we will credit to you as long as we will receive your remittances. If you find the receipt without any error, please pay for the 30 barrels of nails which we will forward you on Capt. Vlaming's ship and which are not ready yet. As for the other 30 barrels, we will have them produced and send them to you at the first opportunity and you will be informed about this. You have seen that, as for the coffee we don't see how to find and send to you the quality you request from us. We will try to search everywhere here if we can obtain it by any chance on the arrival of some ship from Suriname or Martinique and if we succeed, we will let you know. We beg you to continue sending us remittances so that we will be able to carry on forwarding to you the merchandise you desire. As for the cotton, you would have made great profits if you had speculated as we have received excellent cotton from your place and we sold it at 20 florins; but as they are on their way three ships loaded with 1,400 bales and we wait for many others loaded with good quantities, we calculate that these prices will not last and if the prices at your place remain as they have, the reduction will not be considerable. We will keep you informed on what is happening, so that you will be able to organize your speculation. Gallnuts are in high demand, which most likely will further increase. As for the goat's yarn it is found in bad quality here, and it is not advantageous to even think of it. The angora yarn is not in very high demand here, particularly that of second quality. If you have the opportunity to purchase angora yarn from people that you know well and trust, a good connection could provide you with one or two bales for an assessment of the yarn and for this purpose, buy it at a very moderate price, and we believe that it will make a good bargain for you. Enclosed, you will find the up-to-date prices for other commodities.

We commend ourselves to your orders with honour.

Stadsarchief Amsterdam, 332, 1.2.2, vol. 45, p. 32

7. 'We have learned that Mr Raphael Cardamici is preparing to take over the business after Mr Bartholo's death'

Thomas De Vogel to Bartholo Cardamici & Co., Smyrna

23 December 1763

The above is [a] copy of the last letter we sent you and the content of which we refer. Since then, we have learned that Mr Raphael Cardamici is preparing to take over the business after Mr Bartholo's death; may God's will comfort his son and all the other relatives. We hope that we will have an announcement from your part so that we can wind up all our affairs and start new ones with Mr Raphael. You will find herewith enclosed the sales receipt of your 3 bales of sponges of which had return 328.10 florins. We have credited this amount to your account without prejudice.

If you find that the sum of money we return [to] you is appropriate, please be kind to send us a written statement of compliance. We have not yet obtained anything from your insurers. In order to see what we can do, please send us without any delay the invoice for the sponges, the same that you have kept in your books, as it will be indispensable to us. If we cannot get your insurers to respond to our request satisfactorily, then we will await your response.

We have the honour to have your great respect.

Stadsarchief Amsterdam, 332, 1.2.2, vol.47, p. 626

8. 'It is the consumption and the flow of this cotton here that augments its prices and not the prices of the cotton at your place'

Thomas De Vogel to Raphael Cardamici, Constantinople

9 December 1763

We had the honour to write to you all the necessary on the 6th inst. via Vienna and inform you that we have received your letter from Constantinople of the 3rd ult. and the letter from Smyrna from 22 October, when the courier departed. The 600 florins is the insurance of your interest on the 4,900 florins. Capt. Blandauw will carry out the affair and with a following [letter] you will have a response. At present, we have the honour to tell you, in response to your pleasant letter, that since the passing of your uncle we have not received any news, neither from Mr Pavlos nor from Mr N. Chrysogiannis and Michail Masganas. We want their letter so that we can pay attention to follow their orders and everything they want very willingly, so as to continue our association and we greatly value your good intention to liquidate our old accounts, something that we find very positive, as at present, after the passing of Mr Bartholo, this is right and so to restart anew everything the right way is a good thing and you will honour us with your orders. It will give us great pleasure to learn that you have taken into your association Mr Pavlos Cardamici. We await a notice from you. We have the bill of lading for the 3 bales of trimmings and 12 bales of red cotton yarn that you loaded on the *Saint Spiridon* ship of Capt. Paulus Blandauw on our account. Taking notice of their cost and content and in view of their quality, we shall make sure to choose to sell them at the highest price. For what concerns the insurance on the 4,900 florins – please do insure the objects; you should have done so on 8 November. For the 1,600 florins the amount is 74 florins, and for the 1,700 florins the amount is 76.10 florins. The rest involves 1,600 florins – we have succeeded with great difficulty to have the same insurance premium of 4% for this ship as there was a great storm and the same applies for the arrival of Capt. Gerritz to Rotterdam who was in great danger because of this storm too – you will find the account herewith attached for 72 florins of which you will be debited with. Please send to us a written statement of compliance the day after the ship's arrival, of which arrival we congratulate you and may God's benevolence guide the ship in this city, after it will have finished its quarantine, and then we will obtain all the necessary documents and bills of lading.

On the information you have sent us, regarding the cotton and its declining quality; we would have liked it to be otherwise and the quality being high as in the first-quality Kirkağac cotton, because in that case we would have been able to get 18 florins, and now even 19 florins, but this applies only to first-quality cotton, by virtue of its quality. For your 40 bales no one could have made a better price so it was good that you have sent a letter of compliance for what concerned the product and the amount of *avaria* [average damage] received by your insurers. The amount was charged [to] the account of Mr Bartholo Cardamici & Co. It is the consumption and the flow of this cotton here that augments its prices and not the prices of the cotton at your place that we very often see that are pushed up without any reason. The finest cotton is always the best to be put on a sale and right now at 19⅛ florins, as we cannot find any in the market. We see that you have still red cotton yarn in your store, that it was not loaded in time on the ships that departed; we hope you will load it together with other merchandise on the ship of Capt. Pierre De Leeuw and of this we expect your notice.

Customs duties are here always charged on goods arriving from your end on their weight and value and never on each bundle. Therefore, we often find that the captains have untied the bales to better position them; we will thus unbind the bales as there is no need for you to pay excessive duties for them, even if [binding] is necessary for their preservation. As for the orders you gave us for the lead, the porcelain and the mirrors, we have written to you as we could not load the lead on board Capt. Ring's or Capt. Langedyck's ships; the quality of mirrors you ask are not to be found in the city but we will wait for them to arrive and the 20 barrels of nails are being produced so they can be sent to you by spring. We are not sure whether Capt. Kectel will depart this year; he appeared to us to be in a hurry to load the goods that you ordered. When we get to know everything and be sure of his departure, we will send you this shipment without fail, you can be sure of that. We see that you have still made a transfer to Mr Stametz, a 150-dram gold ingot; we have not yet heard anything from him about the one or the other remittances you made to him. We have received your remittances amounting to 650 piastres drawn on Octavio Watson in Livorno which we have negotiated for 88¼%, which is a very favourable exchange rate, and we will credit with you the amount of 1,441.10 florins. Likewise, with 43 florins for the agio on this amount as 3% and on the contrary, we have debited you with 14.15% as our commission on your remittance and 1.10 florins for the brokerage, calculated as 1/1000. Please be kind to send us a letter of compliance and continue to send us your remittances; we would like the goods to be at a better price both here and at your place, but you have to take it as it is. If only we didn't have so many difficulties in this branch of commerce, we could manage our trade business better. We hope to receive from Capt. De Leeuw good shipments of merchandise for our payment and the payment of all old accounts, so we hope to receive good news from you.

We commend ourselves to you.

Stadsarchief Amsterdam, 332, 1.2.2, vol. 47, p. 598

9. 'We have therefore taken the opportunity to sell it at this price as we knew that it was impossible to get a higher one'

Thomas De Vogel to Raphael Cardamici & Co., Smyrna

21 December 1764

We refer to our previous letter, of which you have a copy here above. We announce to you that we have received your dear letter of the 3rd ult. which delivered us a remittance of 1,363.16 florins to be paid to us, [the remittance] has been accepted by the house of C. Van Der Oudermeulen & Son. We will credit it to you once it has been exchanged and will debit you with our commission of 1% amounting to 13.13 florins. And as we have received the 3,000 florins from your remittance, we will also credit it with you and debit you with our commission of 1% amounting 30 florins. Your second letter of the same date brought us your remittance of 600 piastres drawn upon Chasseaud & Co and Antoine & Francisco Filigoni of Livorno. We have negotiated the exchange rate at 88½% and credit it with you the amount of 1,327.10 florins and 43.30 florins for the 3.25% *agio*; we debit your account with 13.14 florins for our commission and 1.70 florins for our brokerage. Please be kind to put in writing a letter of compliance for these two accounts and send it to us. We have continued to try to carry out our duties and sell your 10 bales of goat yarn and if its quality was as it should have been we would have already sold them promptly at a very favourable price. At present it is very hard for us to find a buyer as this quality of goat yarn is not very popular and we have nevertheless taken the affair so far as to succeed in getting an offer of 6.75 florins – we have therefore taken the opportunity to sell it at this price as we knew that it was impossible to get a higher one, as it is already very high. Please send us notice if you have no doubts and you are satisfied with this sale. We hope that the production of the pistols will have finished in a little while and that of the nails towards March and then we hope that we will forward them with the first ship available; you will be informed on the occasion. We wish you for the next new year God's benevolence and everything that you could desire, and we commend ourselves to your orders and we have the honour to be with respect.

Stadsarchief Amsterdam, 332, 1.2.2, vol. 48, p. 582

10. 'We are not in a position to send you the goods you order as we do not have any funds to hand'

Thomas De Vogel to Raphael Cardamici & Co., Constantinople

22 January 1765

Here precedes the copy of our last letter and we refer to its content. We hereby deliver you attached the sales receipt of your 10 bales of goat yarn, the amount produced being 3,497.138 florins. We will credit you this sum without prejudice. If you find no error in the receipt and the money collected, please be kind to put in writing a letter of compliance and pass it to us. We also attach a statement of your current account, the balance of which amounts to 3,528.90 florins. We will credit you this sum without prejudice as well; please be kind to put in writing a letter of compliance for the money collected; hoping to be able to continue our business affairs, we commend ourselves to your orders.

We acknowledge receipt of your two letters from 17 November and 1 December. We took advantage of the first opportunity to send you the goods you ordered . . . We have taken great care and we have no doubt that you will be pleased of the sale of your goat yarn. If the quality was such as you had . . . you would have made good profit, like our friends who received another kind of yarn; being aware that we have not served your interests very well, we want to make you an offer in order to continue our successful commerce; which is to put in production the pistols and the nails and letting you know a little before forwarding them to you so that you could send us the necessary remittances, we know that otherwise you are very reluctant to send remittances too early. We find that method very reasonable and we are willing to make it easier for you, accepting your good intentions; please send us remittances and inform us on their amount, in due time. Otherwise, we are not in a position to send you the goods you order as we do not have any funds in our hands; we do not want to make any advance payments on anyone's account, but if we can, we want to assist our friends. The rest of the commodities ordered can be sent to you with the first departing ship.

We have prepared the 3 barrels of 2½ . . . nails and the other 7 barrels in order to send it to you [at] the beginning of March with the first available ship; we did the same for the 400 pistols and the other 200 pieces made according to the sample that you sent us which will cost . . . florins. These 600 pistols will be produced in a little while and be sent to you with the first available ship. We will also make sure to have the 10 barrels of 2½ . . . nails that you have ordered us and the 50 pistols the English type for the price of . . . florins the piece, ready to be sent altogether with the first available ship. For what concerns the 50 pistols, the Venice type, *Legre* and *Tolci,* we cannot send them to you without your new orders as the price is . . . florins a piece. Moreover, there are two different types of pistols depending on which shape (round or point-shaped) you want the muzzle to be. As you did not tell us anything about it or about the price, which we find to be very high, we did not want to make you pay for it. Waiting for your new orders, we say that the 47 barrels of nails which are being produced and which you will receive at your place with the first available ship, will . . . cost together with the insurance at around . . . 8,000 florins and the 650 pistols will also be onboard together with the insurance at 3,375 florins. In this way, this dispatch will cost a total of approximately 11,375 to 11,400 florins. As we have a debt with you which concerns the product from the sale of the goat yarn which amounts to 3,258.10 florins and we expect also to receive from Capt. Blandauw 2,000 florins – it remains to you to send us with your letter responding to us an amount of 5,000 to 6,000 florins – in order to put us in a position to be able to forward you the above-mentioned goods, otherwise without this transfer nothing will remain saved [in the current account]. We will also send you the sugar loafs and the 300 carrots of St. Vincent tobacco. About the slippers (*sercuke)* we cannot find them in town, and we know this very well; we did receive the orders but we cannot send them as we cannot find them. We have just received you dear letter of 14th ult. by which we see that you have received the bill of lading for the goods sent to you by Capt. De Leeuw and together the acquisition receipt, and you have passed to us a letter of compliance. For the rest we have nothing more to tell you now as you have seen how the dispatch of the nails and pistols will be carried out, we thank you for the shipping arriving from Smyrna and we will pass to you a letter of compliance.

Stadsarchief Amsterdam, 332, 1.2.2, vol. 48, p. 630

11. 'We have not received any remittance from Mr Giovanni Theochari & Co. of Livorno or any letter'

Thomas De Vogel to Raphael Cardamici & Co., Smyrna

7 June 1765

Here above is the copy of your last letter to which we refer to. Since then, we have loaded another 8 barrels of nails on board the ship of Capt. Auke Disma, this week. We only have 5 barrels left to load to carry out your orders. The above-mentioned ship would have left this city if a headwind had not prevented it from leaving; if this situation changes, it will depart in a little while, load the rest of its cargo and pass to the sea the earliest possible. The purchase receipt for these 8 barrels you find it here attached and – comprising the insurance premium – amounts to 2,131.11 florins. This sum is debited to you and please be kind to put [it] in writing and pass to us a letter of compliance. You can now see that we don't waste any time in forwarding to you your orders and we expect your remittances for our payment, as your debit, which as you can see from the accounts we have sent you, is above 4,800 florins – so you should send us good remittances if you haven't done this so far, as without these transfers of funds we do not know what to do; we have told you since the beginning that we need your remittances as we cannot pay and you can send remittances that we will have in our hands before we do any advance payments; after all everything was planned this way – therefore it is up to you, Sir, to take care and get your remittances to us to pay our advances. We are still waiting for the 50 pistols we ordered to be produced and as soon as they arrive, they will be loaded on board the ship as well.

While writing this letter we [received] your letter of 30 April and replying to you we have to tell you that we have not received any remittance from Mr Giovanni Theochari & Co. of Livorno or any letter to draw upon him on your account; if we receive any transfers, be sure that you will be informed. We see that you know about the goods delivered by Capt. De Leeuw in your storehouse; as for the wood we did not find it to be of very good quality – nevertheless, it is the best you can get. As for the peas we do understand your complaints concerning the fact that they are very mouldy and not good, and it hurts us that we haven't been able to find the first quality because we cannot find them anymore [on the market]; those that we sent you now have a different taste and are salted; [. . .] If we receive your new orders we will take care to provide the commodities to you as you wish them to be, as soon as we find them but to get this kind we will be obliged to pay a higher price. We see that the indigo is selling well and, being of a perfect quality, we had no doubt about this. We are very sorry that the loss which is coming to you is causing you harm. May God save you from any bad encounters and spare you from this dangerous evil that holds back Smyrna's trade. As we are at the beginning of it, we will see to send less cargoes to your place. We haven't succeeded much about the cotton yarn that you propose to send us, we do not understand what would please you to tell us with this. For what concerns the cotton, we will be very pleased to have it carried by Capt. Blandauw. We want your instructions about the sale of it in order to get the best price we can. We still have not received the cotton from you, so we do not know anything about it. We are surprised that you did not send any remittances to us as we were expecting them; as you will see we have done nothing recently as we were constraint to take other measures and we do not want to make any advance payments unless we have any funds or goods in our hands, as you are well aware, Sir. It is up to you to satisfy us unless you want us to take any other measures that will be safer for us.

We commend ourselves to your orders.

Stadsarchief Amsterdam, 332, 1.2.2, vol. 49, p. 62

12. 'We should wait for an even higher decline of its price and so there will be an opportunity to speculate'

Thomas De Vogel to Raphael Cardamici & Co., Constantinople

5 August 1766

We refer to your last letter from the 22nd ult. You will find its copy here above and also enclosed [is] the purchase receipt for the commodities you ordered, that have been loaded on board Capt. De Leeuw's ship and herewith attached you have the bill of lading so that you can use it as this ship is ready to depart and expects nothing but a good wind in order to set sail and may God provide this wind and lead it to a safe port. The freight of 44 florins is very cheap . . . as we paid 3½ florins the 1000 . . . nails or one barrel to load them on board of this ship and 8 florins for the textiles without including in this amount the price for the foxskin; you will have to pay 80 florins which proves that we cannot always obtain this kind of service and you should keep this in mind, as we do this gratifying thing just for you. We have loaded on board a quantity of nails and we are still carrying on; don't be worried about their quality, it is completely different [from the previous dispatch] and you will surely appraise that. We are honoured by your last letter of 1st ult., and in reply we have to tell you that both the cloths and the nails will be sent to you and that the 150 pieces of lead haven't been sent because of the quantity of nails [sent]. And so, considering this we hope that you will approve of how we managed the situation and if not, when we receive your orders, we will proceed to the purchase of the remaining 19 barrels of nails which we have promised to deliver to you at the end of next month, when we hope to send them with the first available ship. We have in hand the invoice for the 3 bales of red cotton yarn loaded on Capt. Hans Rave's, ship; we await your orders for the insurance and the bills of lading with the first letter addressed to us.

We have written to Mr Theochari & Co. of Livorno to find out if he wants us to send to us any remittances that will allow us to offer you our services and following their reply and your orders, we will know how to regulate ourselves and give you all the necessary instructions. We have no doubt that Capt. Bakker will have arrived by now at your place; when Capt. Disma's ship will have finished her quarantine we will take care to unload your two bales of silk and examine their quality carefully in order to sell them appropriately, something to which we have always paid particular attention, as you should know. As in your place the price of the silk from Bursa is falling and the harvest is good, we should wait for an even higher decline [in] its price and so there will be an opportunity to speculate, if you could make a profit on the price of 36 florins; we consider that this speculation will not be bad at all. Cotton has not arrived here as all the ships were in quarantine; when we will be able to tell you something more essential, we will send you our instructions. We have sent, by Capt. De Leuuw's ship, addressed to Mr Pavlos Cardamici, a sample of our cloth fabrics which we would like you to examine; we are selling the 9/4 [width] at 88 . . . with a 2% discount and the 8.5/4 [width] at 83 . . . with a 2% discount. If you would like a few bales, we can send them to you in exchange for the commodities you dispatched here to us and it will also be possible to get [them] at a lower price – we have already delivered some to friends.

We remain at your disposal.

Stadsarchief Amsterdam, 332, 1.2.2, vol. 50, p. 46

13. 'As for the 400 cups missing, we are sure that you haven't counted them well'

Thomas De Vogel to Raphael Cardamici & Co., Constantinople

22 August 1766

We refer to our last letter of 5th inst. of which you have a copy here above . . . as well as [attached] the bill of lading for the goods loaded onboard of Capt. De Leuuw's ship, which sailed on 16th inst., and may God lead her to a safe port and you receive a good delivery. We are honoured by your dear letter of the 15 ult. and we have in hand the bill of lading for the red cotton yarn loaded on Capt. Hans Rave's ship; according to your orders we have insured the sum of 2,000 florins corresponding to the account herewith attached, which amounts to 52 florins which we credit with you and we ask you if you could please put in writing and pass to us a letter of compliance if you find it without any error. You had good judgment on the red cotton yarn as the prices were still decent, but this situation has changed as, at the moment, a Greek house has just put up for public sale 40 bales of yarn and another house is also offering 30 bales. Now this is really a way to ruin the turnover of this commodity, but also helps drop its price to 15 or under 20 [florins] we are going to inform you of what will happen at the sale and assess your orders for what concerns the sale of your portion. For what concerns the cotton, the sale of this commodity gives us reason to fear, unless its price declines in Smyrna, but as its price is very high and great quantities of this commodity are arriving here, the output of this product will not change unless its price comes to 20 or 21 florins. As for the silk, the price of the Bursa silk is declining in your place and it would not be a bad idea to speculate, if the price at your place combines to that of its sale price here which is 36 florins. If the quality of the product is good and of the first kind, if you want you can send us 4 bales and the account will be divided between us half-half; and we will pay you our half with cloth from our own factory. We would like to plan this transaction similarly. The money produced by the sale of the cotton in Livorno is very poor according to our friends Mr Theochari & Co. They have informed us that the shipment on our account has arrived and when they have it in their hands, they will handle it properly; and that we can, at the end of this month, draw upon them the sum of 700 piastres and accomplish it after giving you notice. The 19 barrels of nails are being produced and we wait for them to be delivered next week, when we receive them, we will see to load them onboard of a ship and we will let you know of that. For what concerns the porcelain, we hope that you will be happy with it and that you will have the opportunity to sell it well. As for the 400 cups missing, we are sure that you haven't counted them well; after having talked to the vendor he assured us that he had counted them well and put them in packages and so we cannot obtain anything from him without your declaration in a specific form and for this reason we are going to send you one form after you have talked to the vendor if you find that there are still some missing; If you count them and find in the boxes 2,960 cups instead of 3,360, we will do what we can for this. You did well to charge us with the *avaria* [average damage] on the nails and we agree with that.

We commend ourselves to your orders.

Stadsarchief Amsterdam, 332, 1.2.2, vol. 50, p. 74

14. 'God consoles those who have suffered by making them regain their loss twice over'

Thomas De Vogel to Raphael Cardamici & Co., Constantinople

6 November 1767

Here above is the copy of our previous letter and to which we refer. The 14 bales of cotton you sent us are now in our hands. The cotton is no better than the 6 bales received by Capt. De Leuuw but of even more inferior quality and such quality we haven't seen before. We will not be able to get a decent price for it as no one is interested; we will therefore sell it at a public auction hoping to get a good price for it. You must not have paid any attention to our advice, otherwise you would not have sent us such quality of goods, as we are in the same situation with the goat yarn that you have sent us, and they don't want to offer us more than 6 florins. And this is how, Sir, one gets fooled when one sends products of poor quality. We will do our best to get the highest price possible; you will be informed of how things progress. The opposite wind still holds Capt. Pante and Mallaga; may God guide him to a safe port. We have just received your letter of the 1st ult., informing us of the arrival of Capt. Miren. We hope that Capt. Frost will also arrive and that you will receive everything well packaged. As for the porcelain cups, the vendors stated in front of our judges that the 9,400 cups they have sold were actually packed in the three boxes marked VS N. 1–3. In that way we cannot obtain anything from them, as we don't know what has arrived to you or remains to be delivered. You do not need to renew your orders to us; you can stick to the 1% [commission]. But, dear friends, we have not received any remittances and our advance payment is only increasing with all the cargoes sent to you; that is why, in view of the scarcity of money, we are asking you to send us remittances. We do believe that the fire on 20 September caused you much dismay; fortunately, the storehouse is not in the port. God consoles those who have suffered by making them regain their loss twice over. We very much appreciate your notice. We do not doubt that everything will be in good order and with the next courier you will send us remittances. We have the honour of congratulating you on the arrival of Capt. Krimke; may God help him to finish his quarantine and may the ship's cargo provide to your interests.

With honour and respect.

Stadsarchief Amsterdam, 332, 1.2.2, vol. 50, p. 643

15. 'We had these bales remade, and this job was done by an Armenian who has been doing this for over 20 years in the Levant, he is an expert'

Thomas De Vogel to Raphael Cardamici & Co., Constantinople

20 November 1767

We confirm the content of our last letter, a copy of which we enclose.

As the wind continues to be very unfavourable, it keeps the Capts. Mallaga and Pante in Texel; may God help them to have a favourable wind to continue their voyage. Having examined your cottons again, we found some bales among those of very poor quality, of such inferior quality that we do not know what to do in order to sell them. We do not understand why they [customers] should purchase [cotton] from you when there is such a difference in quality. Seeing no way to sell it at a fair price, we have put them up for a public sale on Friday, 25 December. This will be the most advantageous for you, as you recognize the difference in the quality of the bales, and we charge you for them as if we had bought from you high-quality cotton. The shipments you have sent us are detrimental; the shipment of the 6 bales of goat yarn is no better, and as we could not get more than 6 florins, we did not consider it necessary to sell it at this price. As there were several portions inside the bales that were consumed by worms as the old yarn got infested, we had them disassembled – and this portion corresponded to about a third of each of these bales. After the infested part was discarded, we had these bales remade, and this job was done by an Armenian who has been doing this for over 20 years in the Levant, he is an expert. We hope that after the purification, the cotton will be in a better condition and that we can keep the bales safely in the storehouse, knowing that it is a very old yarn of the Benbazar quality. We have done all this for the sake of your interests. We will not fail to continue to ensure your sales at the highest possible price. For what concerns the red cotton yarn, we will have to see what the prices will be like in the spring and then make the sale. In the meantime, we hope to receive good remittances from you and your announcement on the fruit shipments since we learn that Capt. Gerritz will not be coming to Rotterdam and will be making another voyage. We have just received your dear letter of 16th ult., together with the bill of lading for 155 cases of figs and 50 barrels of currants which Mr Van Lennep and Mr Enslie loaded for you on board Capt. Ryndert Everts' ship. We will take out insurance of 1,600 florins that you ordered us to do and with our next letter we will give you notification; with this letter we will answer you in more detail on all issues, as we have run out of time at this moment. The [merchandise] . . . you requested must have been sent to you by Capt. Miren in the VS no. 15 barrel.

We commend ourselves to your orders.

Stadsarchief Amsterdam, 332, 1.2.2, vol. 50, p. 655

16. 'The exchange rate is high and disadvantageous but in order to have an agreement you have either to go beyond that or try to find other opportunities to send us remittances or commodities'

Thomas De Vogel to Raphael Cardamici & Co., Constantinople

5 April 1768

We had the honour to write to you the 18th ult. and you find the copy of this letter here above; we refer to its contents. We were able to sell more than 50 boxes of your figs for 12 florins – as the figs in the rest of the boxes were not that good and were damaged and many of them were black, consumed by humidity, we sold them with difficulty for 10 florins. We could not get a better price for them as their quality was too bad. As for the currants, we sold 13 barrels for 12 florins. For the rest we will continue to serve you as this is the responsibility we have taken on and when everything will be sold, you will get the sales receipt. For what concerns the red yarn, it is impossible for us to sell it because of lack of demand and because of its coarse quality we did not have the occasion to sell the three last bales for a low price at public auction.

Your dear letter of 14 February arrived; we are informed of the arrival of Capt. Pante in Smyrna, and we also hope to hear of his arrival at your place, but the courier has not arrived yet. We hope that our son and brother will visit you and pay their compliments to you. We do not doubt that you will be very happy to get to know them and that they will earn your respect. We would like to thank you beforehand for making us that honour to accept them.

We are surprised that you did not know what to do with the porcelain as it is beautiful and well-assorted. We know that you want to get 2,000 beautiful fine cups together with their plates in order to sell them and we will make sure to provide you with them and also 300 [carrots] of tobacco, half of violet quality and the other half of St Domingue or St Vincent qualities. We cannot obtain any quantity of the St. Martha wood at a price under 17½ florins. We also cannot obtain it at the quality you require; if the price falls to 16 florins or even lower, we will send you 100 pieces.

We haven't forgotten about the tortoiseshell, but until now we could not get it at a reasonable price. Be sure that once we get it, we will send it to you. As for the 20 barrels of nails, they are ready, and we will send them to you; we believe that we will receive them during this month and load them on board the ship *Le Belus* or the *St. Spyridon*, both of which charge the cheapest freights. We will inform you extensively on that in our next letter. Please remember, Sir, to send us some remittances in order to cover our advance payments already made on your account and also those that we will make. The exchange rate is high and disadvantageous but in order to have an agreement, you have either to go beyond that or try to find other opportunities to send us remittances or commodities so that we will be able to pick up our money and utilize it. Truly, Sir, this delay discomforts us extremely as money is very rare here and the storehouses are full of merchandise, so it will please us a lot if you send us some remittances; the one you made through Alexander De Masse has been paid and the amount has been credited with you but more than 30,000 florins have been returned for lack of acceptance as they do not take letters in this place.

We commend ourselves to you with respect.

Stadsarchief Amsterdam, 332, 1.2.2, vol. 51, p. 81

17. 'Truly, Sirs, we are in great pain when the money is very scarce, and you have in your hands many of our resources'

Thomas De Vogel to Raphael Cardamici & Co., Constantinople

7 July 1769

The above is the copy of our last letter and we refer to its content. We have received your letter of 2nd ult. We note, Sir, that you have credited with us 80 florins – paid to Mr Hopker. Everything has now been regulated with him and is in good order. There is nothing else to say as we have your power of attorney, but it is Mr Cardamici of Smyrna who, by being the real shipper of the cargo, should pass to us an attorney; but everything is in order, and we have in our hands the 8 ballots [of yarn]. Three of them are damaged, and the damage will cost 62 florins depending on the tax to be paid. We do not know, as the weight is unknown to us and you haven't sent us a bill of lading, whether the insurers could be charged for this sum. We will therefore proceed [with the sale] of the 8 ballots. We examined the yarn to see its quality and the surprise we felt when we found it so coarse cannot be described in words. We have calculated that its value cannot be more that 16 florins at present so we could get 1,600 florins out of it – freights not included – which makes, Sir, a very big difference and will never reach the amount of 3,000 florins. It will be then insured for the 60% difference that we have lost. Please let us know what you would like us to do with this affair because if we can obtain the price of 16 florins at most and if the circumstances remain as they have been up to now, we will keep it in the storehouse until we receive your reply. We have seen, Sir, with surprise that the pistols you have sent us are of very poor quality, short and mostly damaged. The damage is such that the insurer must look at them, so we need a testimonial and the cost of the taxes charged on their value when damaged and when not damaged and we will see that you will be paid for them. For what concerns their quality we will see that it conforms to your description, and it is indeed the quality that you had asked for and it is the same kind as those you had sent to us herewith. It is useless to take a testimonial from the director as he has no knowledge at all of this issue. The things are exactly as we tell you. The manufacturer is renowned and will be able to send us pistols different from those, and so, Sirs, if you do not find that they conform to your orders, you only have to send them back to us, on the condition that if we find that they do not conform to the orders that we gave him we will resolve the issue with him, but if the pistols conform to our orders, the fault will be yours and we will make you pay the cost for their production, but in a way that you will be free of the costs already paid, as we are sure that after our orders they will be lifted, for the manufacturer is a person of good faith and reputation and we believe in him.

We see that you require 20 florins for the cloths you sent us here and likewise for the 40 quintals of gunpowder of the same quality with the one you sent to us; also, you ordered 100 dozen ordinary shotguns, 10 dozen shotguns but of the finest quality and 12 cases of earthenware plates. But really as you have made a mistake in your request for the nails, you still ordered 15 barrels of nails of 2½ [. . .], 3,000 pieces of Fernambourg wood, 100 pieces of St. Martha wood, 6,000 pieces of Campeachy wood, 80 [. . .] of cloves and 200 units of tobacco of good quality. We will see that the nails are produced and we will try to send all the commodities ordered. The reason that has kept us from forwarding to you the small amount of commodities that you have requested from us, and we were in fact in a great pain to see the ships pass by for your place without us being able to send them to you, is that we find ourselves continually short of your remittances or those already sent are in delay, despite the fact that the one courier passes after the other and other friends sent us some [without any problem]. Truly, Sirs, we are in great pain when the money is very scarce, and you have in your hands many of our resources. The dispatch of 8 bales yarn is not as significant as we thought, and the product will be insured for 60% less. We will see which ship will leave first from here directly for your place but if we don't find one we will have to utilize one of those which have loaded cargoes for Smyrna and when this happens we will let you know.

We have just received your remittance of 2,500 florins upon Rigas, Niotis & Co and we have done everything that was necessary to credit it to you. We hope that you will continue to send us your remittances, considering the advance payments we have made on your account in order to send you the commodities you ordered from us. We are looking forward to it with great respect. Enclosed herewith are letters one from Mrs De Vogel and Enslie and one for Monsieur Falcon of Smyrna and we request you to address them to them.

Stadsarchief Amsterdam, 332, 1.2.2, vol. 52, p. 1

18. 'We thank you for letting this problem pass in view of his death; it is certain, Sirs, that he cared a lot for your interests during his lifetime'

Thomas De Vogel & Son to Raphael Cardamici & Co., Constantinople

23 April 1771

After we have confirmed to you the above copy of our last letter of 22 March, we answer your dear letter of 7 March by which you honoured us by sharing in our loss; may God keep you healthy and offers you his holy benevolence for many years.

As all the business affairs of our late father are coming to an end, and we will give up commerce as well, there is Thomas De Vogel Junior, who will have the honour to see you in Smyrna and Constantinople as the loyal commercial house of De Vogel & Enslie, brother of Mr Enslie of Smyrna, with which you can find an arrangement to serve you in the place of our late father. We have sent you the extract of the statement of your current account – a copy of which is enclosed. The balance of our account is 7,158 florins and since then we have received the 40 barrels of currants which arrived with Capt. Macrielsen and sold them at 127 florins.

As you will see from the attached sales receipt herewith, the net product amounts to 822.10 florins, which amount we have credited with you and please be kind to put it in writing and send to us a letter of compliance. Messrs Van Lennep & Enslie of Smyrna have sent us notice that they have received your remittance for us amounting to 794 piastres but they have never passed this sum to us nor written down the exchange rate, so that we do not know what sum to give you credit with. We kindly ask you to write to them, so that they can send us your remittance and we can thus be able to send the correct balance of account due to you, as according to your letter you have remitted to them 3,059 piastres in addition to the 794 piastres. Having this sum in hand, we could tell you the amount of money corresponding in florins; we are therefore waiting to receive this information after you receive this letter.

Concerning the problem arising from your demand [to receive] a portion of nails . . . that were to be sent to you, we cannot tell you anything else than what our late dear father has already told you. We thank you for letting this problem pass in view of his death; it is certain, Sirs, that he cared a lot for your interests during his lifetime so that he would never do something similar, please consider whether the mistake was entirely yours. We remind you that the pistols were ordered according to your instructions, and we have no doubt that the same applies to the nails. So, Sirs, we thank you in advance for letting this problem pass and hope to have the opportunity to be useful to you; once we receive the Bachra wood we will see to figure out the best we can for your interests and we give you signs of our respect.

Stadsarchief Amsterdam, 332, 1.2.2, vol. 52, p. 721

Notes

Preface

1 Fernand Braudel, *Civilization and Capitalism, 15th–18th Century*, vol. 2, *The Wheels of Commerce* (Berkeley: University of California Press, 1992); Kristof Glamann, 'European Trade, 1500–1750', in *The Fontana Economic History of Europe*, vol. 2, *The Sixteenth and Seventeenth Centuries*, ed. Carlo M. Cipolla (London: Collins/Fontana, 1974), 427–526. For an extensive bibliography on the development of merchant capitalism in Europe, see Eric Mielants, 'Perspectives on the Origins of Merchant Capitalism in Europe', *Review* (Fernand Braudel Center) 23, no. 2 (2000): 229–92.

2 Glamann, 'European Trade', 427.

3 See, in general, Jean Olivia Lindsay, 'Introductory Note', in *The New Cambridge Modern History*, vol. 7, *The Old Regime, 1713–1763*, ed. Jean Olivia Lindsay (Cambridge: Cambridge University Press, 1988), 1–26.

4 The famous and innovative work of Eric J. Hobsbawm, *The Age of Revolution: Europe, 1789–1848* (London: Weidenfeld and Nicolson, 1962), describes with astuteness and clarity this eighteenth-century dynamic.

5 Robert Mantran, 'Commerce maritime et économie dans l'Empire ottoman au XVIIIe siècle', in *Économie et Sociétés dans l'Empire ottoman (fin du XVIIIe–début du XX siècles)*, ed. Jean-Luis Bacqqué-Grammont and Paul Dumont (Paris: CNRS, 1983), 289–96; Bruce Masters, *The Origins of Western Dominance in the Middle East* (New York: New York University Press, 1988); Bruce MacGowan, *Economic Life in Ottoman Europe: Taxation, Trade and the Struggle for Land, 1600–1800* (Cambridge: Cambridge University Press, 1981).

6 Maurits Van den Boogert, *The Capitulations and the Ottoman Legal System: Qadis, Consuls and Beratlis in the 18th Century* (Leiden: Brill, 2005).

7 Traian Stoianovich, 'The Conquering Balkan Orthodox Merchant', *Journal of Economic History* 20, no. 2 (1960): 234–311.

8 Vassilis Kremmydas, '"Τιμιώταται κύρ Κόστα, σας ασπάζομαι αδελφικώς": Η αλληλογραφία ως απόλυτο εργαλείο της εμπορικής πράξης (1800–1850)' [Correspondence as the absolute tool of the commercial act (1800–1850)], in *Επιστημονικό Συμπόσιο Νεοελληνικής Επιστολογραφίας (16ος–19ος αι): Πρακτικά*

[Scientific Symposium on Neohellenic Epistolography (16th–19th centuries): Proceedings], *Μεσαιωνικά και Νέα Ελληνικά* [Medioevalia et Neohellenica] 8 (2006), 317–28.

9 Ibid., 322.

10 Francesca Trivellato, 'Merchants' Letters across Geographical and Social Boundaries', in *Cultural Exchange in Early Modern Europe*, vol. 2, *Correspondence and Cultural Exchange in Europe, 1400–1700*, ed. Francisco Bethencourt and Florike Egmont (Cambridge: Cambridge University Press, 2007), 80–103.

11 Jochen Hoock, Pierre Jeannin and Wolfgang Kaiser, eds, *Ars Mercatoria: Handbücher und Traktate für den Gebrauch des Kaufmanns, 1470–1820/Manuels et traités à l' usage des marchands, 1470–1820 Eine analytische Bibliographie*, vol. 3 (Leiden: Brill, 2001), 37–89; Donald J. Herrald, 'An Education in Commerce: Transmitting Business Information in Early Modern Europe', in *From Early Modern Business Correspondence To Business Week. Information Flows, 1600–2001. Ways and Quantities, Structures and Institutions*, XIV International History Congress, Helsinki, 21–25 August 2006, session 1, 1–8; Richard Van den Berg, 'A Judicious and Industrious Compiler: Mapping Postlethwayt's Dictionary of Commerce', *European Journal History of Economic Thought* 24, no. 6 (2017): 1167–213. Also, Malachy Postlethwayt, *The British Mercantile Academy or the Accomplished Merchant* (London: J. and P. Knapton, 1750).

12 Pierre Jeannin, 'La diffusion de l'information', in *Fiere e Mercati nella Integrazione delle economie europee secc. XIII–XVIII*, ed. Simonetta Cavaciocchi (Florence: Le Monnier, 2001), 231–62.

13 Pierre Jeannin, 'Distinction des compétences et niveaux de qualification: les savoirs négociants dans l'Europe moderne', in *Cultures et formations négociants dans l'Europe modern*, ed. Franco Angiolini and Daniel Roche (Paris: Éditions de l'EHESS, 1995), 363–99; Wolfgang Kaiser and Gilbert Buti, 'Moyens, supports et usages de l'information marchande à l'époque moderne', *Rives nord-méditerranéennes* 27 (2007), accessed 19 March 2020, doi.org/10.4000/rives.1973.

14 Arnaud Bartolomei, Claire Lemercier, Viera Rebolledo-Dhuin and Nadège Sougy, 'Becoming a Correspondent: The Foundations of New Merchant Relationships in Early Modern French Trade (1730–1820)', *Enterprise & Society* 20, no. 3 (2019): 537.

15 Francesca, Trivellato. *The Familiarity of Strangers: The Sephardic Diaspora, Livorno and Cross-Cultural Trade in the Early Modern Period* (New Haven: Yale University Press, 2009), 182.

16 Bartolomei et al., 'Becoming a Correspondent'.

17 Pierre Jeannin, 'La diffusion de manuels de marchands: fonctions et strategies éditoriales', *Revue d'histoire modern et contemporaine, Acteurs et pratiques du commerce dans l'Europe modern* 45, no. 3 (1998): 515–57. For the case of the Ottoman Empire, see Eftychia D. Liata, 'Με "μυστικές γραφές" και "τίμιες" γραφές

οι εντιμότατοι πραγματευτές αλληλογραφούν και νεγκοτσιάρουν τον 18ο αιώνα' [By 'secret' and 'honest' writing the honourable merchants correspond and trade in the 18th century], in *Επιστημονικό Συμπόσιο Νεοελληνικής Επιστολογραφίας*, 301–16, where she refers to the publication of the *Epistolarion* by Spyridon Milias in 1757 and its second edition in Vienna two years later.

18 Trivellato, 'Merchants' Letters', 85. As noted by Trivellato, the edition of *Il Negoziante* by Giovanni Domenico Peri was one of the most advanced Italian commercial guides of the seventeenth century, as it comprised rough and ready instructions on how to compose a letter, while in a separate chapter entitled 'Contracts' referred to the legal status of the business letters. Also Henry Hauser, 'Le "Parfait Négociant" de Jacques Savary', *Revue d'histoire économique et sociale* 13, no. 1 (1925): 1–28.

19 Sylvia Marzagalli, 'La circulation de l'information, révelateur des modalités de fonctionnement propres aux reseaux commerciaux d'Ancien Régime', *Rives nord-méditerranéennes* 27 (2007), http://jaurnals.openedition.org/rives/2073; Trivellato, 'Merchants' Letters', 102–3.

20 Bartolomei et al., 'Becoming a Correspondent', 533–77.

21 Stadsarchief Amsterdam, section 332: Archief van de Familie De Vogel en Aanverwante Families 332, 1.2. 2 Thomas De Vogel, 44–52 Kopieboek, in de Franse taal 1760–1771.

22 Ismail Hakki Kadi, *Ottoman and Dutch Merchants in the Eighteenth Century: Competition and Cooperation in Ankara, Izmir and Amsterdam* (Leiden: Brill, 2012), 184–5.

Chapter 1

1 The Republic of the Netherlands constituted a federation of seven small states: Holland, Zeeland, Utrecht, Gelderland, Ovesijseel, Friesland and Groningen. Each state was independent, had a local administration and comprised a well-organized network of cities. see Fernand Braudel, *Civilization and Capitalism, 15th–18th Century*, vol. 3, *The Perspective of the World* (London: Harper & Row, 1984), 180.

2 Jan de Vries, 'An Inquiry into the Behaviour of Wages in the Dutch Republic and the Southern Netherlands, 1580–1800', *Acta Historiae Neerlandicae*, no. 1 (1978): 79–97.

3 Braudel, *Perspective of the World*, 207.

4 Ibid., 209.

5 Ibid., 207.

6 Clé Lesger, *The Rise of Amsterdam Market and Information Exchange: Merchants' Commercial Expansion and Change in the Spatial Economy of the Low Countries, c. 1550–1630* (Aldershot: Ashgate, 2006).

7 Victor Enthoven, 'Early Dutch Expansion in the Atlantic Region, 1585–1621', in *Riches from Atlantic Commerce: Dutch Transatlantic Trade and Shipping, 1585–1817*, ed. Johannes Postma and Victor Enthoven (Leiden: Brill, 2003), 17–47.

8 For Dutch Mediterranean shipping and trade, see Jonathan I. Israel, *Dutch Primacy in World Trade, 1585–1740* (Oxford: Clarendon, 1989); Israel, *The Dutch Republic: Its Rise, Greatness and Fall, 1477–1806* (Oxford: Clarendon, 1998); and Jan de Vries and Jan van der Woude, *The First Modern Economy: Success, Failure and Perseverance of the Dutch Economy (1500–1815)* (Cambridge: Cambridge University Press, 2007). More specifically, Marie-Christine Engels, *Merchants, Interlopers, Seamen and Corsairs: The 'Flemish' Community in Livorno and Genoa (1615–1635)* (The Hague: Uitgeverij Verloren, 1997), which focuses on the study of Dutch commercial activity in the western Mediterranean region and particularly in Livorno.

9 Braudel, *Perspective of the World*, 190.

10 Charles Henry Wilson, 'The Growth of Overseas Commerce and European Manufacture', in *The Old Regime 1713–1763*, ed. Jean Olivia Lindsay (Cambridge: Cambridge University Press, 1966), 27.

11 Alfred C. Wood, *A History of the Levant Company* (London: Routledge, 2006), 54.

12 Jonathan I. Israel, 'The Dutch Merchant Colonies in the Mediterranean during the Seventeenth Century', *Renaissance and Modern Studies* 30 (1986): 87–108.

13 Richard T. Rapp, 'The Unmaking of the Mediterranean Trade Hegemony: International Trade Rivalry and the Commercial Revolution', *Journal of Economic History* 35, no. 3 (1975): 499–525.

14 Wood, *Levant Company*, 29.

15 Andrea Metrà, *Il mentore perfetto de negozianti ovvero guida sicura de medesimi . . . tomo primo* (Trieste: Giovanni Tommaso Hoechenberger, 1798), 198–9.

16 Israel, *Dutch Republic*, 713–26, 766–76, 796–806. See also James Rees Jones, *The Anglo–Dutch Wars of the Seventeenth Century* (London: Longman, 1996).

17 Sarah Palmer, *Politics, Shipping and the Repeal of the Navigation Laws* (Manchester: Manchester University Press, 1990).

18 Charles Carrière and Marcel Courduriè, 'Les grandes heures de Livourne au XVIII siècle', *Revue Historique* 254, no. 1 (1975): 39–80; Jean Pierre Filippini, 'La navigation entre Livourne et le Levant dans les dernières années de l'Ancien Régime', *Ανάτυπο από το αφιέρωμα στον Νίκο Σβορώνο* [Reprint from the tribute to Nikos Svoronos] (Rethymno: Crete University Press, 1986), 156–79.

19 Jonathan I. Israel, 'Trade, Politics and Strategy. The Anglo–Dutch Wars in the Levant (1647–1675)', in *Friends and Rivals in the East. Studies in Anglo–Dutch Relations in the Levant from the Seventeenth to the Early Nineteenth Century*, ed. Alastair Hamilton, Alexander H. de Groot, and Maurits Van den Boogert (Leiden: Brill, 2000), 11–24.

20 Wilson, 'The Growth of Overseas Commerce and European Manufacture', 42.

21 Ibid., 41–3.

22 Ralph Davis, 'The Rise of Protection in England, 1689–1786', *Economic History Review*, new series, 19, no. 2 (1966): 306–17.

23 Wilson, 'The Growth of Overseas Commerce and European Manufacture', 43.

24 For this period, see Gerard Rudolf and Bosscha Erdbrink, *At the Threshold of Felicity: Ottoman–Dutch Relations during the Embassy of Cornelis Calkoen at the Sublime Porte, 1726–1744* (Ankara: Türk Tarih Kurumu Basimevi, 1975).

25 The same thing had happened previously with Venice and Antwerp and would later happen with London and New York.

26 Jean Baptiste Boyer d'Argens, *Lettres Juives*, vol. 3 (Paris: Paul Gautier, 1738), 194.

27 Braudel, *Perspective of the World*, 266.

28 Daniel Defoe, *A Plan of the English Commerce* (London: C. Rivington, 1728), 192.

29 Mehmet Bulut, *Ottoman–Dutch Economic Relations in the Early Modern Period, 1571–1699* (Hilversum: Uitgeverij Verloren, 2001), 201 and Wood, *Levant Company*, 29.

30 On the history of the foundation of a joint government of the States General, the seven Provinces, following the Union of Utrecht, see Israel, *Dutch Republic*, 184–96.

31 Ari Bülent, 'The First Dutch Ambassador in Istanbul: Cornelis Haga and the Dutch Capitulations of 1612' (PhD diss., Bilkent University, 2003).

32 On the signing, the content and the significance of the English and French capitulations agreements with the Sublime Porte, see Susan A. Skilliter, *William Harborne and the Trade with Turkey, 1578–1582: A Documentary Study of the First Anglo-Ottoman Relations* (Oxford: Oxford University Press, 1977), 86–9. Also, Van den Boogert, *The Capitulations*, 37.

33 Alexander H. de Groot, *The Ottoman Empire and the Dutch Republic: A History of the Earliest Diplomatic Relations, 1610–1630* (Leiden: Nederlands Historisch-Archeologisch Instituut, 1978), 87.

34 Wood, *Levant Company*; Despina Vlami, *Trading with the Ottomans: The Levant Company in the Middle East* (London: I.B. Tauris, 2014); Mortimer Epstein, *The Early History of the Levant Company* (London: George Routledge & Sons, 1908).

35 This was a standard tactic followed by the administration of the Levant Company in the case of the Greek merchants as well. The tactic eventually resulted in the gradual integration of the Greeks into the British trade of the East and the sidelining of the British. Despina Vlami, *Επιχειρηματικότητα και Προστασία στο Εμπόριο της Ανατολής, 1798–1825: Η βρετανική Levant Company και ένας ελληνικός «Δούρειος Ίππος»* [Entrepreneurship and protection in the trade of the East, 1798–1825: The Levant Company and a Greek Trojan horse] (Athens: Academy of Athens, 2017), 264–81.

36 Wood, *Levant Company*, 28.

37 Klaas Heeringa, *Bronnen tot de Geschiedenis van den Levantschen Handel (1590–1726)*, vol. 1 (The Hague: Nijhoff, 1910), 167.

38 Vlami, Επιχειρηματικότητα [Entrepreneurship], 254–64. English shipping laws prohibited foreign merchant fleets from participating in England's trade. Cf. for the negative impact of this policy on Dutch shipping, William Shaw Lindsay, *History of Merchant Shipping and Ancient Commerce*, vol. 2, *1874* (Cambridge: Cambridge University Press 2013), in particularly chap. 5 on 'English Navigation Laws: The Dutch Navigation Seriously Injured'. See also in Palmer, *Politics*.

39 Heeringa, *Bronnen tot de Geschiedenis*, 266–76.

40 Haga is said to have spent 120,000 kurus in gifts after having promised Dutch ships and ammunition to the sultan in order to secure his consent. Wood, *Levant Company*, 46–7. See also in Bulut, *Ottoman–Dutch Economic Relations*, 205.

41 De Groot, *Ottoman Empire*, 117.

42 Bulut, *Ottoman–Dutch Economic Relations*, 206.

43 *The Capitulations and Articles of Peace between the Majesty of the King of Great Britain, France and Ireland etc. and the Sultan of the Ottoman Empire* (London: J.S., 1679).

44 Ibid., 18–20.

45 Vlami, Επιχειρηματικότητα [Entrepreneurship], 43.

46 Ibid., 41–2.

47 Skilitter, *William Harborne*, 86–9 and Vlami, Επιχειρηματικότητα [Entrepreneurship], 43–4.

48 Elena Frangakis-Syrett, 'Commercial Practices and Competition in the Levant: The British and the Dutch in Eighteenth-Century Izmir', in *Friends and Rivals in the East. Studies in Anglo–Dutch Relations in the Levant from the Seventeenth to the Early Nineteenth Century*, ed. Alastair Hamilton, Alexander H. de Groot, Maurits Van den Boogert (Leiden: Brill, 2000), 135–58.

49 Alexander H. de Groot, 'Dragomans' Careers: The Change of Status in some Families Connected with the British and Dutch Embassies at Istanbul, 1785–1829', in *Friends and Rivals in the East: Studies in Anglo–Dutch Relations in the Levant from the Seventeenth to the Early Nineteenth Century*, ed. Alastair Hamilton, Alexander H. de Groot, and Maurits Van den Boogert (Leiden: Brill, 2000), 223.

50 Alexander H. de Groot, 'The Organization of Western European Trade in the Levant', in *Companies and Trade: Essays on Overseas Trading Companies during the Ancien Regime*, ed. Leonard Blussé and Femme Gaastra (The Hague & Leiden: Leiden University Press, 1981), 235. Also Metrà, *Il mentore perfetto*, 183–96.

51 Wood, *Levant Company*, 15–41; Elena Frangakis-Syrett, *The Commerce of Smyrna in the Eighteenth Century, 1700–1820* (Athens: Centre of Asia Minor Studies, 1992), 98.

52 Metrà, *Il mentore perfetto*, 185.

53 Pjan Rietbergen, *A Short History of the Netherlands* (The Hague: Bekking and Blitz, 2019), 92.

54 Hakkı Kadı, *Ottoman and Dutch Merchants*, 145–69. The Council represented in The Hague an agent who handled all the cases that emerged and was in consultation with the central government.

55 Metrà, *Il mentore perfetto*, 183–4. To this end it seems that the governments had placed some restrictions on the export of certain products to North Africa, including the ports of Algiers, Tunis and Tripoli.

56 Wood, *Levant Company*, 218–21; Vlami, *Trading*, 31–42.

57 It was a policy followed respectively by the English, French, Austrian and other European authorities, in Vlami, *Επιχειρηματικότητα* [Entrepreneurship], 48–9.

58 Ab Hoving, *Nicolaes Witsen and Shipbuilding in the Dutch Golden Age* (New York: Texas A&M University Press, 2012), 184, where it is mentioned that in the early seventeenth century each ship's tonnage was measured in lasts, a cargo weight unit equivalent to approximately 2 tons (chap. 1 on 'Ship Measurement').

59 Metrà, *Il mentore perfetto*, 184.

60 Hakki Kadi, *Ottoman and Dutch Merchants*, 237–73.

61 Wilson, 'The Growth of Overseas Commerce and European Manufacture', 27–9.

62 De Groot, *The Ottoman Empire*.

63 Frangakis-Syrett, *Smyrna*, 164–8.

64 Wood, *Levant Company*, 46–7.

65 Mehmet Bulut, 'The Role of the Ottomans and Dutch in the Commercial Integration between the Levant and Atlantic in the Seventeenth Century', *Journal of the Economic and Social History of the Orient* 45, no. 2 (2002): 221.

66 Frangakis-Syrett, *Smyrna*, 164–7.

67 Ibid., 164.

68 Wood, *Levant Company*, 139.

69 Rietbergen, *A Short History*, 121.

70 Wood, *Levant Company*, 149.

71 Ibid., 144.

72 Thierry Allain, 'Les agents économiques et le déclin hollandaise en Méditerranée entre 1763 et 1780', *Rives méditerranéennes* 59 (2019): 96. This interval between 1763 and 1780 can be considered as a vacuum of conflict, except for the declaration of war by the king of Morocco on the Netherlands in April 1772.

73 Allain, 'Agents économiques', 98–9.

74 As early as the second half of the seventeenth century, fifteen to twenty Dutch trading houses had settled in the city. Ibid., 98.

75 Ibid., 102–6. This is an investigation into 478 manifests of Dutch ships recording cargoes carried to and from Smyrna.

76 Ibid., 105–6.

77 The English consul in Smyrna Francis Werry said that Ottoman nationals entered the Dutch trade and managed to open shops in Amsterdam, taking from the hands of the Dutch the trade of the East. The English should not let the same thing happen. Vlami, *Επιχειρηματικότητα* [Entrepreneurship], 271; Hakki Kadi, *Ottoman and Dutch Merchants*, 170–98.

78 Hakki Kadi, *Ottoman and Dutch Merchants*, 198–237.

79 Ben J. Slot, 'Ο Δημήτριος Κουρμούλης και το διεθνές εμπόριο των Ελλήνων κατά έτη 1770–1784' [Dimitrios Kourmoulis and Greek international trade, 1770–1784], *Μνημοσύνη* [Mnimosini], 5 (1974–1975): 115–49.

80 Braudel, *Perspective of the World*, 193–5.

81 The image of the 'Bursa' or the Stock Exchange, as described by a Greek merchant in Amsterdam, Ioannis Prigkos, is indicative. See Vangelis Skouvaras, *Ιωάννης Πρίγκος: Η Ελληνική παροικία του Άμστερνταμ* [Ioannis Prigkos and the Greek community of Amsterdam] (Athens: Istoriki kai Laografiki Etaireia ton Thessalon], 1964), 47–53.

82 Thierry Allain, 'Les Néerlandais et le Marché monétaire levantin dans la seconde moitié du XVII siècle (1648–1701)', *Histoire, Économie et Société* 27, no. 2 (2008): 21–38.

83 Braudel, *Perspective of the World*, 185.

84 Hakki Kadi, *Ottoman and Dutch Merchants*, 149. As Kadı argues, the Dutch authorities did not apply any restrictions to trade of foreign merchants. On the contrary, the Dutch merchants in the ports of the East were free to offer their services to anyone they wished by establishing joint ventures in Ottoman and Dutch ports.

85 Ibid., 161.

86 Frangakis-Syrett, *Smyrna*, 96–103.

87 This is identified as the period between the end of the Seven Years' War and the blockade of Dutch ports by the British navy during the American War of Independence. Ibid., 166.

88 Ibid., 209.

89 Frangakis-Syrett, *Smyrna*, 166. The same tactics were followed during the Seven Years' War when both the French and the British suspended their monopoly laws.

90 Ibid., 99.

91 Fernand Braudel, 'The Expansion of Europe and the "Longue Duree"', in *Expansion and Reaction: Essays on European Expansion and Reaction in Asia and Africa*, ed. Henk L. Wesseling (The Hague: Springer Netherlands, 1978), 17–27; Wilson, 'The Growth of Overseas Commerce and European Manufacture', 44.

92 Hakki Kadi, *Ottoman and Dutch Merchants*, 145–69.

93 Ibid., 43–4.

94 Vlami, *Επιχειρηματικότητα* [Entrepreneurship], 254–91.

95 Metrà, *Il mentore perfetto*, 168–71. Also, Vlami, *Trading*, 161–2.

96 For the organization of the Greek merchant community of Amsterdam, see Skouvaras, *Ιωάννης Πρίγκος* [Ioannis Prigkos]. See also Ismail Hakki Kadi, 'On the Edges of an Ottoman World: Non-Muslim Ottoman Merchants in Amsterdam', in *The Ottoman World*, ed. Christine M. Woodhead (London: Routledge, 2012), 276–88.

97 Philippos Iliou, ed., *Σταμάτης Πέτρου: Γράμματα από το Άμστερνταμ* [Stamatis Petrou. Letters from Amsterdam] (Athens: Ermis, 1976), ν′ [50].

98 Ibid., μη′–μθ′ [48–9]. The Greek community was organized around an Orthodox Church, and several years later, in 1779, it acquired a Greek school for teaching of the Greek language.

99 Ibid., μθ′ [49]. Petrou started his international commercial career as a servant and an assistant to the merchant Adamandios Korais.

100 Skouvaras, *Ιωάννης Πρίγκος* [Ioannis Prigkos], 47–53.

101 Heeringa, *Bronnen tot de Geschiedenis*, 7, 112. See also in Iliou, *Σταμάτης Πέτρου* [Stamatis Petrou], μα′–μβ′ [41–2].

102 Ibid., μθ′–ν′ [49–50].

103 Hakki Kadi, *Ottoman and Dutch Merchants*, 210.

104 Ibid., 202.

105 Iliou, *Σταμάτης Πέτρου* [Stamatis Petrou], μθ′ [49].

106 Hakki Kadi, *Ottoman and Dutch Merchants*, 211.

107 On 6 February 1700, Daniel Jan de Hochepied, Dutch consul in Smyrna, sent to his government the minutes of the discussion that had taken place during a meeting of the Dutch community members in the city.

108 See Ismail Hakki Kadi, *Natives and Interlopers: Competition between Ottoman and Dutch Merchants in the Eighteenth Century* (Leiden: Leiden University Press, 2012); and Hakki Kadi, *Ottoman and Dutch Merchants*, 237–73.

Chapter 2

1 StdAm, 332, 1.2.2, 44/16, Bartholo Cardamici, 7 March 1760.

2 Xavier Lamikiz, 'Social Capital, Networks and Trust in Early Modern Long-Distance Trade: A Critical Appraisal', in *Merchants and Trade Networks in the Atlantic and the Mediterranean, 1550–1800: Connectors of Commercial Maritime Systems*, ed. Manuel Herrero Sánchez and Klemens Kaps (London: Routledge, 2019), 39–61.

3 Sheilagh Ogilvie, *Institutions and European Trade: Merchant Guilds, 1000–1800* (Cambridge: Cambridge University Press, 2011), 315–43.

4 See references to Gerard de Malynes, who in 1622 wrote that 'faith or trust must exist among traders' and also to the Englishman Wyndham Beawes, who in 1752 wrote that the first and most important concern for a merchant should be 'the choice of a representative on whom he can rely', in Xavier Lamikiz, *Trade and Trust in the Eighteenth-Century: Spanish Merchants and their Overseas Networks* (Woodbridge: Boydell 2010), 141 and 162.

5 Diego Gambetta, 'Can We Trust Trust?', in *Trust, Making and Breaking Cooperative Relations*, ed. Diego Gambetta (Oxford: Blackwell, 1988), 217.

6 Sebouh Aslanian, *From the Indian Ocean to the Mediterranean: The Global Trade Networks of Armenian Merchants from New Julfa* (Berkeley: University of California Press, 2014), 17.

7 Tijl Vanneste, *Global Trade and Commercial Networks: Eighteenth-Century Diamond Merchants* (London: Routledge, 2011), 30.

8 Lamikiz, 'Social Capital', 41.

9 A vast bibliography exists on the strategies adopted by the Greek merchant houses in the eighteenth century to promote their businesses abroad. See Despina Vlami, *Το Φιορίνι, το Σιτάρι και η οδός του Κήπου: Έλληνες Έμποροι στο Λιβόρνο 1760–1868* [The Florin, the Grain and via del Giardino: Greek merchants in Livorno, 1760–1868] (Athens: Themelio, 2000), 180–98.

10 Yoram Ben-Porath, 'The F-Connection: Families, Friends, and Firms and the Organization of Exchange', *Population and Development Review* 6, no. 1 (1980): 1–30. See also Richard Grassby, *Kinship and Capitalism: Marriage, Family, and Business in the English-Speaking World, 1580–1740* (Cambridge: Cambridge University Press, 2001).

11 See generally, Ina Baghdiantz McCabe, Gelina Harlaftis and Ioanna Pepelassi Minoglou, eds, *Diaspora Entrepreneurial Networks: Four Centuries of History* (New York: Bloomsbury, 2005).

12 Trivellato, *The Familiarity of Strangers*, 10–16 and 163.

13 Lamikiz, 'Social Capital', 44.

14 Stanley Wasserman and Catherine Faust, *Social Network Analysis: Methods and Applications* (Cambridge: Cambridge University Press, 1994), 20, and Joel M. Podolny and Karen L. Page, 'Network Forms of Organization', *Annual Review of Sociology* 24 (1998): 57–76. For some interesting cases of network analysis applied in the study of international trade during the early modern and modern period, see Marlene Burckhardt, 'Networks as Social Structures in Late Medieval and Early Modern Towns: A Theoretical Approach to Historical Network Analysis', in *Commercial Networks and European Cities, 1400–1800*, ed. Andrea Caracausi and Christof Jeggle (London: Routledge, 2014), 13–43; Vanneste, *Global Trade and Commercial Networks*, 27; and Sheryllynne Haggerty, *Merely for Money? Business Culture in the British Atlantic, 1750–1815* (Liverpool: Liverpool University Press, 2012), 163.

15 Burckhardt, 'Networks', 13.

16 Lamikiz, 'Social Capital', 46.

17 Sylvia Marzagalli, 'Establishing Transatlantic Trade Networks in Time of War: Bordeaux and the United States, 1793–1815', *Business History Review* 79, no. 4 (2005): 838. As Marzagalli argues, the most obvious way to study networks is through the examination and analysis of the activity of one specific company and its representatives.

18 I warmly thank Thierry Allain for providing the valuable material of manifests (1763–70) kept in the Nationaal Archief Den Haag, 1.02.22 *Consulaat Smyrna*, 547 (1763), 554 (1770).

19 Allain, 'Agents économiques', 93–117.

20 For the family organization of Greek merchant enterprises in the eighteenth century and the relation between domestic group and enterprise, see Vlami, *Το Φιορίνι* [The florin], 185–96.

21 For the Mavrogordatos family, see ibid., 296–8.

22 Vlami, *Το Φιορίνι* [The florin], 187–90; Olga Katsiardi-Hering, Ἡ ελληνική παροικία της Τεργέστης, 1751–1830' [The Greek community of Trieste, 1751–1830] (PhD diss., Athens: National and Kapodistrian University of Athens 1986), 414–22.

23 Elena Frangakis-Syrett, 'The Economic Activities of Ottoman and Western Communities in Eighteenth Century Izmir', *Oriente Moderno* 79, no. 1 (1999): 1–26.

24 I would like to extend my deepest thanks to Dr Giannis Spyropoulos of the Institute for Mediterranean Studies in Crete, for finding and translating the Ottoman texts. See Basbakanlik Osmanli Arsivi [BOA], HR.MKT., 12/38: Regarding the payment of a duty by Cardamici from the city of Aivali to İbrahim Edhem, special envoy (moubashir) for the collection of Cardamici's debt. 6 Cemaziyülevvel 1262 (2 May 1846). BOA, A.}DVN., 17/16: Letter from the French consul in Mytilene requesting the release from the prison in Constantinople of the debtor Cardamici so that the French merchant Mr Amir can collect the payment owed to him. For this issue a special envoy was designated (moubashir) who asked for the prisoner to be pardoned. 1 Şaban 1262 (25 June 1846). BOA, A.}MKT.DV., 5/15: Letter from the kaymakam of Metelini regarding the collection, according to the holy law, of all the debts of the bankrupt merchant Cardamici to the Custom House of the city of Aivali. 19 Muharrem 1263 (7 January 1847). BOA, A.}MKT., 145/44: Petition of a 'Merchant of Europe' (Avrupa tüccarlardan) Michalaki for an investigation in the account of Stratis Cardamitsoglou from the city of Aivali and a letter towards the governor of Balikesir and the Kaymakam of the city of Aivali. 3 Şevval 1264 (2 September 1848). BOA, HR.MKT., 30/21: Regarding the delegation of the Cardamitsoglou to the Sublime Porte, because of the disagreements that had arisen between them in relation to their debts. 6 Rebiülahir 1266 (19 February 1850).

25 Vlami, *Το Φιορίνι* [The florin], 185–96; Vlami, 'Γυναίκες, οικογένεια, κοινωνία της εμπορικής διασποράς 18ος–19ος αι.' [Women, family, society of the merchant diaspora, 18th–19th centuries], *Ιστορικά* [Istorika] 23, no. 45 (2006): 243–81.

26 Hakki Kadi, *Ottoman and Dutch Merchants*, 187–98. In his study, Hakki Kadi mainly uses De Vogel's correspondence with members of his family and partners in the family enterprise, other associates and Dutch companies in the East. Also see Frangakis-Syrett, 'The Economic Activities', 1–26.

27 It is interesting that in the lists compiled by Nanninga in 1762, a merchant bearing the surname De Vogel is referred to as a partner in a company called De Vogel & Panajiotti. This is obviously another De Vogel. The relevant lists are presented by Frangakis-Syrett, *Smyrna*, 255–6. See 'List of non-Muslim Merchants who took part in the trade of Smyrna with Holland carried out in Dutch ships, 22 February–22 August 1762' (ARA, Consulaatsarschief, Smirna, 2dd, De Invoer en de Uitvoer met Nederlandschen Scheppen te Smirna, 22 February 1762 to 22 August 1762) in J. G. Nanninga, ed., *Bronnen tot de Geschiedenis van den Levantschen Handel*, vol. 3, *1727–1765* ('S-Gravenhage: s.n., 1952), 715–63) and 'List of non-Muslim merchants who took part in the trade of Smyrna with Holland, carried out in Dutch ships, 22 August 1786 to 22 February 1787' (ARA, 1428–66).

28 There are quite a few references to the Cardamici enterprise in Elena Frangakis-Syrett, 'Commercial Practices', 135–58.

29 Nationaal Archief Den Haag, 1.02.22, *Consulaat Smyrna*, 547 (1763)–563 (1780).

30 Iliou, *Σταμάτης Πέτρου* [Stamatis Petrou], 22.

31 For the operation of Greek trade and maritime networks, see Gelina Harlaftis, 'The "Eastern Invasion": Greeks in the Mediterranean Trade and Shipping in the Eighteenth and Early Nineteenth Centuries', in *Trade and Cultural Exchange in the Early Modern Mediterranean: Braudel's Maritime Legacy*, ed. Maria Fusaro, Colin Heywood, and Mohamed-Salah Omri (London: I.B. Tauris, 2009), 223–52. See also Vlami, *Το Φιορίνι* [The florin], 180–98.

32 These were Georgios Mavrogordatos & Ioannis Anastasis, Manolis Falieros & Avierinos Bros, Vitalis, Zingrilaras & Co, Michail Courmousis, Manolis (son of Iosif) & Co, Georgios Vitalis & Co, Iosif Dimitrakis Mastorakis & Co, Michail Patrikios, Georgios Petritsis & Sons, Nikolaos Pitakos, Georgios Capparis, Georgios Sevastopoulos & Pavlos Psychas, Zingrilaras & Co, Nikolaos Pitakos & Bros, Ioannis Mavroudis, Dimitrios Fronimos and Georgios Capparis & Andreas Bros.

33 Braudel, *Perspective of the World*, 256.

34 This picture of the transactions of Thomas De Vogel & Zoon emerges from a first study of its accounting books by Hakki Kadi, *Ottoman and Dutch Merchants*, 183–4, 283.

35 Ibid., 203–4, 224.

36 Leytstar & Santi, according to my reading.

37 Demestikas, according to my reading.

38 Magaroglou, Kikor son of Carabeth, according to my reading.

39 Hakki Kadi, *Ottoman and Dutch Merchants*, 185–6.

40 Ibid., 113.

41 Ibid., 187–8.

42 See also here in p. 98. In the early 1760s, the all-powerful Dutch financial system faced a series of crises (1763, 1772–3 and 1780–3) that weakened it. These crises had common characteristics and were related to the credit system. The large volume of commercial bills circulating on the market exceeded all limits and led to a series of bankruptcies when many firms began to refuse to pay them back. Braudel, *Perspective of the World*, 267–9.

43 Hakki Kadi, *Ottoman and Dutch Merchants*, 190–1.

44 De Vogel's correspondence with Thomas De Vogel Son & Brother and Van Lennep & Enslie proves also that he continued to trade in the Ottoman Empire. Ibid., 198–234.

45 The De Vogel family businesses that operated in Smyrna during this period, except the Thomas De Vogel & Son, were the Thomas De Vogel Junior, De Vogel Son and Brother, De Vogel Bros and the De Vogel & Enslie. See StdAm, 332, 1.2.2, 50, Raphael Cardamici, 5 October 1766.

46 De Vogel delegated David Van Lennep and his son Thomas De Vogel Junior to control in advance the quality and the value of the goods sent to him by his clients in Smyrna. His main purpose was that the value of the goods addressed to him would exceed the cost of the commodities that had been ordered by his clients to be purchased in Amsterdam for their own account. Van Lennep and De Vogel Junior also took care not to deliver goods to the merchants in Smyrna unless they had loaded Levantine goods on ships proceeding for Amsterdam. Hakki Kadi, *Ottoman and Dutch Merchants*, 187.

47 For the appointment as ambassador in Constantinople and the activity of the British merchant Sir Robert Ainslie, see Vlami, *Trading with the Ottomans*, 91, 120, 157; Wood, *Levant Company*, 171–3.

48 The Van Lennep were connected through marriage with the family of the British general consul in Constantinople, Isaac Morier. They were also British protégés. See Vlami, *Trading with the Ottomans*, 154, 188.

Chapter 3

1 Kristoff Glamann, 'European Trade', 427–9, 439.

2 Immanuel Maurice Wallerstein, Hale Decdeli, and Reşat Kasaba, 'The Incorporation of the Ottoman Empire into the World Economy', in *The Ottoman Empire and the*

World Economy, ed. Huri Ismanoglu Inan (Cambridge: Cambridge University Press, 1987), 88–100.

3 Braudel, *Perspective of the World,* 471–4 and 483. For the advance of Ottoman manufacture, see Donald Quataert, *Ottoman Manufacture in the Age of Industrial Revolution* (Cambridge: Cambridge University Press, 2002). For the extensive consumption of Ottoman products within Ottoman society, see Elif Akçetin and Suraiya Faroqhi, eds, *Living the Good Life: Consumption in the Qing and Ottoman Empires of the Eighteenth Century* (Leiden: Brill, 2017).

4 Frangakis-Syrett, *Smyrna*, 9.

5 Elena Frangakis-Syrett, 'Izmir and the Ottoman Maritime World of the Eighteenth Century', *Oriente Moderno*, new series, 81, no. 1 (2001): 121. An interesting question posed by Braudel is whether these merchants functioned within the Ottoman Empire as architects of the survival of the Ottoman economy or as 'mice' ready to leave the sinking ship. Braudel, *Perspective of the World*, 482.

6 Slot, 'Δημήτριος Κουρμούλης' [Dimitrios Kourmoulis], 115–49.

7 Metrà, II mentore perfetto, 171.

8 As early as the eighteenth-century goods began to be transported via land and sea routes that bypassed Amsterdam, in Braudel, *Perspective of the World*, 237.

9 According to Metrà, by the end of the eighteenth century the Dutch had begun to lose the lead in this area of business as well. Many similar commercial companies offering brokerage services had moved and established themselves in Hamburg, as well as in the North, where the trade charges on imports and exports were much lower than in the ports of the Netherlands, Metrà, *Il Mentore*, 183–96.

10 Braudel, *Perspective of the World*, 241.

11 Iliou, *Σταμάτης Πέτρου* [Stamatis Petrou], 14–15. As already mentioned, the negotiation for the sale of the goods was done on the Amsterdam Stock Exchange, where the Greek Ottoman merchants had their own 'column', where they stood during the negotiation of buying and selling prices of various commodities.

12 Hakki Kadi, *Ottoman and Dutch Merchants*, 185–8.

13 StdAm, 332, 1.2.2, 49/62, Raphael Cardamici, 7 June 1765, and 50/677, Raphael Cardamici, 4 December 1766. Pavlos Cardamici also received cargoes from Amsterdam as an independent merchant through Van Lennep & Enslie, which he then forwarded to his uncle Raphael Cardamici.

14 Braudel, *Perspective of the World*, 236.

15 Ibid., 238. The same thing was happening in the duty-free port of Livorno, in Vlami, *Το Φιορίνι* [The florin], 134–59.

16 Braudel, *Perspective of the World*, 238.

17 Iliou, *Σταμάτης Πέτρου* [Stamatis Petrou], 4–48, and Skouvaras, *Ιωάννης Πρίγκος* [Ioannis Prigkos], 47. Among them, Stathis Thomas, Rigas & Niotis and Sechir Jasegiroglou, all persons and companies mentioned in Stamatis Petrou's letters,

have the primary position, along with Zingrilaras. Petrou was an employee of Stathis Thomas sent to Amsterdam as an assistant/servant of Thomas's commercial representative in the international port, Adamantios Korais.

18 Iliou, *Σταμάτης Πέτρου* [Stamatis Petrou], 73.

19 Metrà characteristically mentions tsekinia from Hungary and other coins, such as the lion's thaler, a silver coin minted in Holland with a value of 42 stubers called by the Ottomans the aslan because it had on it engraved the coat of arms of the Republic of Holland, coins from Mexico that had been transferred from New Spain via Cadiz, coins from Seville that were minted in Seville and named pezze da 8 reali, coins from Emden, Deventer, Campe and Zwol called isolotti in the East. See Metrà, II mentore perfetto, 183–96.

20 Katsiardi-Hering, *Η Ελληνική Παροικία της Τεργέστης* [The Greek Community of Trieste]; Vlami, *Το Φιορίνι* [The florin].

21 Kirkağac is a town in one of the most important cotton-producing areas that had close commercial contacts with Smyrna.

22 The specialization of the Greeks in the trade of cotton integrated them into the international cotton trade networks and provided them with capitals and foreign protection; see above.

23 Hakki Kadi, *Ottoman and Dutch Merchants*, 196.

24 Iliou, *Σταμάτης Πέτρου* [Stamatis Petrou], 37, 47.

25 StdAm, 332,1.2.2, 44/16, Bartholo Cardamici, 7 March 1760, and 44/39, Bartholo Cardamici, 21 March 1760; 45/355, Bartholo Cardamici, 22 September 1761; 50/122, Raphael Cardamici, 23 September 1766; 44/117, Bartholo Cardamici, 6 May 1760; 51/420, Raphael Cardamici, 4 November 1768; 46/527, Raphael Cardamici, 19 November 1762.

26 On the sale process of goods in public auctions when demand was low see, Metrà, II mentore perfetto, 285.

27 StdAm, 332, 1.2.2, 44/92, Bartholo Cardamici, 22 April 1760 and 52/46, Raphael Cardamici, 8 August 1769.

28 De Vogel himself traded red cotton yarn in Amsterdam. For what concerns his fixation with the good quality of this product, see Hakki Kadi, *Ottoman and Dutch Merchants*, 224.

29 StdAm, 332, 1.2.2, 52/105, Raphael Cardamici, 22 September 1769.

30 StdAm, 332, 1.2.2, 44/576, Bartholo Cardamici, 29 December 1760; 48/503, Raphael Cardamici, 2 November 1764; 50/266, Raphael Cardamici, 6 February 1767.

31 StdAm, 332, 1.2.2, 45/32, Bartholo Cardamici, 7 April 1761.

32 StdAm, 332, 1.2.2, 46/526, Bartholo Cardamici, 19 November 1762.

33 StdAm, 332, 1.2.2, 46/555, Bartholo Cardamici, 3 December 1762.

34 StdAm, 332, 1.2.2, 44/16, Bartholo Cardamici, 7 March 1760, and 44/92, 22 April 1760; 45/320, Bartholo Cardamici, 4 September 1761.

35 Apparently the Cardamicis supplied military equipment to the Ottoman army and navy during the Russo-Turkish war of 1768–74. For the Constantinople market and the consumption of a specific type of commodities by the upper classes of the empire, see Akçetin and Faroqhi, *Living the Good Life*, 474–92.

36 StdAm, 332, 1.2.2, 46/555, Bartholo Cardamici, 3 December 1762.

37 StdAm, 332, 1.2.2, 47/366, Raphael Cardamici, 23 August 1763.

38 StdAm, 332, 1.2.2, 50/299–300, Ambrosio Mavrogordatos, 5 March 1767.

39 StdAm, 332, 1.2.2, 47/366, Raphael Cardamici, 23 August 1763.

40 StdAm, 332, 1.2.2, 44/399, Bartholo Cardamici, 12 September 1760.

41 Raphael's decision to trade in a variety of new commodities may have resulted from the fact that from the mid-eighteenth century Constantinople appeared to shift again towards the centre of the Ottoman economy; see in Braudel, *Perspective of the World*, 469.

42 For the trade of diamonds in the capital of the Ottoman Empire, see Hedda Reindl-Kiel, 'Diamonds are a Vizier's Best Friend or: Merzifonlu Kara Mustafa's Jewelry Assets', in Akçetin and Faroqhi, *Living the Good Life*, 409–32.

43 StdAm, 332, 1.2.2, 47/219, Raphael Cardamici, 11 June 1763.

44 StdAm, 332, 1.2.2, 48/299, Raphael Cardamici, 6 July 1764.

45 StdAm, 332, 1.2.2, 48/346, Raphael Cardamici, 7 August 1764.

46 StdAm, 332, 1.2.2, 48/630, Raphael Cardamici, 22 January 1765.

47 StdAm, 332, 1.2.2, 49/742, Raphael Cardamici, 6 July 1766.

48 StdAm, 332, 1.2.2, 49/570, Raphael Cardamici, 21 March 1766.

49 StdAm, 332, 1.2.2, 50/135, Raphael Cardamici, 7 October 1766.

50 StdAm, 332, 1.2.2, 50/266, Raphael Cardamici, 6 February 1767.

51 StdAm, 332, 1.2.2, 51/521, Raphael Cardamici, 3 January 1769.

52 StdAm, 332, 1.2.2, 52/46, Raphael Cardamici, 8 August 1769, and 52/237, 22 December 1769.

53 For the introduction of new food products that came from Western and new world markets in the market of Constantinople, see Arif Bilgin, 'From Artichoke to Corn: New Fruits and Vegetables in the Istanbul Market (Seventeenth to Nineteenth Centuries)', in Akçetin and Faroqhi, *Living the Good Life*, 259–82.

54 Braudel, *Perspective of the World*, 471.

55 At this time, social imperatives regarding mealtime, table setting, food presentation and behaviour during lunch became the subject of guides of good behaviour and etiquette, addressed to members of the upper middle class, and were very widespread. See Maxine Berg, *Luxury and Pleasure in Eighteenth-Century Britain* (Oxford: Oxford University Press, 2005), 228. For the consumption of luxury goods in the Ottoman Empire, see Colette Establet, 'Consuming Luxurious and Exotic Goods in Damascus around 1700', in Akçetin and Faroqhi, *Living the Good Life*, 236–57. See also Suraiya Faroqhi, 'Women, Wealth and the Textiles in 1730 Bursa', in Akçetin and Faroqhi, *Living the Good Life*, 213–35.

56 As Berg mentions, the rituals of breakfast and tea were new habits in the eighteenth century. The appearance of these rituals coincided with that of hot drinks such as tea, coffee and chocolate as well as ceramic, silvery or glass utensils that accompanied their serving. See Maxine Berg, *Luxury*, 237. Also, Lawrence E. Klein, 'Coffeehouse Civility, 1660–1714: An Aspect of Post-Courtly Culture in England', *Huntington Library Quarterly* 59 (1997): 30–51.

57 European merchants contributed to the development of this culture with their activity, which flourished in the eighteenth century. Of particular interest is the luxurious and semi-luxurious making of most of these goods, as the significant demand for similar goods in the markets of the Ottoman Empire at that time is confirmed. See Edhem Eldhem, *French Trade in Istanbul in the Eighteenth Century* (Leiden: Brill, 1999) and Charles Carrière and Michel Morineau, 'Draps du Languedoc et commerce du Levant au XVIII siècle', *Revue d'Histoire Économique et Sociale* 46 (1968): 108–21.

58 The new aesthetics and culture included the use of not only precious and decorated ceramic and porcelain crockery but also silver and gold-plated dinnerware, precious cutlery, special ways of behaving during lunch, various ways of serving food and finally the new habits of drinking coffee, tea and chocolate. See Berg, *Luxury*, 228; Amanda Vickery, 'Women and the World of Goods: A Lancashire Consumer and Her Possessions, 1751–1781', in *Consumption and the World of Goods*, ed. John Brewer and Roy Porter (London: Routledge, 1994), 274–304.

59 The plethora of luxurious and semi-luxurious fabrics and materials intended for garments, lining pillows, mattresses and sofas, packaging, curtains or for adorning spaces, furniture and clothing confirms the importance and spread of a 'culture of fabric', a term used by Suraiya Faroqhi to describe the aesthetics of interiors in Ottoman residences. See Suraiya Faroqhi, *Κουλτούρα και καθημερινή ζωή στην Οθωμανική Αυτοκρατορία: Από τον Μεσαίωνα ως τις αρχές του 20ου αιώνα* [Culture and everyday life in the Ottoman Empire: From the Middle Ages to the beginning of the 20th century], trans. Katerina Papakonstantinou (Athens: Exandas, 2000), 198.

60 Furs were considered a very luxurious object, whatever their use, as garments or decorative items, as a gift or as a commodity to be sold and bring profit. Their presence inside a household or as part of one's attire gave an image of a luxurious way of life; see Despina Vlami, 'Το υλικό περιβάλλον και ο οικιακός χώρος ενός Άγγλου εμπόρου στη Θεσσαλονίκη στα τέλη του 18ου με αρχές του 19ου αιώνα' [Material environment and the domestic space of an English merchant in Thessaloniki in the end of the eighteenth and the beginning of the nineteenth centuries], *Μνήμων* [Mnimon] 30 (2009): 89.

61 Markus Koller, 'Istanbul Fur Market in the Eighteenth Century', in *Living in the Ottoman Community*, ed. Vera Constantini and Markus Koller (Leiden: Brill, 2008), 127–8.

62 Neil McKendrick, John Brewer and John H. Plumb, eds, *The Birth of a Consumer Society: The Commercialization of Eighteenth-Century England* (Bloomington: Indiana University Press, 1982), 100–45.

63 Dimitris Papastamatiou, *Wealth Distribution, Social Stratification and Material Culture in an Ottoman Metropolis: Thessaloniki According to the Probate Inventories of the Muslim Court (1761–1770)* (Istanbul: Isis, 2017).

64 Müge Fatma Göçek, *Rise of the Bourgeoisie, Demise of the Empire: Ottoman Westernization and Social Change* (New York: Oxford University Press, 1996), 98.

65 Ibid., 99. The osmosis of European and Ottoman material culture was particularly visible in the dressing habits of members of foreign diplomatic missions in Istanbul. See Malcolm Jack, *The Turkish Embassy Letters: Lady Mary Wortley Montagu*, intro. Anita Desai (London: Virago, 1999).

66 Papastamatiou, *Wealth Distribution*, 99, 107.

Chapter 4

1 Hakki Kadi, *Ottoman and Dutch Merchants*, 210.

2 For a comprehensive presentation of European maritime law at the beginning of the nineteenth century, see Joseph Chitty, *Lex Mercatoria or, a Complete Code of Commercial Law; being a General Guide to all Men in Business*, 2 vols (London: Nabu, 2011).

3 Daniel Panzac, 'Le contrat d' affrètement maritime en Méditerranée: Droit maritime et pratique commerciale entre Islam et chrétienté (XVII-XVIII siècles)', *Journal of the Economic and Social History of the Orient* 45 (2002): 342–62.

4 Ibid., 220.

5 Richard W. Unger, 'Technology and Industrial Organisation: Dutch Shipbuilding to 1800', *Business History* 17, no. 1 (1975): 56–72.

6 Mary Lindemann, *The Merchant Republics: Amsterdam, Antwerp, and Hamburg, 1648–1790* (Cambridge: Cambridge University Press, 2014), 223.

7 Ibid., 220. Also, Sabine C. P. J. Go, 'The Amsterdam Chamber of Insurance and Average: A New Phase in Formal Contract Enforcement (Late Sixteenth and Seventeenth Centuries)', *Enterprise and Society* 14 (2013): 518, 520, 535.

8 Metrà, *Il mentore perfetto*, 364. The Dutch last was a unit for the measurement of weight and corresponded to 1,976.4 kilograms. Meaning literally a 'load', it was also equivalent to 120 cubic feet of shipping space.

9 The *cappa* (in French *chape* or *chapeau*) was a bonus offered to the captain as a gift and was calculated as a percentage of the total weight of the goods. Ibid., 367. See also Patrick Boulanger, 'Salaires et revenues des équipages de navires marchandes provençaux durant le XVIII siècle', *Provence Historique* 30, no. 132 (1980): 421–2.

10 Metrà, II *mentore perfetto*, 366–72.

11 The manifest differed from the bill of lading. It was a document which was handed over to the captain by the *sensale* when the ship was about to set sail. In each manifest all the packages, stamped and numbered, were listed, together with the names of the merchants who dispatched the cargoes and those who received them. The manifests were examined by the local authorities of each port who then issued a certificate that each captain, in case he was arrested for any reason during the voyage, could present an official, certified description of the cargo he was carrying. See Vlami, *Trading with the Ottomans*, 41.

12 Ibid., 370. The captain signed three or four copies of the bill of lading, one of which he kept himself, one was delivered to the charterer and the rest was sent to the person responsible for delivering the cargo to the port of destination of the ship or to the merchant-owner of the cargo. The delivery of copies of the bill of lading to each of the agents involved in the process of chartering, transporting and receiving the goods offered legal protection against any attempt at counterfeiting, theft and illegality. The bill of lading was issued in different languages and supplemented by interested parties.

13 StdAm, 332, 1.2.2, 46/80, Bartholo Cardamici, 23 April 1762.

14 StdAm, 332, 1.2.2, 46/256, Bartholo Cardamici, 23 July 1762.

15 Hakki Kadi, *Ottoman and Dutch Merchants*, 210.

16 For a description of a captain's responsibilities and obligations, see Jack Savary de Bruslons, *Dictionnaire Universel du Commerce*, vol. 2 (Paris: Estienne, 1729), 1166–7.

17 See also Gilbert Buti, Christopher Denis-Delacour, Luca Lo Basso, and Olivier Raveaux, 'Introduction', in *Entrepreneurs des mers: Capitaines et mariniers du XVIe au XIXe siècle*, ed. Gilbert Buti, Luca Lo Basso, and Olivier Raveux (Paris: Riveneuve, 2017), 7–15. On the question of whether ship captains were exclusively acting as organizers or could interfere in the negotiations and the progress of an enterprise, see Gilbert Buti, 'Capitaines et patron provençaux de navires marchands au XVIII siècle: Exécutants où entrepreneurs de mers', in Buti, Lo Basso and Raveux, *Entrepreneurs des mers*, 39–57.

18 For an interesting review of the tasks and responsibilities of a ship's captain during the operation of organizing and completing a voyage, from the seventeenth to the nineteenth centuries, see Jann M. Witt, '"During the Voyage every Captain is a Monarch of the Ship": The Merchant Captain from the Seventeenth to the Nineteenth Century', *International Journal of Maritime History* 13, no. 2 (2001): 166–84. For a comprehensive study of the same issue, see Buti, Lo Basso and Raveux, *Entrepreneurs des mers*.

19 See also a relevant remark in a letter addressed by De Vogel to Cardamici: 'We will talk about the lead with Capt. Marten Pante to finally agree on the lowest freight', in StdAm, 332, 1.2.2, 50/505, Raphael Cardamici, 7 August 1767.

20 Panzac, 'Le contrat d' affrètement', 357. Panzac underlines the multidimensional role and the great freedom of action of the European captains who participated in the Ottoman trade in Daniel Panzac, *La caravane maritime: Marins européens et marchands ottomans en Méditerranée (1690–1830)* (Paris: CNRS, 2004), 87–94.

21 Buti, 'Capitaines', 43. Often, a network consisted of people from the same maritime family or 'dynasty' of captains and shipowners.

22 Studying a significant number of Dutch captains' testimonies before the Insurance Council, following accidents at sea, Allain maintains that, in general, captains took over the responsibilities associated with the navigation and the governance of the ship for each voyage. See Thierry Allain, 'Les capitaines d' Amsterdam et l'économie maritime méditerranéenne au XVIII siècle au prisme du récit de la future de mer', in Buti, Lo Basso and Raveaux, *Entrepreneurs de mers*, 19–37.

23 Buti, 'Capitaines', 50.

24 On the 'business dimension' of marine professionals and their contribution to the development of international trade in the eighteenth century, see Maria Fusaro et al., 'Entrepreneurs at Sea: Trading Practices, Legal Opportunities and Early Modern Globalization', *International Journal of Maritime History* 28, no. 4 (2016): 774–86; see in particular the contribution of Tijl Vanneste, 'Maritime Entrepreneurship between an Old Sea and a New Republic: The Commercial Activities of the Dutch Seafarers in the Early Modern Mediterranean', in 'Entrepreneurs at Sea. Trading Practices, Legal Opportunities and Early Modern Globalization', *International Journal of Maritime History* 28, no. 4 (2016): 774–86, edited by Maria Fusaro et al., 780–6.

25 StdAm, 332, 1.2.2, 44/399, Bartholo Cardamici, 12 September 1760.

26 StdAm, 332, 1.2.2, 49/649, Raphael Cardamici, 6 May 1766.

27 StdAm, 332, 1.2.2, 50/154, Raphael Cardamici, 24 October 1766. 'We try to get the lowest freights, but we don't always know how to do it, as in the case of the Capt. Andriessen, who claims a freight of 100 florins for 20 barrels of nails, thinking he is doing a favour.'

28 On the involvement of captains in commercial enterprises, see Buti, 'Capitaines', 50–7.

29 StdAm, 332, 1.2.2, 47/331, Bartholo Cardamici, 5 August 1763.

30 Ibid.

31 Nationaal Archief Den Haag, 1.02.22, *Consulaat Smyrna*, 547 (1763)–563 (1780). This material was elaborated and organized in tables by Thierry Allain. For the purpose of my research, I have utilized the material for the period 1763–71.

32 See, among others, Carrière and Courdurié, 'Les grandes heures', 38–80; and the more recent Corey Tazzara, *The Free Port of Livorno and the Transformation of the Mediterranean World, 1574–1790* (New York: Oxford University Press, 2017), in particular the chapter 'Brokering Trade in Central Mediterranean'.

33 When the recorded numbers of Dutch ships do not coincide, it is obviously because some ships did not pay customs duties at the Dutch consulate in Smyrna.

34 StdAm, 332, 1.2.2, 52/390–401, Raphael Cardamici, May 1770.

35 StdAm, 332, 1.2.2, 51/469, Raphael Cardamici, 6 December 1768.

36 StdAm, 332, 1.2.2, 51/502, Raphael Cardamici, 23 December 1768.

37 StdAm, 332, 1.2.2, 48/42, Raphael Cardamici, 21 February 1764.

38 StdAm, 332, 1.2.2, 47/751, Raphael Cardamici, 7 February 1764.

39 StdAm, 332, 1.2.2, 51/445, Raphael Cardamici, 22 November 1768.

40 StdAm, 332, 1.2.2, 50/154, Raphael Cardamici, 24 October 1766.

41 StdAm, 332, 1.2.2, 44/731, Bartholo Cardamici, 10 March 1761.

42 StdAm, 332, 1.2.2, 45/32, Bartholo Cardamici, 7 April 1761. See in Appendix, letter 6.

43 StdAm, 332, 1.2.2, 51/604, Raphael Cardamici, 3 March 1769.

44 StdAm, 332, 1.2.2, 47/598, Raphael Cardamici, 9 December 1763.

45 StdAm, 332, 1.2.2, 49/82, Raphael Cardamici, 21 June 1765.

46 StdAm, 332, 1.2.2, 45/234, Bartholo Cardamici, 24 July 1761.

47 StdAm, 332, 1.2.2, 48/477, Raphael Cardamici, 23 October 1764.

48 StdAm, 332, 1.2.2, 48/733, Raphael Cardamici, 5 April 1765.

49 StdAm, 332, 1.2.2, 51/502, Raphael Cardamici, 23 December 1768.

50 See generally, Panzac, *La caravane,* 87–104, for the costs of the freights in the cabotage of the Eastern Mediterranean.

51 StdAm, 332, 1.2.2, 45/1, Bartholo Cardamici, 21 March 1761, 'Freights in Constantinople are very expensive . . . now we cannot find an opportunity for a good price . . . and we were obliged to pay those high freights to Capt. Kectel.'

52 StdAm, 332, 1.2.2, 48/166, Raphael Cardamici, 20 April 1764.

53 StdAm, 332, 1.2.2, 45/479, Bartholo Cardamici, 20 November 1761.

54 StdAm, 332, 1.2.2, 45/576, Bartholo Cardamici, 5 January 1762.

55 StdAm, 332, 1.2.2, 49/62, Raphael Cardamici, 7 June 1765.

56 StdAm, 332, 1.2.2, 48/109, Raphael Cardamici, 23 March 1764.

57 StdAm, 332, 1.2.2, 48/551, Raphael Cardamici, 3 December 1764.

58 StdAm, 332, 1.2.2, 50/186, Raphael Cardamici, 21 November 1766.

59 StdAm, 332, 1.2.2, 47/751, Raphael Cardamici, 7 February 1764.

60 StdAm, 332, 1.2.2, 48/191, Raphael Cardamici, 8 May 1764.

61 StdAm, 332, 1.2.2, 47/219, Bartholo Cardamici, 11 June 1763.

62 StdAm, 332, 1.2.2, 45/389, Bartholo Cardamici, 6 October 1761.

63 StdAm, 332, 1.2.2, 45/32, Bartholo Cardamici, 7 April 1761.

64 StdAm, 332, 1.2.2, 52/460, Raphael Cardamici, 29 July 1770.

65 StdAm, 332, 1.2.2, 52/351, Raphael Cardamici, 23 March 1770.

66 StdAm, 332, 1.2.2, 44/39, Bartholo Cardamici, 21 March 1760.

67 StdAm, 332, 1.2.2, 44/399, Bartholo Cardamici, 12 September 1760. See Appendix, letter 4.

68 Metrà, II mentore perfetto, 367.

69 StdAm, 332, 1.2.2, 50/229, Raphael Cardamici, 19 December 1766.

70 StdAm, 332, 1.2.2, 49/8, Raphael Cardamici, 23 April 1765.

71 StdAm, 332, 1.2.2, 50/266, Raphael Cardamici, 6 February 1767.

72 StdAm, 332, 1.2.2, 52/46, Raphael Cardamici, 8 August 1769.

73 StdAm, 332, 1.2.2, 50/154, Raphael Cardamici, 24 October 1766.

74 StdAm, 332, 1.2.2, 50/285, Raphael Cardamici, 20 February 1767.

75 Amsterdam remained throughout the eighteenth century the centre of European maritime insurance, even though, from that time, London also was a major competitor in this field. See Wilson, 'The Growth of Overseas Commerce and European Manufacture', 44.

76 Savary de Bruslons, *Dictionnaire*, vol. 1, 176–7, where we find the entry *assurance* (insurance) and *police d'assurance* which refers to *polizza*, the Italian expression most commonly used in the sector.

77 For Livorno, see Vlami, *Το Φιορίνι* [The florin], 162–4. In Odessa, the first insurance company was founded in 1816. See Vassilis A. Kardasis, *Έλληνες Ομογενείς στη νότιο Ρωσία, 1775–1861* [Greek expatriates in southern Russia, 1775–1861] (Athens: Alexandria, 1998), 193.

78 For what concerns the institutional framework of the Amsterdam insurance market, see Metrà, Il mentore perfetto, 200–3.

79 Ibid., 200–3. Gold and silver cut into coins or not, jewellery, pearls and other valuable items, ammunition and weapons was to be declared and described in the insurance policy.

80 Metrà, Il mentore perfetto, 200–3.

81 StdAm, 332, 1.2.2, 48/733, Raphael Cardamici, 5 April 1765.

82 StdAm, 332, 1.2.2, 48/477, Raphael Cardamici, 23 October 1764.

83 StdAm, 332, 1.2.2, 46/85, Bartholo Cardamici, 23 April 1762.

84 StdAm, 332, 1.2.2, 47/709, Raphael Cardamici, 24 January 1764.

85 StdAm, 332, 1.2.2, 50/266, Raphael Cardamici, 6 February 1767.

86 StdAm, 332, 1.2.2, 50/673, Raphael Cardamici, 29 May 1766.

87 StdAm, 332, 1.2.2, 51/2, Raphael Cardamici, 5 February 1768.

88 StdAm, 332, 1.2.2, 48/188, Raphael Cardamici, 3 May 1764.

89 StdAm, 332, 1.2.2, 46/256, Bartholo Cardamici, 23 July 1762.

90 StdAm, 332, 1.2.2, 50/13, Raphael Cardamici, 22 July 1766.

Chapter 5

1 Pit Dehing and Marjolein 't Hart, 'Linking the Fortunes: Currency and Banking, 1550–1800', in *A Financial History of the Netherlands*, ed. Marjolein 't Hart, Joost Jonker and Jan Luiten van Zanden (Cambridge: Cambridge University Press 1997), 37–63.

2 See also above, p. 15.

3 Jacques Accarias de Sérionne, *La Richesse de la Hollande* (London: au depens de la Compagnie 1778), 345–63.

4 Braudel, *The Perspective of the World*, 241–2.

5 StdAm, 332, 1.2.2, 44/576, Bartholo Cardamici, 29 December 1760 and 332, 1.2.2, 50/154, Raphael Cardamici, 24 October 1766.

6 See Appendix.

7 The Seven Years' War (1756–63) was followed by a period of great progress for the Netherlands, which throughout remained neutral and did not get involved in the hostilities but did serve the belligerent countries in the sectors of trade and transport. See Alice Clare Carter, 'The Dutch as Neutrals in the Seven Years' War', *International and Comparative Law Quarterly* 12, no. 3 (1963): 818–34. Also, in Braudel, *Perspective of the World*, 269.

8 Craig Muldrew, *The Economy of Obligation: The Culture of Credit and Social Relations in Early Modern England* (New York: Palgrave Macmillan 1998), 173–95. Historians have considered, generally, the development of the international financial system and credit services as a positive trend in global economy. However, in the late seventeenth and eighteenth centuries, the procedure for granting and receiving credit caused great concern to traders and society and the debts associated with it made it an unreliable process.

9 Lindemann, *Merchant Republics*, 224.

10 Ibid., 267.

11 Braudel, *Perspective of the World*, 269. In August 1763 the bankruptcy of the Neufville commercial house in 1763 was associated with the onset of the crisis.

12 Ibid., 271.

13 Ibid., 269.

14 Muldrew, *The Economy of Obligation*, 123–47. Also in Julian Hoppit, 'The Use and Abuse of Credit in Eighteenth Century England', in *Business Life and Public Policy: Essays in Honour of D.C. Coleman*, ed. Neil McKendrick and Brian Outhwaite (Cambridge: Cambridge University Press 1986), 65, 78.

15 Braudel, *Perspective of the World*, 243.

16 Metrà, II mentore perfetto, 283–4.

17 Wilson, 'The Growth of Overseas Commerce and European Manufacture', 44–5.

18 James Steve Rogers, *The Early History of the Law of Bills and Notes: A Study of the Anglo-American Commercial Law* (Cambridge: Cambridge University Press 1995), 94–9. Also, Jacques Savary de Brûlons, *Dictionnaire universel*, 253. See also Lindemann, *Merchant Republics*, 227–8.

19 Geoffrey Parker, 'The Emergence of Modern Finance in Europe, 1500–1750', in Cipolla, *Fontana Economic History of Europe*, vol. 2, 540.

20 Lindemann, *Merchant Republics*, 226, and Francesca Trivellato, 'Credit, Honor and the Early Modern French Legend of the Jewish Investment of Bills of Exchange', *Journal of Modern History* 84, no. 2 (2012): 289–334, esp. 290–3. Where she

confirms that exchange rates were trading tools that allowed abuse, exploitation and fraud. Trade of bills brought therefore the 'stain of usury', associated with the myth that it had been invented by the Jews during the Middle Ages.

21 Metrà, II mentore perfetto, 284, on the redemption of bills of exchange and cheques on the Amsterdam market.

22 Parker, 'The Emergence', 542.

23 Ibid.

24 StdAm, 332, 1.2.2, 51/445, Raphael Cardamici, 22 November 1768.

25 StdAm, 332, 1.2.2, 49/294, Raphael Cardamici, 22 October 1765.

26 StdAm, 332, 1.2.2, 48/503, Raphael Cardamici, 2 November 1764.

27 StdAm, 332, 1.2.2, 48/705, Bartholo Cardamici, 20 January 1764.

28 StdAm, 332, 1.2.2, 48/166, Raphael Cardamici, 20 April 1764.

29 StdAm, 332, 1.2.2, 51/329, Raphael Cardamici, 6 September 1768.

30 StdAm, 332, 1.2.2, 50/505, Raphael Cardamici, 7 August 1767.

31 StdAm, 332, 1.2.2, 49/143, Raphael Cardamici, 6 August 1765.

32 StdAm, 332, 1.2.2, 50/302, Raphael Cardamici, 6 March 1767.

33 StdAm, 332, 1.2.2, 49/82, Raphael Cardamici, 21 June 1765.

34 StdAm, 332, 1.2.2, 50/285, Raphael Cardamici, 20 February 1767.

35 StdAm, 332, 1.2.2, 50/442, Raphael Cardamici, 23 June 1767.

36 A similar role was played by Thomas De Vogel Son & Brother in Smyrna. See @@@.

37 StdAm, 332, 1.2.2, 50/704, Raphael Cardamici, 7 August 1767.

38 StdAm, 332, 1.2.2, 50/704, Raphael Cardamici, 22 December 1767.

39 StdAm, 332, 1.2.2, 52/460, Raphael Cardamici, 29 July 1770.

40 StdAm, 332, 1.2.2, 51/469, Raphael Cardamici, 6 December 1768.

41 StdAm, 332, 1.2.2, 52/656, Raphael Cardamici, 22 January 1771.

42 StdAm, 332, 1.2.2, 52/706, Raphael Cardamici, 22 March 1771.

43 Hakki Kadi, *Ottoman and Dutch Merchants*, 215–23, describes the life, activity and bankruptcy of the Armenian trader Alexander De Masse in Amsterdam.

44 According to Hakki Kadi, Alexander De Masse was one of Thomas De Vogel's major competitors in Eastern trade whose activity the Dutch merchant watched closely and commented on the letters he exchanged with his associates. Ibid., 217.

45 StdAm, 332, 1.2.2, 44/575, Raphael Cardamici, 29 December 1760.

46 StdAm, 332, 1.2.2, 44/576, Bartholo Cardamici, 29 December 1760.

47 On Zingrilaras, see Maurits Van den Boogert, 'Ottoman Greeks in the Dutch Levant Trade: Collective Strategy and Individual Practice (C. 1750–1821)', *Oriente Moderno*, new series, 86, no. 1 (2006): 131–2.

48 StdAm, 332, 1.2.2, 44/642, Bartholo Cardamici, 23 January 1761.

49 StdAm, 332, 1.2.2, 48/477, Raphael Cardamici, 23 October 1764.

50 StdAm, 332, 1.2.2, 48/346, Raphael Cardamici, 7 August 1764.

51 StdAm, 332, 1.2.2, 50/285, Raphael Cardamici, 20 February 1767.

52 StdAm, 332, 1.2.2, 51/329, Raphael Cardamici, 6 September 1768.

53 StdAm, 332, 1.2.2, 45/624, Bartholo Cardamici, 22 January 1762.

54 StdAm, 332, 1.2.2, 46/320, Raphael Cardamici, 24 August 1762.

55 StdAm, 332, 1.2.2, 51/239, Raphael Cardamici, 8 July 1768.

56 StdAm, 332, 1.2.2, 51/370, Raphael Cardamici, 7 October 1768.

57 StdAm, 332, 1.2.2, 48/503, Raphael Cardamici, 2 November 1764.

58 StdAm, 332, 1.2.2, 45/119, Bartholo Cardamici, 22 May 1761. Skouvaras, *Ιωάννης Πρίγκος* [Ioannis Prigkos], 47–53, mentions that the merchant Ioannis Prigkos lived in Zingrilaras' house when he arrived in Amsterdam from the Greek village of Zagora in Epiros.

59 StdAm, 332, 1.2.2, 51/360, Raphael Cardamici, 23 September 1768, for the company Stathis Thomas of Isaias & Co., see also Iliou, *Σταμάτης Πέτρου* [*Stamatis Petrou*], νδ.

60 StdAm, 332, 1.2.2, 52/1, Raphael Cardamici, 7 July 1769, for the company Rigas, Niotis & Co., see also Ibid., 11.

61 Van den Boogert, 'Ottoman Greeks', 129–47. On the Sechir Jasegiroglou mentioned several times by De Vogel in his letters, see Iliou, *Σταμάτης Πέτρου* [Stamatis Petrou], 27.

62 In general, on the presence of Greek trading houses in Amsterdam since the beginning of the eighteenth century see Hakki Kadi, *Ottoman and Dutch Merchants*, 198–234, which refers in general to the activity of Ottoman trading houses and their relations with Dutch trading houses.

63 However, De Vogel maintained correspondence with De Bok and when De Masse went bankrupt, he contacted him in order to find out if he was in trouble, see Ibid., 221.

64 Ibid., 191.

65 StdAm, 332, 1.2.2, 49/143, Raphael Cardamici, 6 August 1765.

66 StdAm, 332, 1.2.2, 49/322, Raphael Cardamici, 5 November 1765.

67 StdAm, 332, 1.2.2, 48/503, Raphael Cardamici, 2 November 1764.

68 On the commercial and financial activity of the Greek commercial companies of Vienna during the eighteenth century, see Vaso Seirinidou, 'Οι Έλληνες στη Βιέννη, 1780–1850' '[The Greeks of Vienna, 1780–1850]' (PhD diss., National and Kapodistrian University of Athens, 2002), 146–64.

69 StdAm, 332, 1.2.2, 44/117, Bartholo Cardamici, 6 May 1760.

70 StdAm, 332, 1.2.2, 44/117, Bartholo Cardamici, 6 May 1760.

71 StdAm, 332, 1.2.2, 48/709, Raphael Cardamici, 24 January 1764.

72 StdAm, 332, 1.2.2, 44/117, Bartholo Cardamici, 6 May 1760.

73 StdAm, 332, 1.2.2, 44/531, Bartholo Cardamici, 21 November 1760.

74 StdAm, 332, 1.2.2, 48/706, Raphael Cardamici, 20 January 1764.

75 StdAm, 332, 1.2.2, 47/363, Raphael Cardamici, 22 November 1763.

76 There is an extensive bibliography on Livorno's position in the international system of maritime and financial transactions during the eighteenth century, a very significant contribution to which is the Tazzara, *The Free Port of Livorno*.

77 StdAm, 332, 1.2.2, 46/576, Bartholo Cardamici, 5 January 1762.

78 StdAm, 332, 1.2.2, 48/751, Raphael Cardamici, 7 February 1764.

79 StdAm, 332, 1.2.2, 47/363, Raphael Cardamici, 22 November 1763.

80 StdAm, 332, 1.2.2, 48/42, Raphael Cardamici, 21 February 1764.

81 StdAm, 332, 1.2.2, 48/166, Raphael Cardamici, 20 April 1764.

82 StdAm, 332, 1.2.2, 49/8, Raphael Cardamici, 23 April 1765.

83 StdAm, 332, 1.2.2, 48/582, Raphael Cardamici, 21 December 1764.

84 StdAm, 332, 1.2.2, 48/42, Raphael Cardamici, 21 February 1764.

85 StdAm, 332, 1.2.2, 50/154, Raphael Cardamici, 24 October 1766.

86 Christoforos Bonis was one of the first merchants of Greek origin to settle in Livorno. In 1763, together with the merchants Theodoros Xenos and Stefanos Skaramangas, he raised money for the construction of the first Greek Orthodox Church in Livorno. See Vlami, *To Φιορίνι* [The florin], 74.

87 StdAm, 332, 1.2.2, 48/109, Raphael Cardamici, 23 March 1764.

88 Theocharis did not belong to the group of the most affluent Greek merchants of Livorno. However, he appears to have had a dynamic presence in community's organization and life. Therefore, in 1760 he was among the seven Greek merchants (Ioannis Bezos, Ioannis Argyris Vrettos, Christodoulos Kostakis, Georgios Ioannou Lambros, Evangelos Adamopoulos, Spyridon Zacharias and Ioannis Theocharis) who proposed the establishment of a permanent tax system that would ensure the financial means to finance the activity of the Greek community's Confraternity of the Holy Trinity and will meet the needs of the local Orthodox Church. See Vlami, *To Φιορίνι* [The florin], 287.

89 StdAm, 332, 1.2.2, 50/154, Raphael Cardamici, 24 October 1766.

90 StdAm, 332, 1.2.2, 48/411, Raphael Cardamici, 13 September 1764.

91 StdAm, 332, 1.2.2, 49/229, Raphael Cardamici, 19 December 1766.

92 StdAm, 332, 1.2.2, 50/302, Raphael Cardamici, 6 March 1767.

93 Lindemann, *Merchant Republics*, 224.

Chapter 6

1 Malachy Postlethwayt, *The Merchant's Public Counting-House: or, New Mercantile Institution: Wherein is Shewn, the Necessity of Young Merchants being Bred to Trade with Greater Advantages than they Usually are* (London: John & Paul Knapton, 1751), 21.

2 Trivellato, *The Familiarity of Strangers*, 10–16.

3 Margaret C. Jacob and Catherine Secretan, eds., *The Self-Perception of Early Modern Capitalists* (New York: Palgrave Macmillan, 2008), 5.

4   Jochen Hoock, 'Professional Ethics and Commercial Rationality at the Beginning of the Modern Era', in *The Self-Perception of Early Modern Capitalists*, ed. Margaret C. Jacob and Catherine Secretan (New York: Palgrave Macmillan 2008), 147–59.

5   Trivellato, 'Merchants' letters', 80–103.

6   Although it should be taken for granted, judging by the handwriting and spelling, that the letters were written by more than one secretary-employee of the company, the style and content of the letters presents an impressive uniformity and continuity, which indicates that the person who dictated them remained the same.

7   Clé Lesger, 'Merchants in Charge: The Self-Perception of Amsterdam Merchants, ca. 1550–1700', in *The Self-Perception of Early Modern Capitalists*, ed. Margaret C. Jacob and Catherine Secretan (New York: Palgrave Macmillan, 2008), 79. Particularly in Amsterdam, wealthy and powerful traders were accustomed to imposing their views on both business and politics, administration, justice and social affairs.

8   Ibid., 82.

9   Ibid., 78. As far as Dutch traders are concerned, Julia Adams notes, in *The Familial State: Ruling Families and Merchant Capitalism in Early Modern Europe* (Ithaca: Cornell University Press, 2005), their professional identity, self-esteem and their mentality and behaviour included the principles of patriarchal honour and pride that came from their place in the hierarchy of family and business. In order to reach the economic and social scale of Amsterdam, Dutch traders relied on family solidarity, cooperation and identity and thereby achieved business recognition that lasted for many generations.

10 For this issue see generally, Mark Casson, 'The Economics of the Family Firm', *Scandinavian Economic History Review* 47, no. 1 (1999): 10–23.

11 Mary Lindemann, 'The Anxious Merchant, the Bold Speculator and the Malicious Bankrupt: Doing Business in the Eighteenth-Century Hamburg', in *The Self-Perception of Early Modern Capitalists,* ed. Margaret C. Jacob and Catherine Secretan (New York: Palgrave Macmillan, 2008), 161–82.

12 StdAm, 332, 1.2.2, 46/134, Bartholo Cardamici, 16 May 1762.

13 StdAm, 332, 1.2.2, 52/84, Raphael Cardamici, 2 September 1769.

14 StdAm, 332, 1.2.2, 44/16, Bartholo Cardamici, 7 March 1760.

15 StdAm, 332, 1.2.2, 44/39, Bartholo Cardamici, 21 March 1760.

16 StdAm, 332, 1.2.2, 44/399, Bartholo Cardamici, 12 September 1760.

17 StdAm, 332, 1.2.2, 45/140, Bartholo Cardamici, 5 June 1761.

18 GAS, 332, 1.2.2, 47/503, Raphael Cardamici, 25 October 1763.

19 Lesger, 'Merchants in Charge', 77.

20 Jacob and Secretan, *The Self-Perception*, 7–8.

21 Hoock, 'Professional Ethics', 147–59.

22 StdAm, 332, 1.2.2, 48/706, Raphael Cardamici, 20 January 1764.

23 StdAm, 332, 1.2.2, 44/576, Bartholo Cardamici, 29 December 1760.

24 StdAm, 332, 1.2.2, 52/460, Raphael Cardamici, 29 July 1770.

25 StdAm, 332, 1.2.2, 44/204, Bartholo Cardamici, 20 June 1760.

26 StdAm, 332, 1.2.2, 44/307, Raphael Cardamici, 5 August 1760.

27 StdAm, 332, 1.2.2, 49/673, Raphael Cardamici, 29 May 1766.

28 Jacob and Secretan, *The Self-Perception*, 6–7. The ethics of hard work comprised the value of ceaseless and tireless effort.

29 Ibid., 7.

30 Lindemann, 'The Anxious Merchant', 165–6.

31 StdAm, 332, 1.2.2, 44/16, Bartholo Cardamici, 7 March 1760.

32 StdAm, 332, 1.2.2, 44/16, Bartholo Cardamici, 7 March 1760.

33 StdAm, 332, 1.2.2, 44/399, Bartholo Cardamici, 12 September 1760.

34 StdAm, 332, 1.2.2, 44/92, Bartholo Cardamici, 22 April 1760.

35 StdAm, 332, 1.2.2, 48/477, Raphael Cardamici, 23 October 1764.

36 StdAm, 332, 1.2.2, 44/642, Bartholo Cardamici, 23 January 1761.

37 StdAm, 332, 1.2.2, 45/119, Bartholo Cardamici, 22 May 1761.

38 StdAm, 332, 1.2.2, 45/140, Bartholo Cardamici, 5 June 1761.

39 StdAm, 332, 1.2.2, 46/526, Bartholo Cardamici, 19 November 1762.

40 StdAm, 332, 1.2.2, 47/503, Raphael Cardamici, 25 October 1763.

41 StdAm, 332, 1.2.2, 50/206, Raphael Cardamici, 5 December 1766.

42 StdAm, 332, 1.2.2, 44/642, Bartholo Cardamici, 23 January 1761.

43 StdAm, 332, 1.2.2, 49/258, Raphael Cardamici, 8 October 1765.

44 StdAm, 332, 1.2.2, 51/469, Raphael Cardamici, 6 December 1768.

45 StdAm, 332, 1.2.2, 51/502, Raphael Cardamici, 23 December 1768.

46 StdAm, 332, 1.2.2, 49/109, Raphael Cardamici, 5 July 1765.

47 StdAm, 332, 1.2.2, 50/240, Raphael Cardamici, 6 January 1767.

48 StdAm, 332, 1.2.2, 44/307, Bartholo Cardamici, 5 August 1760.

49 StdAm, 332, 1.2.2, 44/576, Bartholo Cardamici, 29 December 1760.

50 StdAm, 332, 1.2.2, 44/642, Bartholo Cardamici, 23 January 1761.

51 StdAm, 332, 1.2.2, 51/19, Raphael Cardamici, 19 February 1768.

52 StdAm, 332, 1.2.2, 50/154, Raphael Cardamici, 24 October 1766.

53 StdAm, 332, 1.2.2, 50/677, Raphael Cardamici, 4 December 1767.

54 StdAm, 332, 1.2.2, 51/701, Raphael Cardamici, 23 May 1769.

55 StdAm, 332, 1.2.2, 44/751, Raphael Cardamici, 29 March 1761.

56 StdAm, 332, 1.2.2, 50/154, Raphael Cardamici, 24 October 1766.

57 StdAm, 332, 1.2.2, 50/505, Raphael Cardamici, 7 August 1767.

58 StdAm, 332, 1.2.2, 51/645, Raphael Cardamici, 7 April 1769.

59 StdAm, 332, 1.2.2, 48/42, Raphael Cardamici, 21 February 1764.

60 StdAm, 332, 1.2.2, 46/526, Bartholo Cardamici, 19 November 1762.

61 StdAm, 332, 1.2.2, 47/598, Raphael Cardamici, 9 December 1763.

62 StdAm, 332, 1.2.2, 46/461, Bartholo Cardamici, 22 October 1762.

63 StdAm, 332, 1.2.2, 47/207, Raphael Cardamici, 7 June 1763.

64 StdAm, 332, 1.2.2, 44/576, Bartholo Cardamici, 29 December 1760.

65 Lindemann, 'The Anxious Merchant', 165–6.

66 Ibid., 162.

67 Despite his collaboration with De Masse, De Vogel considered him a competitor. Regarding De Masse's bankruptcy and De Vogel's reaction, see Hakki Kadi, *Ottoman and Dutch Merchants*, 215–23.

68 De Masse owed a large sum of money to Haim Coen Hemzy. This fact had particularly alarmed De Vogel, who feared a possible bankruptcy of the Jewish merchant, which would also affect him through the collaboration that Hemzy had with David Van Lennep. See ibid., 188.

69 StdAm, 332, 1.2.2, 51/284, Raphael Cardamici, 5 August 1768.

70 StdAm, 332, 1.2.2, 44/642, Bartholo Cardamici, 23 January 1761 and 45/263, 7 August 1761.

71 StdAm, 332, 1.2.2, 48/477, Raphael Cardamici, 23 October 1764.

72 StdAm, 332, 1.2.2, 50/618, Raphael Cardamici, 23 October 1767.

73 StdAm, 332, 1.2.2, 50/571, Raphael Cardamici, 22 September 1767.

74 See Lesger, *The Rise of the Amsterdam Market*, 164–5, and also Lesger, 'The "Visible Hand": Views on Entrepreneurs and Entrepreneurship in Holland, 1580–1850', in *Small Business Entrepreneurs in Asia and Europe: Towards a Comparative Perspective*, ed. Mario Rutten and Carol Upadhya (New Delhi: Thousand Oaks, 1997), 255–77.

75 StdAm, 332, 1.2.2, 45/32, Bartholo Cardamici, 7 April 1761.

76 See generally in Mark Casson, *Entrepreneurship. Theory, Networks, History* (Cheltenham: Edward Elgar, 2010), a compilation of the most important articles on entrepreneurship by Casson himself or in collaboration with other academics and researchers.

77 Lindemann, 'The Anxious Merchant', 174.

78 StdAm, 332, 1.2.2, 45/263, Bartholo Cardamici, 7 August 1761.

79 StdAm, 332, 1.2.2, 46/394, Raphael Cardamici, 24 September 1762.

80 StdAm, 332, 1.2.2, 46/526, Bartholo Cardamici, 19 November 1762.

81 StdAm, 332, 1.2.2, 50/186, Raphael Cardamici, 21 November 1766.

82 StdAm, 322, 1.2.2, 52/351, Raphael Cardamici, 23 March 1770.

83 StdAm, 332, 1.2.2, 50/742, Raphael Cardamici, 6 July 1766.

84 StdAm, 332, 1.2.2, 45/119, Bartholo Cardamici, 22 May 1761.

85 StdAm, 332, 1.2.2, 44/117, Bartholo Cardamici, 6 May 1760.

Bibliography

Manuscript sources

Stadsarchief Amsterdam [StdAm]
Archief van de Familie De Vogel en Aanverwante Families 332
1.2.2 Thomas De Vogel
44–52 Kopieboek, in de Franse taal 1760–1771
Nationaal Archief Den Haag
1.02.22, *Consulaat Smyrna*
547 (1763)–563 (1780)

Printed primary sources

Accarias de Sérionne, Jacques. *La Richesse de la Hollande*. London: au depens de la Compagnie, 1778.

Boyer d'Argens, Jean Baptiste. *Lettres Juives*. Paris: Paul Gautier, 1738.

Defoe, Daniel. *A Plan of the English Commerce*. London: C. Rivington, 1728.

Metrà, Andrea. *Il mentore perfetto de negozianti ovvero guida sicura de medesimi . . . tomo primo*. Trieste: Giovanni Tommaso Hoechenberger, 1798.

Postlethwayt, Malachy. *The British Mercantile Academy or the Accomplished Merchant*. London: J. and P. Knapton, 1750.

Postlethwayt, Malachy. *The Merchant's Public Counting-House: Or, New Mercantile Institution: Wherein is Shewn, the Necessity of Young Merchants being Bred to Trade with Greater Advantages than they Usually are*. London: John & Paul Knapton, 1751.

Savary de Brûlons, Jacques. *Dictionnaire Universel du Commerce*, vol. 1. Paris: Estienne, 1742.

Savary de Brûlons, Jacques. *Dictionnaire Universel du Commerce*, vol. 2. Paris: Estienne, 1729.

The Capitulations and Articles of Peace between the Majesty of the King of Great Britain, France and Ireland etc. and the Sultan of the Ottoman Empire. London: J.S., 1679.

Secondary sources

Adams, Julia. *The Familial State: Ruling Families and Merchant Capitalism in Early Modern Europe*. Ithaca: Cornell University Press, 2005.

Akçetin, Elif and Suraiya Faroqhi, eds. *Living the Good Life: Consumption in the Qing and Ottoman Empires of the Eighteenth Century*. Leiden: Brill, 2017.

Allain, Thierry. 'Les agents économiques et le déclin hollandaise en Méditerranée entre 1763 et 1780'. *Rives Méditerranéennes* 59 (2019): 93–117.

Allain, Thierry. 'Les capitaines d' Amsterdam et l'économie maritime méditerranéenne au XVIII siècle au prisme du récit de la future de mer'. In *Entrepreneurs des mers: Capitaines et mariniers du XVIe au XIXe siècle*, edited by Gilbert Buti, Luca Lo Basso, and Olivier Raveux, 19–37. Paris: Riveneuve, 2017.

Allain, Thierry. 'Les Néerlandais et le Marché monétaire levantin dans la seconde moitié du XVII siècle (1648–1701)'. *Histoire, Économie et Société* 27, no. 2 (2008): 21–38.

Aslanian, Sebouh. *From the Indian Ocean to the Mediterranean: The Global Trade Networks of Armenian Merchants from New Julfa*. Berkeley: University of California Press, 2014.

Baghdiantz McCabe, Ina, Gelina Harlaftis, and Ioanna Pepelassi Minoglou, eds. *Diaspora Entrepreneurial Networks: Four Centuries of History*. New York: Bloomsbury, 2005.

Bartolomei, Arnaud, Claire Lemercier, Viera Rebolledo-Dhuin, and Nadège Sougy. 'Becoming a Correspondent: The Foundations of New Merchant Relationships in Early Modern French Trade (1730–1820)'. *Enterprise & Society* 20, no. 3 (2019): 533–74.

Ben-Porath, Yoram. 'The F-Connection: Families, Friends, and Firms and the Organization of Exchange'. *Population and Development Review* 6, no. 1 (1980): 1–30.

Berg, Maxine. *Luxury and Pleasure in Eighteenth-Century Britain*. Oxford: Oxford University Press, 2005.

Bilgin, Arif. 'From Artichoke to Corn: New Fruits and Vegetables in the Istanbul Market (Seventeenth to Nineteenth Centuries)'. In *Living the Good Life: Consumption in the Qing and Ottoman Empires of the Eighteenth Century*, edited by Akçetin, Elif and Suraiya Faroqhi, 259–82. Leiden: Brill, 2017.

Boulanger, Patrick. 'Salaires et revenues des équipages de navires marchandes provençeaux durant le XVIII siècle'. *Provence Historique* 30, no. 132 (1980): 421–2.

Braudel, Fernand. *Civilization and Capitalism, 15th–18th Century. The Perspective of the World*, vol. 3. London: Harper & Row, 1984.

Braudel, Fernand. *Civilization and Capitalism, 15th–18th Century. The Wheels of Commerce*, vol. 2. Berkeley: University of California Press, 1992.

Braudel, Fernand. 'The Expansion of Europe and the "Longue Duree"'. In *Expansion and Reaction: Essays on European Expansion and Reaction in Asia and Africa*, edited by Henk L. Wesseling, 17–27. The Hague: Springer Netherlands, 1978.

Bülent, Ari. 'The First Dutch Ambassador in Istanbul: Cornelis Haga and the Dutch Capitulations of 1612' (PhD diss., Bilkent University, 2003).

Bulut, Mehmet. *Ottoman–Dutch Economic Relations in the Early Modern Period, 1571–1699*. Hilversum: Uitgeverij Verloren, 2001.

Bulut, Mehmet. 'The Role of the Ottomans and Dutch in the Commercial Integration between the Levant and Atlantic in the Seventeenth Century'. *Journal of the Economic and Social History of the Orient* 45, no. 2 (2002): 197–230.

Burckhardt, Marlene. "Networks as Social Structures in Late Medieval and Early Modern Towns: A Theoretical Approach to Historical Network Analysis". In *Commercial Networks and European Cities, 1400–1800*, edited by Andrea Caracausi and Christof Jeggle, 13–43. London: Routledge, 2014.

Buti, Gilbert. 'Capitaines et patron provençaux de navires marchands au XVIII siècle: Exécutants où entrepreneurs de mers'. In *Entrepreneurs des mers: Capitaines et mariniers du XVIe au XIXe siècle*, edited by Gilbert Buti, Luca Lo Basso, and Olivier Raveux 39–57. Paris: Riveneuve, 2017.

Buti, Gilbert, Christopher Denis-Delacour, Luca Lo Basso, and Olivier Raveaux. "Introduction". In *Entrepreneurs des mers: Capitaines et mariniers du XVIe au XIXe siècle*, edited by Gilbert Buti, Luca Lo Basso, and Olivier Raveux, 7–15. Paris: Riveneuve, 2017.

Carrière, Charles and Marcel Courdurié. 'Les grandes au XVIII siècle: L'example de la guerre de Sept Ans'. *Revue historique* 254, no. 1 (1975): 38–80.

Carrière, Charles and Michel Morineau. 'Draps du Languedoc et commerce du Levant au XVIII siècle'. *Revue d'Histoire Économique et Sociale* 46 (1968): 108–21.

Carter, Alice Clare. 'The Dutch as Neutrals in the Seven Years' War'. *International and Comparative Law Quarterly* 12, no. 3 (1963): 818–34.

Casson, Mark. 'The Economics of the Family Firm'. *Scandinavian Economic History Review* 47, no. 1 (1999): 10–23.

Casson, Mark. *Entrepreneurship. Theory, Networks, History*. Cheltenham: Edward Elgar, 2010.

Chitty, Joseph. *Lex Mercatoria or, a Complete Code of Commercial Law; being a General Guide to all Men in Business*, 2 vols. London: Nabu, 2011.

Davis, Ralph. 'The Rise of Protection in England, 1689–1786'. *Economic History Review*, new series, 19, no. 2 (1966): 306–17.

De Groot, Alexander H. 'Dragomans' Careers: The Change of Status in Some Families Connected with the British and Dutch Embassies at Istanbul, 1785–1829'. In *Friends and Rivals in the East: Studies in Anglo–Dutch Relations in the Levant from the Seventeenth to the Early Nineteenth Century*, edited by Alastair Hamilton, Alexander H. de Groot, and Maurits Van den Boogert, 223–46. Leiden: Brill, 2000.

De Groot, Alexander H. 'The Organization of Western European Trade in the Levant'. In *Companies and Trade: Essays on Overseas Trading Companies during the Ancien Regime*, edited by Leonard Blussé and Femme Gaastra, 231–41. The Hague and Leiden: Leiden University Press, 1981.

De Groot, Alexander H. *The Ottoman Empire and the Dutch Republic. A History of the Earliest Diplomatic Relations, 1610–1630*. Leiden: Brill, 1978.

De Vries, Jan. 'An Inquiry into the Behaviour of Wages in the Dutch Republic and the Southern Netherlands, 1580–1800'. *Acta Historiae Neerlandicae*, no. 1 (1978): 79–97.

De Vries, Jan and Jan van der Woude. *The First Modern Economy: Success, Failure and Perseverance of the Dutch Economy (1500–1815)*. Cambridge: Cambridge University Press, 2007.

Dehing, Pit and Marjolein't Hart. 'Linking the Fortunes: Currency and Banking, 1550-1800'. In *A Financial History of the Netherlands*, edited by Marjolein't Hart, Joost Jonker, and Jan Luiten van Zanden, 37–63. Cambridge: Cambridge University Press, 1997.

Eldhem, Edhem. *French Trade in Istanbul in the Eighteenth Century*. Leiden: Brill, 1999.

Engels, Marie-Christine. *Merchants, Interlopers, Seamen and Corsairs: The 'Flemish' Community in Livorno and Genoa (1615–1635)*. The Hague: Uitgeverij Verloren, 1997.

Enthoven, Victor. 'Early Dutch Expansion in the Atlantic Region, 1585–1621'. In *Riches from Atlantic Commerce: Dutch Transatlantic Trade and Shipping, 1585–1817*, edited by Johannes Postma and Victor Enthoven, 17–47. Leiden: Brill, 2003.

Epstein, Mortimer. *The Early History of the Levant Company*. London: George Routledge & Sons, 1908.

Establet, Colette. 'Consuming Luxurious and Exotic Goods in Damascus Around 1700'. In *Living the Good Life: Consumption in the Qing and Ottoman Empires of the Eighteenth Century*, edited by Akçetin, Elif and Suraiya Faroqhi, 236–57. Leiden: Brill, 2017.

Faroqhi, Suraiya. *Κουλτούρα και καθημερινή ζωή στην Οθωμανική Αυτοκρατορία: Από τον Μεσαίωνα ως τις αρχές του 20ου αιώνα* [Culture and everyday life in the Ottoman Empire: From the Middle Ages to the beginning of the 20th century]. Translated by Katerina Papakonstantinou. Athens: Exandas, 2000.

Faroqhi, Suraiya. 'Women, Wealth and the Textiles in 1730 Bursa'. In *Living the Good Life: Consumption in the Qing and Ottoman Empires of the Eighteenth Century*, edited by Akçetin, Elif and Suraiya Faroqhi, 213–35. Leiden: Brill, 2017.

Filippini, Jean Pierre. 'La Navigation entre Livourne et le Levant dans les dernières années de l'Ancien Régime'. In *Ανάτυπο από το αφιέρωμα στον Νίκο Σβορώνο* [Reprint from the tribute to Nikos Svoronos], 156–79. Rethymno: Crete University Press, 1986.

Frangakis-Syrett, Elena. *The Commerce of Smyrna in the Eighteenth Century, 1700–1820*. Athens: Centre of Asia Minor Studies, 1992.

Frangakis-Syrett, Elena. 'Commercial Practices and Competition in the Levant: The British and the Dutch in Eighteenth-Century Izmir'. In *Friends and Rivals in the East. Studies in Anglo–Dutch Relations in the Levant from the Seventeenth to the early Nineteenth Century*, edited by Alastair Hamilton, Alexander H. de Groot, and Maurits Van den Boogert, 135–58. Leiden: Brill, 2000.

Frangakis-Syrett, Elena. 'The Economic Activities of Ottoman and Western Communities in Eighteenth Century Izmir'. *Oriente Moderno* 79, no. 1 (1999): 1–26.

Frangakis-Syrett, Elena. 'Izmir and the Ottoman Maritime World of the Eighteenth Century'. *Oriente Moderno new series* 81, no. 1 (2001): 109–28.

Fusaro, Maria et al. 'Entrepreneurs at Sea: Trading Practices, Legal Opportunities and Early Modern Globalization'. *International Journal of Maritime History* 28, no. 4 (2016): 774–86.

Gambetta, Diego. 'Can We Trust Trust?'. In *Trust, Making and Breaking Cooperative Relations*, edited by Diego Gambetta, 213–37. Oxford: Blackwell, 1988.

Gerard, Rudolf and Bosscha Erdbrink. *At the Threshold of Felicity: Ottoman–Dutch Relations during the Embassy of Cornelis Calkoen at the Sublime Porte, 1726-1744*. Ankara: Türk Tarih Kurumu Basimevi, 1975.

Glamann, Kristof. 'European Trade, 1500-1750'. In *The Fontana Economic History of Europe, vol. 2, The Sixteenth and Seventeenth Centuries*, edited by Carlo M. Cipolla, 427–526. London: Collins/Fontana, 1974.

Go, Sabine C. P. J. 'The Amsterdam Chamber of Insurance and Average: A New Phase in Formal Contract Enforcement (Late Sixteenth and Seventeenth Centuries)'. *Enterprise and Society* 14 (2013): 511–43.

Göçek, Müge Fatma. *Rise of the Bourgeoisie, Demise of the Empire: Ottoman Westernization and Social Change*. New York: Oxford University Press, 1996.

Grassby, Richard. *Kinship and Capitalism: Marriage, Family, and Business in the English-Speaking World, 1580-1740*. Cambridge: Cambridge University Press, 2001.

Haggerty, Sheryllynne. *Merely for Money? Business Culture in the British Atlantic, 1750-1815*. Liverpool: Liverpool University Press, 2012.

Hakki Kadi, Ismail. *Natives and Interlopers: Competition between Ottoman and Dutch Merchants in the Eighteenth Century*. Leiden: Leiden University Press, 2012.

Hakki Kadi, Ismail. 'On the Edges of an Ottoman World: Non–Muslim Ottoman Merchants in Amsterdam'. In *The Ottoman World*, edited by Christine M. Woodhead, 276–88. London: Routledge, 2012.

Hakki Kadi, Ismail. *Ottoman and Dutch Merchants in the Eighteenth Century: Competition and Cooperation in Ankara, Izmir and Amsterdam*. Leiden: Brill, 2012.

Harlaftis, Gelina. 'The "Eastern Invasion": Greeks in the Mediterranean Trade and Shipping in the Eighteenth and Early Nineteenth Centuries'. In *Trade and Cultural Exchange in the Early Modern Mediterranean: Braudel's Maritime Legacy*, edited by Maria Fusaro, Colin Heywood, and Mohamed-Salah Omri, 223–52. London: I.B. Tauris, 2009.

Hauser, Henry. 'Le "Parfait Négociant" de Jacques Savary'. *Revue d'histoire économique et sociale* 13, no. 1 (1925): 1–28.

Heeringa, Klaas. *Bronnen tot de Geschiedenis van den Levantschen Handel (1590-1726)*. vol. 1. The Hague: Nijhoff, 1910.

Herrald, Donald J. 'An Education in Commerce: Transmitting Business Information in Early Modern Europe'. In *From Early Modern Business Correspondence To*

Business Week. Information Flows, 1600–2001. Ways and Quantities, Structures and Institutions, XIV International History Congress, Helsinki, 21–25 August 2006, session 1, 1–8.

Hobsbawm, Eric J. *The Age of Revolution: Europe, 1789–1848*. London: Weidenfeld and Nicolson, 1962.

Hoock, Jochen. 'Professional Ethics and Commercial Rationality at the Beginning of the Modern Era'. In *The Self-Perception of Early Modern Capitalists*, edited by Margaret C. Jacob and Catherine Secretan, 147–59. New York: Palgrave Macmillan, 2008.

Hoock, Jochen, Pierre Jeannin, and Wolfgang Kaiser, eds. *Ars Mercatoria: Handbücher und Traktate für den Gebrauch des Kaufmanns, 1470–1820/Manuels et traités à l'usage des marchands, 1470–1820 Eine analytische Bibliographie*, vol. 3. Leiden: Brill, 2001.

Hoppit, Julian. 'The Use and Abuse of Credit in Eighteenth Century England'. In *Business Life and Public Policy: Essays in Honour of D.C. Coleman*, edited by Neil McKendrick and Brian Outhwaite, 64–78, Cambridge: Cambridge University Press, 1986.

Hoving, Ab. *Nicolaes Witsen and Shipbuilding in the Dutch Golden Age*. New York: Texas A&M University Press, 2012.

Iliou, Philippos, ed. *Σταμάτης Πέτρου: Γράμματα από το Άμστερνταμ* [Stamatis Petrou. Letters from Amsterdam]. Athens: Ermis, 1976.

Israel, Jonathan I. 'The Dutch Merchant Colonies in the Mediterranean during the Seventeenth Century'. *Renaissance and Modern Studies* 30 (1986): 87–108.

Israel, Jonathan I. *Dutch Primacy in World Trade, 1585–1740*. Oxford: Clarendon, 1989.

Israel, Jonathan I. *The Dutch Republic: Its Rise, Greatness and Fall, 1477–1806*. Oxford: Clarendon, 1998.

Israel, Jonathan I. 'Trade, Politics and Strategy. The Anglo–Dutch Wars in the Levant (1647–1675)'. In *Friends and Rivals in the East. Studies in Anglo–Dutch Relations in the Levant from the Seventeenth to the Early Nineteenth Century*, edited by Alastair Hamilton, Alexander H. de Groot, and Maurits Van den Boogert, 11–24. Leiden: Brill, 2000.

Jack, Malcom. *The Turkish Embassy Letters: Lady Mary Wortley Montagu*. London: Virago, 1999.

Jacob, Margaret C. and Catherine Secretan, eds, *The Self-Perception of Early Modern Capitalists*. New York: Palgrave Macmillan, 2008.

Jeannin, Pierre. 'Distinction des compétences et niveaux de qualification: les savoirs négociants dans l'Europe Modern'. In *Cultures et formations négociants dans l'Europe modern*, edited by Franco Angiolini and Daniel Roche, 363–99. Paris: Éditions de l'EHESS, 1995.

Jeannin, Pierre. 'La diffusion de l'information'. In *Fiere e Mercati nella Integrazione delle economie europee secc. XIII–XVIII*, edited by Simonetta Cavaciocchi, 231–62. Florence: Le Monnier, 2001.

Jeannin, Pierre. 'La diffusion de manuels de marchands: fonctions et strategies éditoriales'. *Revue d'histoire modern et contemporaine, Acteurs et pratiques du commerce dans l'Europe moderne* 45, no. 3 (1998): 515–57.

Kaiser, Wolfgang and Gilbert Buti, 'Moyens, supports et usages de l'information marchande à l'époque Modern'. *Rives nord-méditerranéennes* 27 (2007), accessed 19 March 2020, doi.org/10.4000/rives.1973.

Kardasis, Vassilis A. *Έλληνες Ομογενείς στη νότιο Ρωσία, 1775–1861* [Greek expatriates in southern Russia, 1775–1861]. Athens: Alexandria, 1998.

Katsiardi-Hering, Olga. 'Η ελληνική παροικία της Τεργέστης, 1751–1830' [The Greek community of Trieste, 1751–1830] (PhD diss., Athens: National and Kapodistrian University of Athens 1986).

Klein, Lawrence E. 'Coffeehouse Civility, 1660–1714: An Aspect of Post-Courtly Culture in England'. *Huntington Library Quarterly* 59 (1997): 30–51.

Koller, Markus. 'Istanbul Fur Market in the Eighteenth Century'. In *Living in the Ottoman Ecumenical Community*, edited by Vera Constantini and Markus Koller, 115–29. Leiden: Brill, 2008.

Kremmydas, Vassilis. "'Τιμιώταται κύρ Κόστα, σας ασπάζομαι αδελφικώς": Η αλληλογραφία ως απόλυτο εργαλείο της εμπορικής πράξης (1800–1850)' [Correspondence as the absolute tool of the commercial act (1800–1850)], in *Επιστημονικό Συμπόσιο Νεοελληνικής Επιστολογραφίας (16ος–19ος αι): Πρακτικά* [Scientific Symposium on Neohellenic Epistolography (16th–19th centuries): Proceedings], *Μεσαιωνικά και Νέα Ελληνικά* [Medioevalia et Neohellenica] 8 (2006): 317–28.

Lamikiz, Xavier. 'Social Capital, Networks and Trust in Early Modern Long-Distance Trade: A Critical Appraisal'. In *Merchants and Trade Networks in the Atlantic and the Mediterranean, 1550–1800: Connectors of Commercial Maritime Systems*, edited by Manuel Herrero Sánchez and Klemens Kaps, 39–61. London: Routledge, 2019.

Lamikiz, Xavier. *Trade and Trust in the Eighteenth-Century: Spanish Merchants and their Overseas Networks*. Woodbridge: Boydell 2010.

Lesger, Clé. 'Merchants in Charge: The Self-Perception of Amsterdam Merchants, ca. 1550–1700'. In *The Self-Perception of Early Modern Capitalists*, edited by Margaret C. Jacob and Catherine Secretan, 75–97. New York: Palgrave Macmillan, 2008.

Lesger, Clé. *The Rise of Amsterdam Market and Information Exchange: Merchants' Commercial Expansion and Change in the Spatial Economy of the Low Countries, c. 1550–1630*. Aldershot: Ashgate, 2006.

Lesger, Clé. *The Rise of the Amsterdam Market and Information Exchange: Merchants, Commercial Expansion and Change in the Spatial Economy of the Low Countries, c. 1550–1630*. London: Routledge, 2006.

Lesger, Clé. 'The "Visible Hand": Views on Entrepreneurs and Entrepreneurship in Holland, 1580–1850'. In *Small Business Entrepreneurs in Asia and Europe: Towards a Comparative Perspective*, edited by Mario Rutten and Carol Upadhya, 255–77. New Delhi: Thousand Oaks, 1997.

Liata, Eftychia D. 'Με "μυστικές γραφές" και "τίμιες" γραφές οι εντιμότατοι πραγματευτές αλληλογραφούν και νεγκοτσιάρουν τον 18ο αιώνα' [By 'secret' and 'honest' writing the honorable merchants correspond and trade in the 18th century], in *Πρακτικά Επιστημονικό Συμπόσιο Νεοελληνικής Επιστολογραφίας* [Scientific Symposium on Neohellenic Epistolography (16th–19th centuries): Proceedings], *Με σαιωνικά και Νέα Ελληνικά* [Medioevalia et Neohellenica] 8 (2006): 301–16.

Lindemann, Mary. 'The Anxious Merchant, the Bold Speculator and the Malicious Bankrupt: Doing Business in the Eighteenth-Century Hamburg'. In *The Self-Perception of Early Modern Capitalists*, edited by Margaret C. Jacob and Catherine Secretan, 161–82. New York: Palgrave Macmillan, 2008.

Lindemann, Mary. *The Merchant Republics: Amsterdam, Antwerp, and Hamburg, 1648–1790*. Cambridge: Cambridge University Press, 2014.

Lindsay, Jean Olivia. 'Introductory Note'. In *The New Cambridge Modern History, vol. 7, The Old Regime, 1713–1763*, edited by Jean Olivia Lindsay, 1–26. Cambridge: Cambridge University Press, 1988.

MacGowan, Bruce. *Economic Life in Ottoman Europe: Taxation, Trade and the Struggle for Land, 1600–1800*. Cambridge: Cambridge University Press, 1981.

Mantran, Robert. 'Commerce maritime et économie dans l'Empire ottoman au XVIIIe siècle'. In *Économie et Sociétés dans l'Empire ottoman (fin du XVIIIe–début du XX siiècles)*, edited by Jean-Luis Bacqqué-Grammont and Paul Dumont, 289–96. Paris: CNRS, 1983.

Marzagalli, Sylvia. 'Establishing Transatlantic Trade Networks in Time of War: Bordeaux and the United States, 1793–1815'. *Business History Review* 79, no. 4 (2005): 811–44.

Marzagalli, Sylvia. 'La circulation de l'information, révelateur des modalités de fonctionnement propres aux reseaux commerciaux d'Ancien Régime'. *Rives nord-méditerranéennes* 27 (2007), http://jaurnals.openedition.org/rives/2073.

Masters, Bruce. *The Origins of Western Dominance in the Middle East*. New York: New York University Press, 1988.

McKendrick, Neil, John Brewer, and John H. Plumb, eds. *The Birth of a Consumer Society: The Commercialization of Eighteenth-Century England*. Bloomington: Indiana University Press, 1982.

Mielants, Erik. 'Perspectives on the Origins of Merchant Capitalism in Europe'. *Review (Fernand Braudel Center)* 23, no. 2 (2000): 229–92.

Muldrew, Craig. *The Economy of Obligation: The Culture of Credit and Social Relations in Early Modern England*. New York: Palgrave Macmillan, 1998.

Nanninga, J. G., ed. *Bronnen tot de Geschiedenis van den Levantschen Handel, 1727–1765*, vol. 3. 'S-Gravenhage, 1952.

Ogilvie, Sheilagh. *Institutions and European Trade: Merchant Guilds, 1000–1800*. Cambridge: Cambridge University Press, 2011.

Palmer, Sarah. *Politics, Shipping and the Repeal of the Navigation Laws*. Manchester: Manchester University Press, 1990.

Panzac, Daniel. *La caravane maritime: Marins européens et marchands ottomans en Méditerranée (1690–1830)*. Paris: CNRS, 2004.

Panzac, Daniel. 'Le contrat d' affrètement maritime en Méditerranée: Droit maritime et pratique commerciale entre Islam et chrétienté (XVII-XVIII siècles)'. *Journal of the Economic and Social History of the Orient* 45 (2002): 342–62.

Papastamatiou, Dimitris. *Wealth Distribution, Social Stratification and Material Culture in an Ottoman Metropolis: Thessaloniki According to the Probate Inventories of the Muslim Court (1761–1770)*. Istanbul: Isis, 2017.

Parker, Geoffrey. 'The Emergence of Modern Finance in Europe, 1500–1750'. In *Fontana Economic History of Europe*, vol. 2, edited by Carlo Cipolla, chapter 7. New York: Barnes & Noble, 1976.

Podolny, Joel M. and Karen L. Page. 'Network Forms of Organization'. *Annual Review of Sociology* 24 (1998): 57–76.

Quataert, Donald. *Ottoman Manufacture in the Age of Industrial Revolution*. Cambridge: Cambridge University Press, 2002.

Rapp, Richard T. 'The Unmaking of the Mediterranean Trade Hegemony: International Trade Rivalry and the Commercial Revolution'. *Journal of Economic History* 35, no. 3 (1975): 499–525.

Rees Jones, James. *The Anglo–Dutch Wars of the Seventeenth Century*. London: Longman, 1996.

Reindl-Kiel, Hedda. 'Diamonds are a Vizier's Best Friend or: Merzifonlu Kara Mustafa's Jewelry Assets'. In *Living the Good Life: Consumption in the Qing and Ottoman Empires of the Eighteenth Century*, edited by Elif Akçetin and Suraiya Faroqhi, 409–32. Leiden: Brill, 2017.

Rietbergen, Pjan. *A Short History of the Netherlands*. The Hague: Bekking and Blitz, 2019.

Rogers, James Steve. *The Early History of the Law of Bills and Notes: A Study of the Anglo-American Commercial Law*. Cambridge: Cambridge University Press, 1995.

Seirinidou, Vaso. 'Οι Έλληνες στη Βιέννη, 1780–1850' [The Greeks of Vienna, 1780–1850]'(PhD diss., National and Kapodistrian University of Athens, 2002).

Shaw Lindsay, William. *History of Merchant Shipping and Ancient Commerce, 1874*, vol. 2. Cambridge: Cambridge University Press, 2013.

Skilliter, Susan A. *William Harborne and the Trade with Turkey, 1578–1582: A Documentary Study of the First Anglo–Ottoman Relations*. Oxford: Oxford University Press, 1977.

Skouvaras, Vangelis. *Ιωάννης Πρίγκος: Η Ελληνική παροικία του Άμστερνταμ* [Ioannis Prigkos and the Greek community of Amsterdam]. Athens: Istoriki kai Laografiki Etaireia ton Thessalon, 1964.

Slot, Ben J. 'Ο Δημήτριος Κουρμούλης και το διεθνές εμπόριο των Ελλήνων κατά έτη 1770–1784' [Dimitrios Kourmoulis and Greek international trade, 1770–1784]. *Μνη μοσύνη* [Mnimosini] 5 (1974–1975): 115–49.

Stoianovich, Traian. 'The Conquering Balkan Orthodox Merchant'. *Journal of Economic History* 20, no. 2 (1960): 234–311.

Tazzara, Corey. *The Free Port of Livorno and the Transformation of the Mediterranean World, 1574–1790*. Oxford: Oxford University Press, 2017.

Trivellato, Francesca. 'Credit, Honor and the Early Modern French Legend of the Jewish Investment of Bills of Exchange'. *Journal of Modern History* 84, no. 2 (2012): 289–334.

Trivellato, Francesca. *The Familiarity of Strangers: The Sephardic Diaspora, Livorno and Cross-Cultural Trade in the Early Modern Period*. New Haven: Yale University Press, 2009.

Trivellato, Francesca. 'Merchants' Letters across Geographical and Social Boundaries'. In *Cultural Exchange in Early Modern Europe, vol. 2, Correspondence and Cultural Exchange in Europe, 1400–1700*, edited by Francisco Bethencourt and Florike Egmont, 80–103. Cambridge: Cambridge University Press, 2007.

Unger, Richard W. 'Technology and Industrial Organisation: Dutch Shipbuilding to 1800'. *Business History* 17, no. 1 (1975): 56–72.

Van den Berg, Richard. 'A Judicious and Industrious Compiler: Mapping Postlethwayt's Dictionary of Commerce'. *European Journal History of Economic Thought* 24, no. 6 (2017): 1167–213.

Van den Boogert, Maurits. *The Capitulations and the Ottoman Legal System: Qadis, Consuls and Beratlis in the 18th Century*. Leiden: Brill, 2005.

Van den Boogert, Maurits. 'Ottoman Greeks in the Dutch Levant Trade: Collective Strategy and Individual Practice (C. 1750–1821)'. *Oriente Moderno*, new series, 86, no. 1 (2006): 131–2.

Vanneste, Tijl. *Global Trade and Commercial Networks: Eighteenth-Century Diamond Merchants*. London: Routledge, 2011.

Vanneste, Tijl. 'Instruments of Trade or Maritime Entrepreneurs? The Economic Agency of Dutch Seamen in the Golden Age'. *Journal of Social History* 52, no 4 (Summer 2019): 1132–64.

Vanneste, Tijl. 'Maritime Entrepreneurship between an Old Sea and a New Republic: The Commercial Activities of Dutch Seafarers in the Early Modern Mediterranean'. In 'Entrepreneurs at Sea: Trading Practices, Legal Opportunities and Early Modern Globalization'. *International Journal of Maritime History* 28, no. 4 (2016): 774–86, edited by Maria Fusaro et al., 780–6.

Vickery, Amanda. 'Women and the World of Goods: A Lancashire Consumer and Her Possessions, 1751–1781'. In *Consumption and the World of Goods*, edited by John Brewer and Roy Porter, 274–304. London: Routledge, 1994.

Vlami, Despina. *Επιχειρηματικότητα και Προστασία στο Εμπόριο της Ανατολής, 1798–1825: Η βρετανική Levant Company και ένας ελληνικός «Δούρειος Ίππος»* [Entrepreneurship and protection in the trade of the East, 1798–1825: The Levant Company and a Greek Trojan horse]. Athens: Academy of Athens, 2017.

Vlami, Despina. 'Γυναίκες, οικογένεια, κοινωνία της εμπορικής διασποράς 18ος–19ος αι'. [Women, family, society of the merchant diaspora, 18th–19th centuries]. *Ιστορικά* [Istorika] 23, no. 45 (2006): 243–81.

Vlami, Despina. 'Το υλικό περιβάλλον και ο οικιακός χώρος ενός Άγγλου εμπόρου στη Θεσσαλονίκη στα τέλη του 18ου με αρχές του 19ου αιώνα' [Material environment and the domestic space of an English merchant in Thessaloniki in the end of the eighteenth and the beginning of the nineteenth centuries]. *Μνήμων* [Mnimon] 30 (2009): 61–105.

Vlami, Despina. *Το Φιορίνι, το Σιτάρι και η οδός του Κήπου: Έλληνες Έμποροι στο Λιβόρνο 1760-1868* [The Florin, the Grain and via del Giardino: Greek merchants in Livorno, 1760-1868]. Athens: Themelio, 2000.

Vlami, Despina. *Trading with the Ottomans: The Levant Company in the Middle East.* London: I.B. Tauris, 2014.

Wallerstein, Immanuel Maurice, Hale Decdeli, and Reşat Kasaba, 'The Incorporation of the Ottoman Empire into the World Economy'. In *The Ottoman Empire and the World Economy*, edited by Huri Ismanoglu Inan, 88–100. Cambridge: Cambridge University Press, 1987.

Wasserman, Stanley and Catherine Faust. *Social Network Analysis: Methods and Applications.* Cambridge: Cambridge University Press, 1994.

Wilson, Charles H. 'The Growth of Overseas Commerce and European Manufacture'. In *The New Cambridge Modern History, vol. 7, The Old Regime, 1713-1763*, edited by Jean Olivia Lindsay, 27–49. Cambridge: Cambridge University Press, 1966.

Witt, Jann M. "'During the Voyage every Captain is a Monarch of the Ship'": The Merchant Captain from the Seventeenth to the Nineteenth Century'. *International Journal of Maritime History* 13, no. 2 (2001): 166–84.

Wood, Alfred C. *A History of the Levant Company.* London: Routledge, 2006.

Index

Milton Keynes UK
Ingram Content Group UK Ltd.
UKHW022007281124
451744UK00004B/52